T0323675

SOCIAL NORMS AND THE THEORY OF THE FIRM

For decades, the economic theory of the firm referred to as agency theory has dominated business research and education in the United States. Although agency theory has been influential in accounting, finance, and managerial economics, it lacks informal and nonfinancial controls. Douglas Stevens resolves to enhance this theory through the incorporation of social norms. Drawing on historical context related to the firm, the theory of the firm, and social norm theory related to the firm, he demonstrates the importance of social norms in the formation and development of free-market capitalism and the firm. He also describes the latest theoretical, experimental, and archival evidence to exhibit the growing body of research that incorporates social norms into the theory of the firm. These foundations enable Stevens to create a comprehensive roadmap of agency theory that will have strong implications for practice and public policy.

Douglas E. Stevens studied experimental economics at Indiana University while completing his PhD in accounting. His experimental and theoretical research demonstrates how incorporating social norms enhances the theory of the firm. His research has been published in leading academic journals including *The Accounting Review*; *Contemporary Accounting Research*; *Accounting, Organizations and Society*; *Experimental Economics*; *Journal of Business Ethics*; *Journal of Management Accounting Research*; and *Behavioral Research in Accounting*.

Social Norms and the Theory of the Firm

A Foundational Approach

DOUGLAS E. STEVENS

Georgia State University

CAMBRIDGE
UNIVERSITY PRESS

University Printing House, Cambridge CB2 8BS, United Kingdom

One Liberty Plaza, 20th Floor, New York, NY 10006, USA

477 Williamstown Road, Port Melbourne, VIC 3207, Australia

314–321, 3rd Floor, Plot 3, Splendor Forum, Jasola District Centre,
New Delhi – 110025, India

79 Anson Road, #06–04/06, Singapore 079906

Cambridge University Press is part of the University of Cambridge.

It furthers the University's mission by disseminating knowledge in the pursuit of
education, learning, and research at the highest international levels of excellence.

www.cambridge.org
Information on this title: www.cambridge.org/9781108423328
DOI: 10.1017/9781108525824

First published 2019

Printed in the United States of America by Sheridan Books, Inc.

A catalogue record for this publication is available from the British Library.

Library of Congress Cataloging-in-Publication Data
Names: Stevens, Douglas E., author.
Title: Social norms and the theory of the firm : a foundational approach / Douglas E. Stevens.
Description: Cambridge, United Kingdom : New York, NY : Cambridge
University Press, 2019. | Includes bibliographical references and index.
Identifiers: LCCN 2018015244 | ISBN 9781108423328 (hardback : alk. paper)
Subjects: LCSH: Industrial organization (Economic theory) | Social norms. |
Industrial sociology.
Classification: LCC HD2326 .S768 2019 | DDC 338.501–dc23
LC record available at https://lccn.loc.gov/2018015244

ISBN 978-1-108-42332-8 Hardback
ISBN 978-1-108-43745-5 Paperback

To my wife Carol

and my daughter Heather,

two special women who have blessed my life

Contents

Preface

This book is the culmination of more than twenty years of research, but it reflects many insights learned from everyday life. Thus, a little background may be in order. I graduated in 1981 with an undergraduate degree in music from a small liberal arts college in southern Michigan where my father was a business professor. I had married my college sweetheart my senior year and the few music-related jobs I could find did not pay the bills. So, I tried my hand at a number of sales jobs, including restaurant supplies, insurance and investments, and commodity futures. My insurance and investment experience finally helped me land a job at a small bank in northern Indiana as a loan officer. As I strived to work my way up at the bank, however, I found that my Achilles heel was always my lack of coursework in accounting and finance. To fill this hole in my knowledge, I resigned my position at the bank in the fall of 1987 and entered an MBA program at Purdue University (Krannert). So it is that this artsy-fartsy guy ended up in business school with a bunch of engineers. After seeing a suggested reading list for MBAs, I purchased Adam Smith's classic book on economics and public policy, *The Wealth of Nations*. I carefully read every page, underlining important passages. It was my first taste of economic thought, and it ended up being a good preparation for my graduate studies in business.

My classmates and I began our MBA program at Purdue with the normal fanfare and high hopes of capturing one of the coveted manufacturing jobs that the engineer-dominated school was known for. As a former banker, I especially enjoyed our first finance class. Taught by an energetic young professor, we learned modern finance theory dominated by rational expectations and the efficient market hypothesis. One Tuesday morning, however, the normally punctual professor was mysteriously absent at the beginning of class. After what seemed like an eternity, the classroom door finally opened and in shuffled our young professor, his lifeless eyes glued to the floor. He reached his desk at the front of the room and slowly sat down. After gathering himself enough to speak, he stated that stock markets around the world were crashing. He mumbled something about there not being any jobs for us at the end of our program and the need for us to rethink our choice of leaving the workforce to get a graduate degree in business. Given the events unfolding on world markets, he said, the topic for the day seemed irrelevant. Eerily shaken and filled with despair, he canceled class and shuffled back out of the room.

The previous day was October 19, 1987 – what was to become infamously known as Black Monday. On that day, a panic sent stock markets around the world plummeting, beginning in Hong Kong and spreading west through Europe before crossing the Atlantic. When the panic hit the United States, the Dow Jones Industrial Average dropped 22.6% – the steepest one-day percentage drop in stock market history. None of this made sense to any of us eager MBA students. The modern finance theory that dominated our classes in accounting and finance left no room for market inefficiencies. What was unfolding on world markets, therefore, seemed beyond belief. Fortunately, the markets stabilized and recovered their precrash levels by the time we graduated in 1989. I had earned good grades and acquired an attractive job offer from Caterpillar. Therefore, I did end up with one of the highly sought-after manufacturing jobs out of Purdue. Above all, I had taken enough accounting and finance courses to sit for the CPA exam a few years later, so the hole in my knowledge had been filled. My transformation from a musician to a financial professional was complete. However, my MBA degree had only whet my appetite for knowledge. After receiving a doctoral fellowship from Coopers & Lybrand (now PricewaterhouseCoopers), I entered a PhD program in accounting at Indiana University after one summer at Caterpillar.

I found the same strong influence of modern finance theory among the faculty at Indiana. In contrast to Purdue, however, the school had a prominent group of accounting faculty who applied behavioral theory in their research. Instead of applying theory in economics assuming that individuals were fully rational, they applied theory in psychology suggesting that individuals exhibited irrational biases and heuristics in their decision making. These behavioral accounting researchers sought to explain market bubbles and crashes and other economic phenomena inconsistent with neoclassical economic theory. While thoroughly trained in rational expectations and the efficient market hypotheses, I could not forget Black Monday. Therefore, I was initially attracted to the new behavioral theory in accounting. One seminar in experimental economics from Professor Arlington Williams in the economics department, however, changed all of that. A former PhD student of Vernon Smith's at Arizona, Arlie taught me that it was not necessary to abandon neoclassical economic theory in my experimental research. I learned that experimental researchers in economics were using lab experiments to test and extend neoclassical economic theory. I was hooked. I spent more and more time in the economics department honing my new research specialty in experimental economics.

It turns out that my graduate school days at Purdue and Indiana were at the height of the influence of a neoclassical theory of the firm that emerged out of the University of Chicago in the 1960s (Khurana 2007, Fourcade and Khurana 2013). From this rigorous economic perspective, managers of the firm were assumed to be self-interested opportunists motivated solely by their own wealth and leisure. This was not a real concern, however, because markets were also assumed to be fully efficient and able to discipline manager behavior that conflicted with the wishes of shareholders. From this perspective, the interests of other stakeholders of the firm such as employees, suppliers, and local communities did not matter. As is true of a fully developed research paradigm (Kuhn 1962), few researchers attempted to challenge these underlying assumptions during the heady days of the 1980s and 1990s. Top academic positions and journal editorships went to those who were steeped in the dominant paradigm out of Chicago. The powerful influence of hiring and tenure decisions, along with publication decisions at the top journals, perpetuated the paradigm. It would take nearly two more decades of conflicting evidence, including the 2000 dot-com market crash and the 2008 market meltdown, for the dominant paradigm to be sufficiently challenged.

In addition to studying experimental economics with Arlie Williams in the economics department, I studied trading volume behavior with Orie Barron in the accounting department. I soon found out, however, that my research put me at odds with the dominant paradigm from the Chicago school. If markets were fully efficient from an informational perspective, then trading volume could play little role in the financial markets. All that mattered was stock price. In fact, the dominant paradigm left no role for information asymmetry or disagreement among investors, and the market could be characterized as a single investor. To complicate things further, I developed a dissertation topic examining the effects of reputation and ethics on budgetary slack in participative budgeting. This had many faculty at Indiana wondering if I had torched my academic career by the end of my doctoral program. Looking back now, I was certainly swimming against the current. Rather than receiving one of the coveted research university positions upon graduation in 1995, I began my academic career at a small public university in New England where I was given a heavy teaching load and few resources to conduct my research.

My first publication used a noisy rational expectations model to demonstrate how characteristics of analyst forecasts captured their heterogeneous beliefs and important aspects of their information environment (Barron, Kim, Lim, and Stevens 1998). It became one of the most heavily cited papers in *The Accounting Review*. My second publication used an experimental market setting to show that market prices and traders' subject beliefs underreacted to new information, and that trading volume reflected heterogeneous beliefs and capital gains expectations among traders (Gillette, Stevens, Watts, and Williams 1999). These early publications allowed me to secure a visiting faculty position at the University of Arizona in 1998 and an assistant professor position at Syracuse University in 1999. I was finally teaching doctoral seminars and advising PhD students in accounting. However, it would be three more years before I got my dissertation published (Stevens 2002). It was just too big a leap at the time. Recently, my research incorporating social norms into the theory of the firm has appeared in top academic journals (Davidson and Stevens 2013, Douthit and Stevens 2015, Abdel-Rahim and Stevens 2018). I have also published the first review paper of trading volume research with Linda Bamber and Orie Barron (Bamber, Barron, and Stevens 2011). Thus, in contrast to early expectations, I have been successful at publishing my research challenging the dominant paradigm out of Chicago.

Despite the strong current it generated against my research early in my career, I am grateful for the economic theory of the firm that emanated from the Chicago school. It is hard to imagine where we would be today without the rich insights garnered from that powerful theory. Rather than ignore these insights, or attempt to lay a new foundation based on behavioral biases and heuristics, my research builds upon the foundation laid by neoclassical economic theory. Over my academic career, I have had the privilege of working with prominent experimental economists while at Indiana University, the University of Arizona, Florida State University, and now Georgia State University. These economists have demonstrated that it is possible to expand neoclassical economic theory without abandoning rational expectations or the rich insights from expected utility theory. While the Chicago school used Adam Smith's second book to advance a neoclassical theory of the firm based upon opportunistic self-interest, researchers have recently returned to Adam Smith's first book to incorporate social norms into the theory. This research has expanded the descriptive validity and usefulness of the theory of the firm. However, this research effort is still young, and there is much work yet to be done.

The purpose of this book is to stimulate research incorporating social norms into the theory of the firm. I take an incremental, foundational approach that builds upon the rich insights of neoclassical economic theory. In the first half of the book, I develop a foundation for this research by presenting history and fundamental theory related to both the firm and social norms. In the second half of the book, I present theoretical, experimental, and archival evidence regarding the ability of social norms to control opportunistic behavior within the firm. Throughout the book, I also present the latest insights regarding Adam Smith from my semester in 2011 as a visiting scholar at the Adam Smith Research Foundation at the University of Glasgow. Neoclassical economists at the Chicago school relied heavily on Smith's second book when forming and defending their economic theory of the firm. Smith's first book, however, contains a comprehensive moral theory based on culture and social norms. My study of Adam Smith has convinced me that the same author to whom neoclassical researchers turned when developing the theory of the firm can be turned to again when incorporating social norms into that theory.

Acknowledgments

I am indebted to many people who have supported my research career and influenced my thinking over the years. First of all, I owe a great debt of gratitude to my immediate and extended family. I wish to thank most of all my wife Carol, who helped an old widower get up off the mat and enjoy life again. I could never have finished this book without her unwavering love and support. I also wish to thank my daughter Heather, who has endured many years of graduate school and the death of her mother after a long battle with breast cancer. She has been with me from the very beginning of my career and has been a constant encouragement through the good times and the bad. Of course, I am also heavily indebted to my loving and supportive parents, who instilled in me a strong sense of morals and a desire to leave this world better off than I found it. Through it all, I am the same guy who majored in music and minored in philosophy/religion during my undergraduate studies and had a very difficult time choosing between graduate studies in music and business. I think I made the right choice.

I owe a special debt to my home academic institution of Georgia State University (GSU), where I have been granted generous time and resources to conduct my research. This includes summer research grants from the Robinson College of Business and the GSU School of Accountancy. I have also received generous research funding as a fellow at the Center for the Economic Analysis of Risk (CEAR) at GSU, which has come with the rich insights of the center director, Glenn Harrison. I would especially like to acknowledge the generous financial support I have received as the James E. & Patricia W. Copeland Deloitte Chair in Accountancy. My research has benefitted from conversations with accounting faculty at Georgia State and at nearby Emory University, Georgia Tech, and the University of Georgia. I would especially like to thank John Campbell, Jeff Hales, Frank Heflin,

Jason Kuang, Jeremy Lill, Michael Majerczyk, Ivo Tafkov, Kristy Towry, Greg Waymire, and Flora Zhou for their helpful insights. The talented research community in Atlanta suffered a serious loss when Bryan Church of Georgia Tech passed away suddenly last spring. His behavioral research in accounting was ground-breaking in many ways, and I shall greatly miss his friendship and insights.

Over the years, I have received invaluable help from the constructive comments of editors and reviewers of my work. I am especially indebted to the editor behind my dissertation paper at the *Journal of Management Accounting Research*, Harry Evans, who insisted that my dissertation was more about extending traditional agency theory than about finding another behavioral anomaly that it could not explain. He was absolutely correct, of course, and thus began my journey to extend the neoclassical theory of the firm. I am also grateful to the many other journal editors who have skillfully critiqued my work over the years, including Robert Bloomfield, Lynn Hannan, Steve Kachelmeier, Steve Kaplan, Joan Luft, Don Moser, Steve Salterio, Katherine Schipper, Mike Shields, Michael Williamson, and Rick Young. Finally, I am deeply indebted to the many anonymous reviewers who have reviewed my work, whether they recommended rejection or eventual acceptance. They will find much of their constructive criticism addressed in this book.

I owe a special debt of gratitude to my dissertation co-chairs at Indiana University, Joe Fisher and Mike Tiller. I first developed an interest in social norms under their guidance and inspiration. Of course, I never would have been able to take this journey without the training I received in experimental economics under Arlie Williams. Arlie programmed Vernon Smith's early market experiments as a PhD student at Arizona. After listening to Vernon's inspiring keynote address at a recent meeting of the Economic Science Association (Tucson, Arizona, 2016), I realized what an intellectual debt I owe him. Of course, all research in experimental economics can be traced back to Vernon's early market experiments in the 1960s. I also owe a debt of gratitude to other leading experimental economists who have crossed my path at Arizona, Florida State, and Georgia State, including David Cooper, Jim Cox, Glenn Harrison, and Mark Isaac. These economists conduct experimental research because they take seriously the underlying assumptions and predictions of neoclassical economic theory. I have also benefitted greatly from other accounting researchers trained in experimental economics, including Joyce Berg, John Dickhaut, Steve Kachelmeier, Ron King, Kevin McCabe, Don

Moser, Bill Rankin, Jeff Schatzberg, Shyam Sunder, Bill Waller, David Wallin, and Rick Young.

I am also indebted to the many courageous researchers who have extended the boundaries of the theory of the firm. First of all, I thank Linda Bamber and Orie Barron for exposing me to trading volume research. Our review paper (Bamber, Barron, and Stevens 2011) demonstrates how far we have come yet how far we have to go to understand the large and increasing volume of trade around public financial disclosures. My recent research with Orie and Richard Schneible suggests that much of the market reaction to earnings announcements is in trading volume and not stock price (Barron, Schneible, and Stevens 2018). Thus, we really don't know as much about financial markets as we think we do. I also thank the theoretical researchers who have recently incorporated social norms into the theory of the firm, including Paul Fischer, Steve Huddart, Brian Mittendorf, Mark Penno, and Alex Thevaranjan. Your comments, insights, and models have heavily impacted my thinking. I especially thank Mark Penno for admonishing me to "go deep" in this book. I also thank Bill Mayew for making me aware of the growing literature related to social and moral norms in archival capital markets research.

I am deeply indebted to the many PhD students who have attended my doctoral seminars over the years. Many of them became my research assistants and co-authors. They include Heba Abdel-Rahim, Alisa Brink, Bruce Davidson, Jeremy Douthit, Eric Gooden, Linwood Kearney, Mark Mellon, Richard Schneible Jr., Minsup Song, James Wilhelm, and Ke Xu. Your questions and insights challenged me to go deeper and come up with better answers. I hope I also convinced you how tentative our current answers really are, and how much further research is needed to incorporate social norms into the theory of the firm. I look forward to your future contributions to the literature. Some of the content of this book has also crept into my MBA and graduate management accounting courses. I am particularly grateful for the practical implications and insights gleaned from my MBA students at New Hampshire, Syracuse, Florida State, and Georgia State.

I have attempted to expand my perspective over the course of my academic career by presenting my research at conferences and workshops in multiple disciplines, including accounting, economics, finance, and business ethics. I have also served as an anonymous reviewer for academic journals related to these disciplines. This multidisciplinary exposure has convinced me how limited my own perspective is regarding many of the research topics covered in this book. I apologize up front for the need to focus primarily on economics-related research. I concluded early on that incorporating social norms into the theory of the firm would require a rigorous foundation that is faithful both to neoclassical economic theory and social norm theory related to the firm. I found Christi Bicchieri's (2006) model of social norm activation, which was motivated by results in experimental tests of game theory, particularly helpful in this regard. Nevertheless, I highly value varying perspectives and have benefitted greatly from reading widely in social psychology and moral philosophy. Due to space and time constraints, and the limitations of the author, I have also focused on my own theoretical, experimental, and archival research in this book.

I want to thank two anonymous referees whose detailed comments and suggestions pushed me to include more detail regarding the theory of the firm in economics. I owe a special debt to the editorial staff at Cambridge University Press, especially Karen Maloney, Stephen Acerra, and Kristina Deusch, who walked me through the entire process of this book project from the initial prospectus to the finished product. I also owe a debt of gratitude to project manager Krishna Prasath and copyeditor Kathleen Allain. I also thank graphic artist Christian Coppoletti for his art and design work on the book cover. Finally, I would like to thank my agent D. J. Snell at the Legacy Agency, who provided much encouragement and legal advice and became a personal friend during this project.

1

The Importance of Behavioral Assumptions
in Economic Theory

INTRODUCTION

Milton Friedman wrote a methodological essay in 1953 that was highly influential in the fields of economics, accounting, and finance. Entitled *The Methodology of Positive Economics*, it is required reading in my philosophy of science seminar along with other classics such as Adam Smith's (1795) *The History of Astronomy*, Karl Popper's (1934) *The Logic of Scientific Discovery*, and Thomas Kuhn's (1962) *The Structure of Scientific Revolutions*. I find Friedman's essay worthy of study for new doctoral students because it is the most heavily cited methodological work in economics, and arguably the most controversial (Mäki 2009a). Importantly, the essay raises a rich array of theoretical issues and helps me explain economic theory-building within its historical and social context. Friedman became a prominent economist at the University of Chicago at about the same time that academics and administrators joined a major initiative to make American business education "scientific" (see Chapter 3). Thus, the influence of his methodological essay quickly spread from economics to economics-based research in accounting and finance. Accounting researchers were so influenced by Friedman's essay that they named their application of his research methodology *positive accounting theory* (Watts and Zimmerman 1986).[1]

Some researchers view economics as a scientific success thanks to its adherence to the methodology outlined in Friedman's essay. Others, however, view Friedman's methodology as "deeply flawed, even dangerous for

[1] My own view of Friedman's methodological essay began to change after discussions with experimental economists at Florida State University during my time on the faculty there. I thank David Cooper, Mark Isaac, and Tim Salmon for helping rid me of the simplistic view of Friedman's essay frequently held in accounting and finance.

the cognitive aspirations and social responsibilities of economics" (Mäki 2009a, 47). To be sure, Friedman's essay shaped economists' conceptions of what constituted good theory and good empirical evidence. After his essay, representative research in the top economic journals became "more *formal* – more mathematical, more analytical, less historical, less institutional, more standardized, and more narrow regarding admissible priors" (Hands 2009, 145, italics in the original). At the time of Friedman's essay, the theory of the firm was "an imperiled embryo" with multiple forces pulling it in different directions (Reder 2009). Friedman's essay narrowed the discussion space and pushed many formerly prominent topics to the periphery (Backhouse 2009, Williamson 2009). Consistent with Kuhn's (1962) characterization of scientific advancement, Friedman's essay helped the theory of the firm develop into a focused research paradigm. Thus, any book that proposes to introduce social norms into the theory of the firm must address the theoretical and methodological issues raised in Friedman's essay.

In this chapter I use Friedman's essay to stress the importance of behavioral assumptions in economic theory. Some may find this surprising given that Friedman has been credited with taking the opposite position in his essay. It is my view that Friedman's essay has largely been misunderstood in this regard, to the detriment of the theory of the firm. Thus, I begin by summarizing Friedman's theoretical and methodological arguments with the goal of yielding the most straightforward interpretation. For this task, I borrow insights from other classic works in the philosophy of science (Smith 1795, Popper 1934, Kuhn 1962). Similar to Mäki (2009b), I find ample evidence in Friedman's statements and subsequent behavior to support the opposite conclusion for which he is so often credited. In particular, I find ample support in his essay for the importance of behavioral assumptions in economic theory and a cost/benefit approach to the realism of such assumptions. I follow this summary of Friedman's essay with a brief cost/benefit analysis of incorporating social norms into the theory of the firm. I conclude by introducing the topics covered in the remaining chapters of this book.

FRIEDMAN'S METHODOLOGY OF POSITIVE ECONOMICS

Milton Friedman, like many economists of his generation, was attracted to the field of economics because of the suffering he witnessed during the Great Depression (Snowdon and Vane 1999). After completing his graduate studies at the University of Chicago in 1935, Friedman was initially unable to find academic employment. Thus, he found himself in

Washington, DC, working at the National Resources Committee (NRC). While at the NRC, Friedman was part of a task force assigned to providing a statistical answer to the debate over the causes of the Great Depression (Serrano and Bonilla 2009). Roosevelt's New Deal policies required government intervention in the US economy on a scale never seen before, and statistical analysis at the NRC was used to justify such intervention. In addition to giving Friedman valuable experience in data analysis, his experience at the NRC allowed him to witness first-hand how economic analysis could be used to serve a normative, political purpose. In 1941, Friedman was appointed as the principal economist at the Treasury's division of tax research, where he took direct part in policy-making debates. In 1946, Friedman completed his PhD from Columbia University and joined the faculty at the University of Chicago where his views of government intervention soon changed from being thoroughly Keynesian to laissez-faire (Friedman and Friedman 1998).

By the time his methodological essay was published in 1953, therefore, Friedman had overcome his modest beginnings and had gained extensive experience in public policy and data analysis. In particular, he had amassed an impressive résumé of policy-related research as a member of the NRC task force researching the influence of consumer behavior on the Great Depression and later as the principal economist at the Treasury's division of tax research. Friedman was part of a small cohort of US economists who had been attracted to the profession because of the Great Depression and had spent time in Washington shaping public policy to help fight it. This background gave Friedman a unique perspective regarding theoretical arguments for government intervention in the economy and the data used to justify such intervention. It also made him well qualified to write an essay about research methodology and the foundations of economic theory.

The chief aim of Friedman's essay was to promote a more scientifically based research methodology in economics. The 1940s had witnessed an explosion of advances in science and mathematics, and these advances were changing the way economics was practiced. John von Neumann and Oskar Morgenstern had published their *Theory of Games and Economic Behavior* in 1944 and Paul Samuelson had published his *Foundations of Economic Analysis* in 1947. The Cowles Commission, founded in Colorado in 1932, had moved to the University of Chicago in 1939 to make Chicago a mecca for mathematical economics. Cowles sponsored conferences and published papers deepening the rigor of economic theory in conference monographs and a new academic journal called *Econometrica*. While the theory of the firm was becoming more mathematically rigorous, however, it was also becoming narrower. Thus, other forces pushed back against this trend in neoclassical economics. Prominent economists of the day criticized the simplified behavioral assumptions underlying the theory of the firm, calling for greater realism (Gordon 1948). Further, developments in psychology led some to conclude that the theory was outmoded and needed to be reconstructed in line with such developments (Friedman 1953, 30).[2]

Friedman's essay made some of the same arguments as Popper (1934) regarding what constitutes a testable hypothesis and how to develop formal tests of theory. In fact, some researchers have credited Friedman with introducing Popper's philosophy of science to economists (Walters 1987). For example, Friedman argued that factual evidence can never "prove" a hypothesis; it can only fail to disprove it. This falsification standard causes researchers to state that a given hypothesis has been "supported" or "confirmed" by the data and never "proven." Friedman also made a distinction between positive theory and normative theory, with the former relating to the scientific quest for "what is" and the latter relating to the often values-driven quest for "what ought to be." As the title of his essay suggests, Friedman promoted the advancement of positive theory in economics as a precursor to good public policy. Given Friedman's background and future role in public policy, however, it is unlikely that he ever advocated a complete retreat from normative theory.[3]

By characterizing the field of economics as a "positive science," Friedman set the boundaries of what constitutes good economics. He identified the ultimate goal of a positive science as "the development of a 'theory' or 'hypothesis' that yields valid and meaningful (i.e., not truistic) predictions about phenomena not yet observed" (Friedman 1953, 7). Friedman also identified two elements of such a theory: (1) it provides a language that is designed to promote systematic and organized methods of reasoning, and (2) it provides a body of substantive hypotheses designed to abstract essential features of complex reality. Friedman argued that as a language, the function of a theory "is to serve as a filing system for

[2] This movement eventually led to Cyert and March's (1963) behavioral theory of the firm. Cyert and March applied the concept of bounded rationality from psychology to propose that real firms aimed at satisficing rather than maximizing their results.

[3] As I discuss below, some researchers in accounting and finance used Friedman's (1953) essay on positive theory to justify retreating from normative theory relevant to public policy.

organizing empirical material and facilitating our understanding of it" (Friedman 1953, 7). As a positive science, therefore, good economics involves the search for theories that are able to explain "what is" and predict what one would expect to find given the right conditions.

While he promoted a more rigorous, scientifically based view of economic theory, Friedman readily acknowledged the role of subjective beliefs and tastes in theory development. As a language, theory defines the discussion space and helps determine what researchers in a field perceive as "acceptable." Friedman (1953, 29–30) acknowledged that the "single-minded pursuit of pecuniary self-interest" is a behavioral assumption that is more acceptable to a trained economist than to a sociologist, and repeated the popular view that economics "is a 'dismal' science because it assumes man to be selfish and money-grubbing." Further, he acknowledged the common criticism that economic theory rests on "outmoded psychology," and the desire on the part of some social scientists that the theory "be reconstructed in line with each new development in psychology." Friedman (1953, 31) argued, however, that "criticism of this type is largely beside the point unless supplemented by evidence that a hypothesis differing in one or another of these respects from the theory being criticized yields better predictions for as wide a range of phenomena."

The view that scientific theory is socially constructed was not new at the time of Friedman's essay, nor was it confined to the social sciences. A similar view appears in Adam Smith's account of the development of scientific theory in *The History of Astronomy* (Smith 1795). Smith argued that scientific theory is as much a work of the imagination as of empirical evidence.[4] He traced the theory of the heavens from Aristotle to Ptolemy, Copernicus, Galileo, and Newton. In praising Isaac Newton's recent discovery of the principle of gravity and its ability to explain the motions of heavenly bodies, Smith warned of the temptation to characterize Newton's new system as "true." While the new theory was capable of accounting for observed phenomena in terms of a smaller number of principles and could successfully predict future movement, Smith argued that it was still a mere product of the imagination.

Friedman (1953, 12) emphasized the importance of empirical evidence in theoretical work: "Empirical evidence is vital at two different, though closely related, stages: in constructing hypotheses and in testing their

---

[4] Adam Smith referred to science as "natural philosophy" and to scientists as "philosophers." The labels "science" and "scientists" were not widely used prior to 1839 (Wightman 1982, 13).

validity." Besides suggesting new hypotheses, empirical evidence assures that a given hypothesis explains what it sets out to explain. Friedman acknowledged, however, that empirical evidence itself is not a sufficient criterion for choosing among hypotheses. "If there is one hypothesis that is consistent with the available evidence, there are always an infinite number that are" (Friedman 1953, 9). Because hypothesis choices are underdetermined by the evidence, therefore, there is room for subjective judgments and social constraints in the development of economic theory (Mäki 2009b, 113). Friedman (1953, 23) was pragmatic about this underdetermination and the need for subjective judgment in economic theory: "Yet the continued use and acceptance of the hypothesis over a long period, and the failure of any coherent, self-consistent alternatives to be developed and be widely accepted, is strong indirect testimony to its worth."

Similarly, Adam Smith (1795) spoke of "prejudices" of the imagination in the development of scientific theory. He identified a number of prejudices that generated a resistance to new theoretical developments in astronomy, including prejudices of background and education. This prejudice of the imagination can explain why researchers in different fields prefer different behavioral assumptions in their theory and generally resist new assumptions. This resistance to new theoretical developments is a major theme in Thomas Kuhn's (1962) classic work, *The Structure of Scientific Revolutions*. Kuhn emphasized the role of the scientific community in the development of scientific theory. According to Kuhn, a given community of scholars makes a commitment to a given theory and commits resources and institutions to perpetuate that theory, even to the extent of ignoring inconsistent evidence. Over time, however, evidence inconsistent with the accepted theory begins to mount, perhaps due to advances in measurement and data availability. At some point, this process generates a crisis at which time a new theory can emerge and become the new research paradigm for the community of scholars.[5]

Given the presence of underdetermination in theory development (the fact that multiple theories can explain the same set of data), Friedman provided a list of virtues to guide economic researchers in choosing among theories. The list includes, foremost, simplicity and fruitfulness: "A theory is 'simpler' the less the initial knowledge needed to make a prediction within a given field of phenomena; it is 'fruitful' the more precise the resulting prediction, the wider the area within which the theory yields predictions, and the more additional lines for further research it suggests"

---

[5] I discuss research paradigms and paradigm shifts more fully in Chapter 7.

(Friedman 1953, 10). Logical completeness and consistency are also listed as important, although they play a subsidiary role to Friedman. Adam Smith (1795) emphasized that one theory may be preferred over another because it is simpler. When it comes to scientific theory, therefore, Smith and Friedman agree that less is more (Occam's razor). But by far the most important virtue, according to Friedman, is the usefulness of the theory for prediction. This is also consistent with Smith, who argued that a theory is satisfactory to the imagination only if it is coherent and capable of accounting for observed appearances.

In an often-quoted passage, however, Friedman (1953, 14) appears to discount the importance of the underlying behavioral assumptions of a theory: "Truly important and significant hypotheses will be found to have 'assumptions' that are wildly inaccurate descriptive representations of reality, and, in general, the more significant the theory, the more unrealistic the assumptions." This statement not only takes the view that the realism of underlying behavioral assumptions is irrelevant; it also turns the unrealism of such assumptions into a theoretical virtue (Mäki 2009b). This statement was controversial from its inception, and it continues to draw strong criticism from researchers in philosophy and economics (Mäki 2009a). Some researchers view Friedman's statement defending the use of unrealistic assumptions as the "weak spot" of his essay and some have even labeled his arguments in this regard as "philosophically amateurish" (Mayer 2009, 122). Other researchers have attributed Friedman's strong statement to the author's tendency to "revel in controversy" or "overreach" (Williamson 2009, 242). So many researchers have found this statement unacceptable and outrageous on its face, that a straightforward interpretation must be wrong.

Friedman's strong statement regarding the virtue of unrealistic assumptions has been interpreted as: "*economic theories should not be judged by their assumptions but by their predictive implications* – and in particular, *the unrealisticness of the assumptions of a theory is no reason for complaint or worry about the theory*" (Mäki 2009b, 93–94, italics in the original). Consistent with this interpretation, Friedman's essay has been used to justify simplifying behavioral assumptions in game theory and mathematical economics. His essay has also been used, however, to beat back attempts to enhance the realism of underlying behavioral assumptions in the theory of the firm. To the extent that this was Friedman's original goal, he has been largely successful. This is particularly true of economics-based research in accounting and finance. Some researchers in accounting and finance have used Friedman's essay not only to keep more realistic behavioral assumptions out of the theory of the firm, but also to justify retreating altogether from normative theory relevant to public policy. This is highly unfortunate, but it appears to be the outcome of an overly simplistic interpretation of Friedman's positions.

AN ALTERNATIVE INTERPRETATION OF FRIEDMAN'S POSITION ON BEHAVIORAL ASSUMPTIONS

To be sure, Friedman (1953) devoted a large portion of his essay debating the importance of unrealistic assumptions to economic theory. Many of his arguments appear at odds with Adam Smith's (1795) argument that a theory is more pleasing to the imagination if it is stated in terms of assumptions that are at least plausible. To understand why Friedman would devote so much space defending the use of unrealistic assumptions, it is important to recall the environment in which he wrote his essay. Prominent economists at the time were critical of the realism of the assumptions underlying the neoclassical theory of the firm (Gordon 1948). Further, developments in psychology were exposing the theory of the firm to the criticism that it was outmoded and needed to be reconstructed in line with such developments (Friedman 1953, 30). Friedman initially developed his essay as a response to the 1946–1947 marginalist controversy that had broken out between Lester, Machlup, and Stigler, where he questioned Lester's view of theory and Machlup and Stigler's view of empirical evidence (Backhouse 2009). His main target, however, was the emerging theory of monopolistic competition. While objecting to the claim that the theory could prove the basis for a more general theory, Friedman particularly objected to the claim that it represented an improved theory because of the increased realism of its underlying assumptions (Williamson 2009).

These developments posed a potential threat to the neoclassical theory of the firm. As such, Friedman's defense of the use of unrealistic behavioral assumptions can be viewed as a defense of the neoclassical theory of the firm from its detractors. In light of Kuhn's (1962) classic work on the philosophy of science, Friedman's defense is symptomatic of a strong theoretical paradigm. According to Kuhn, normal science functions within a given theoretical paradigm. In particular, normal science involves the laborious process of accumulating detail in accord with the established theory, without questioning or challenging the underlying assumptions of that theory. In essence, Friedman was concerned that critics had gone too far in questioning the underlying assumptions of the established neoclassical theory of the firm. Rather than question these assumptions, he argued for getting on with the task of accumulating more detail in accord with the established theory. From this perspective, Friedman's essay performed a valuable service in preserving the accepted neoclassical paradigm for future researchers.

Recent scholarship regarding Friedman's (1953) methodological essay, however, suggests that his position regarding the importance of behavioral assumptions has largely been misunderstood. Why would Friedman devote most of his methodological essay to the underlying assumptions of a theory if such assumptions were unimportant? Given this unevenness in treatment, some researchers have argued that the main message of Friedman's essay is really the importance of a theory's assumptions (Mäki 2009b). For example, Friedman attacks Edward Chamberlin's theory of monopolistic competition based on its criticism of the neoclassical theory's assumption of "perfect competition" rather than on its inferior ability to predict. His criticism of Chamberlin's theory conveys the opposite position for which Friedman is credited in his essay. In fact, Friedman's essay and future behavior suggest that the underlying assumptions of a theory really do matter (Mäki 2009b).

One simplifying assumption dominates all others in neoclassical economic theory. This assumption is called "rational expectations" or "rationality." These labels capture the overarching assumption that individuals or firms have a well-defined utility function and attempt to maximize their utility through their decisions and behavior. Economic research, therefore, can be described as the study of rational behavior on the part of individuals, groups, or firms to maximize their utility given a set of information and a world of limited resources. In this regard, there is considerable overlap between the descriptive goal of economic theory (positive theory) and the prescriptive goal of economic theory (normative theory). In particular, the rationality assumption is used by economists both to describe what economic agents *actually do* and to prescribe what they *should do* given a specific economic setting. In developing both positive and normative economic theory, therefore, economists have found it convenient to assume rationality on the part of both individuals and firms. The importance of the rationality assumption to economic theory emphasizes the point that the assumptions of a theory do matter, and very much.

It has been my experience that the underlying assumptions of a theory are very important. Although my research training is in experimental economics, I have joined with theorists to publish a noisy rational expectations model of the information environment of market analysts (Barron, Kim, Lim, and Stevens 1998) and a principal-agent model demonstrating how incorporating a social norm for promise-keeping improves the descriptive, prescriptive, and pedagogical usefulness of the model (Stevens and Thevaranjan 2010).[6] The review process at top academic journals has convinced me of the importance of underlying assumptions. As any theorist knows, simplifying assumptions are not only critical for mathematical tractability; they also drive the results of an economic model. In addition to providing mathematical proofs, therefore, journal editors and reviewers require theorists to justify the underlying assumptions of their models. This is why theorists typically begin with a model that is already firmly established in the literature and then make small, incremental changes.[7] Thus, while Friedman's theoretical virtues of simplicity and fruitfulness (unifying power) are certainly important to an economic theory, and mathematical elegance is a plus, the realism of a theory's assumptions is also very important.

Melvin Reder (2009, 173) identifies another theoretical virtue to help researchers select among theories: "consilience of a theory with other beliefs, especially those associated with other theories, that have wide acceptance." Researchers have long promoted the merits of enhancing neoclassical economic theory with insights from the other social sciences such as psychology (Cyert and March 1963, Wilson 1998). The incorporation of behavioral assumptions from other successful research paradigms, while potentially fruitful, is commonly resisted due to prejudices of the imagination (Smith 1795) and socialization in a community of researchers (Kuhn 1962). I have experienced this resistance first-hand in my own research in the theory of the firm. In the course of my academic career, I have presented my research before audiences trained in diverse research paradigms from economics, accounting, and finance to psychology and moral philosophy. The prejudices in the various research disciplines are inbred and deep, and include prejudices of methodology as well as behavioral assumptions.

---

[6] I consider myself neither a mathematician nor a statistician, although I have taken graduate courses in both fields and have taught statistics and research methodology seminars. (I was tempted to write, "but I did sleep in a Holiday Inn Express last night," but thought better of it.)

[7] As Joel Demski once told me, an established model is a theorist's playground. When pressed to justify one of the underlying assumptions of his model at a research workshop, he admitted that his model was just "a toy."

Experimental research has greatly expanded our understanding of the rationality assumption in economic theory. Upon winning the Nobel Prize in Economic Science in 2002, in large part for his role in making economics an "experimental science," Vernon Smith wrote a book summarizing emerging insights from this research (Smith 2008). Smith emphasizes two forms of systematic or "rational" behavior that have emerged in experimental tests of economic theory. In addition to traditional economic rationality, which he calls "constructivist rationality," Smith identifies a second form of rationality based on the works of Adam Smith, David Hume, and more recently Friedrich Hayek. Called "ecological rationality," this maximizing behavior emerges as a result of social interaction and situational cues present in the economic setting. These cues appear to activate social norms that control opportunistic behavior and yield cooperative results that dominate narrowly defined economic self-interest. Norm-based behavior that has been demonstrated in the laboratory includes fairness, reciprocity, honesty, and trustworthiness. Rather than view these findings as "anomalies" that threaten the validity of traditional neoclassical theory, however, Smith views them as opportunities to advance the theory.

Oliver Williamson (2009) argues that Friedman's methodological essay set overly strict constraints that needlessly restricted the future development of the theory of the firm. For example, Friedman (1953, 31) characterized criticisms of the theory as "largely beside the point" unless the detractor can produce an alternative theory that "yields better predictions for as wide a range of phenomena." This unnecessarily limited the menu of possible theories to large, overly general theories. Upstart contenders, however, do not have the benefit of "successive extensions, applications, and refinements" of neoclassical theory (Williamson 2009, 243). Such upstart theories may be crude, as most new theories are, but they may provide better predictions for a limited range of phenomena. Further, such upstart theories may direct our attention to a whole new set of phenomena. Thus, Friedman's insistence on a single, all-purpose theory may have limited future developments in the theory of the firm.

Many researchers, fortunately, have not limited themselves to Friedman's directive regarding alternative theories. In particular, researchers in the theory of the firm have already added alternative behavioral assumptions to the theory. For example, Baumol (1959) postulated that large firms maximized revenues subject to a minimum profit constraint, Marris (1964) advanced a growth maximization hypothesis, and Williamson (1964) added managerial staff and emoluments to the objective function of the firm. All three of these models describe the firm as a production function as in neoclassical theory but restate the objective function of the firm to reflect alternative managerial purposes besides straight profit maximization. All three of these models, however, preserve the behavioral assumption of rational expectations. Cyert and March (1963) took an entirely different approach. In their behavioral theory of the firm, they assumed bounded rationality and satisficing behavioral rather than rational expectations and maximizing behavior. They also incorporated the concept of organizational slack as a stabilizing and adaptive force.

Uskali Mäki (2009b) argues that Friedman's (1953) position regarding the realism of a theory's underlying assumptions can be better described as a "cost/benefit" approach. This cost/benefit approach is reflected in the following two passages:

To put this point less paradoxically, the relevant question to ask about the 'assumptions' of a theory is not whether they are descriptively 'realistic,' for they never are, but whether they are sufficiently good approximations for the purpose in hand (Friedman 1953, 15).

Complete "realism" is clearly unattainable, and the question whether a theory is realistic 'enough' can be settled only by seeing whether it yields predictions that are good enough for the purpose in hand or that are better than predictions from alternative theories (Friedman 1953, 41).

As discussed above, researchers have already increased the realism of the underlying assumptions of the theory of the firm, and have generated many useful insights regarding the behavior of managers and firms. Due to their efforts, we have multiple theories with multiple assumptions that have yielded superior predictions over certain classes of phenomena (Williamson 2009). These theories look beyond observed behavior to underlying causes that have extended the boundaries of the theory of the firm. To date, however, researchers have been slow to incorporate social norm behavior. It appears that cost/benefit issues have made doing so prohibitive up to this point. The purpose of this book is to encourage further advances in this important research area. Before outlining the content of this book, therefore, I discuss potential costs and benefits to incorporating social norms into the theory of the firm.

A COST/BENEFIT ANALYSIS TO INCORPORATING SOCIAL NORMS

There are certainly potential costs to incorporating social norms into the theory of the firm, and I have borne many of them myself. But I am not unique in this regard. Many researchers have attempted to extend the "dismal science" to include other motivations besides pecuniary self-interest only to find that theorists are generally content with the *homo economicus* view of human motivation. The road to enriching the theory of the firm by incorporating social norm behavior, however, goes both ways. In the course of my academic career I have presented my research before audiences trained in accounting, economics, finance, psychology, and moral philosophy. The theoretical prejudices across the disciplines are inbred and deep, and generate conflicts involving methodology as well as behavioral assumptions. In the course of my career I have experienced strong prejudice against social norm theory from economists, but I have also experienced strong prejudice against neoclassical economic theory from those trained in psychology and moral philosophy.[8]

Twenty-plus years of attempting to incorporate social norms into the theory of the firm have convinced me that the prejudice against expanding the underlying assumptions of the theory is stronger in economics-based research in accounting and finance than in economics itself. Top academic journals in accounting and finance continue to be influenced by the powerful research paradigm of the Chicago school and narrow interpretations of Friedman's methodological essay. For example, top economics-based journals in accounting continue to publish little experimental research and resist efforts to increase the realism of underlying assumptions of neoclassical economic theory. Unfortunately, tenure and promotion decisions in accounting are often determined by the number of publications appearing in such journals. Thus, there is a potential cost to one's career for incorporating social norms into the theory of the firm.

The potential cost of bridging the literatures in social norms and the theory of the firm can also be very high due to the large gap between theory in social psychology and economics. Nevertheless, my experimental and theoretical research suggests that this gap can be bridged to the benefit of theory in both disciplines. Since the publication of Friedman's (1953) influential essay, researchers in accounting and finance have been hesitant to incorporate social norms into the theory of the firm because of the belief that doing so would be purely "normative." The results emerging from experimental tests of game theory and agency theory, however, suggest that

---

[8] The strongest reaction I ever received to a paper I presented was at an ethics conference in accounting. While presenting an early version of my theory paper with Alex Thevaranjan (Stevens and Thevaranjan 2010), the discussion devolved into a shouting match between members of the audience who either approved or disapproved of our use of the neoclassical theory of the firm to develop a social norm solution to the moral hazard problem.

incorporating norm-based behavior can increase the descriptive validity of the theory of the firm and therefore advance positive theory. Correspondingly, social norm theory has advanced in ways that make it more useful to neoclassical economic theory. For example, Bicchieri's (2006) model of social norm activation is a positive theory that was developed in part to explain emerging results in experimental tests of economic game theory. This makes the model readily applicable to neoclassical economic theory.

Theorists in economics and accounting have recently demonstrated how social norm behavior can be incorporated into the theory of the firm in a rigorous way that advances the descriptive validity of the theory. For example, Alex Thevaranjan and I use insights from Bicchieri's model to introduce a norm for promise-keeping into the traditional principal-agent model, and find that the ability of the model to describe contracting behavior in the firm is increased (Stevens and Thevaranjan 2010). We preserve all of the traditional assumptions of the principal-agent model but add a disutility for providing less than a previously agreed-upon standard of effort. The disutility increases in the sensitivity of the agent to the norm and the difference between the actual effort provided and the standard. We find that a work ethic arises endogenously in the model that controls the opportunism of the agent and grants a fixed contract the power to induce effort. When comparing the predictions of our model with the traditional principal-agent model, we find that our model explains a fuller range of contracting behavior within the organization than the traditional model that is void of social norms.

Due to recent advances in theory and empirical evidence, the potential cost of incorporating social norms into the theory of the firm has gone down dramatically. Furthermore, these advances have revealed that the potential benefit of this research initiative is significant. Friedman (1953, 31) concluded that criticisms of the realism of behavioral assumptions are largely beside the point unless supplemented by evidence that enriching the behavioral assumptions in some regard results in better predictions. Given the predictive power demonstrated in economic models incorporating social norms (Stevens and Thevaranjan 2010), and norm-based behavior emerging from experimental tests of game theory and agency theory, criticisms of the "greedy money grubbing" assumption in the neoclassical theory of the firm are no longer beside the point. Indeed, they are valid criticisms worth pursuing to the benefit of the theory. This research initiative has commenced in earnest in the experimental literature in managerial accounting.[9] Archival capital market researchers have also begun to examine the effects of social norms on firm behavior (Dyreng, Hanlon, and Maydew 2010, Dyreng, Mayew, and Williams 2012).

I am convinced that this research initiative is capable of generating many new and useful insights, to the benefit of both practice and theory. Friedman identified two elements of a theory: (1) it provides a language that is designed to promote systematic and organized methods of reasoning, and (2) it provides a body of substantive hypotheses designed to abstract essential features of complex reality. Incorporating social norms in a precise and theoretically valid way, therefore, will aid researchers in both their reasoning and research design. Regarding the former, this research program will give theorists a foundation to build new theoretical predictions and hypotheses. Regarding the latter, this research program will give empirical researchers a better idea of what to test and what variables are important as independent or control variables in a given study. I have found that incorporating social norm behavior can help explain previous anomalies that have puzzled researchers in management accounting (Douthit and Stevens 2015, Abdel-Rahim and Stevens 2018) and auditing (Blay, Gooden, Mellon, and Stevens 2018).

The assumption that agents are motivated by social norms has implications for both positive and normative theory. In particular, social norm preferences can easily be added to the utility function of economic agents to both describe what they *actually do* and prescribe what they *should do* in an economic setting. Regarding positive theory, the neoclassical theory of the firm has no explanation for such organizational controls as codes of ethics or certification requirements (Davidson and Stevens 2013). By reducing organizational control to contracting and financial incentives, the neoclassical theory of the firm provides little support for informal or nonfinancial incentives that are ever present in the firm (Abdel-Rahim and Stevens 2018). More generally, the neoclassical theory of the firm provides little explanation for the existence of nonprofit firms where financial incentives are nonexistent or very weak (Stevens and Thevaranjan 2010). Regarding normative theory, the neoclassical theory of the firm provides little support for following any standards or social norms other than "greedy, money-grubbing" behavior. Because of this lack of support for anything other than opportunistic behavior, the theory has been blamed for irresponsible and unethical behavior that has plagued businesses, industries, and the economy (Khurana 2007, Miles 2016).

---

[9] For a review of this experimental evidence, see Blay, Gooden, Mellon, and Stevens (2017).

Regarding its implications for organizational control, the neoclassical theory of the firm provides little support for popular controls such as participative budgeting or the balanced scorecard. Regarding the former, agency researchers have argued that involving managers in the formation of their budget is inefficient because it only encourages them to lie (Jensen 2001). Regarding the latter, agency researchers have argued that setting nonfinancial goals in the balanced scorecard is inefficient because only financial goals have motivational power (Jensen 2002). This limited perspective reflects the continuing influence of the powerful research paradigm that emanated from the Chicago school and the narrow interpretation of Friedman's methodological essay. An overemphasis on financial incentives can lead to dysfunctional organizational behavior such as the recent scandal at Wells Fargo Bank, where overly strong financial incentives for cross-selling led employees at the bank to open accounts for customers without their knowledge. This scandal is consistent with experimental evidence showing that financial incentives can "crowd-out" intrinsic motivation and social norm behavior.

A FOUNDATIONAL APPROACH

In this book, I provide a foundational approach to incorporating social norms into the theory of the firm. In particular, I provide an historical, theoretical, and empirical perspective that should prove useful to researchers, practitioners, and policy-makers. In this first chapter, I have argued that Friedman's (1953) methodological essay supports a cost/benefit approach to the realism of behavioral assumptions, and have presented a cost/benefit analysis suggesting that the potential benefits of incorporating social norms into the theory of the firm outweigh the potential costs. In the following three chapters, I provide a foundation for this new and potentially fruitful research initiative. In Chapter 2, I present a history of the firm that incorporates social norms. This narrative emphasizes the importance of culture, institutions, and social norms in the birth of free-market capitalism and the development of the firm. In Chapter 3, I present the theory of the firm and its historical development within the university-based business school. This chapter emphasizes key developments in the theory over time and summarizes key insights from classical and neoclassical economic theory. In Chapter 4, I present social norm theory related to the firm, from Adam Smith's two classic works to the latest theory in social norm activation (Bicchieri 2006). This chapter emphasizes the ability of social norm theory to fit within the traditional neoclassical framework.

Throughout the rest of the book, I build on this historical and theoretical foundation by presenting the latest research in norm-based behavior related to the firm. In Chapter 5, I present the formal neoclassical theory of the firm that emanated out of the Chicago school and demonstrate how it has been successfully expanded by theorists to incorporate social norms. I begin by analyzing the behavioral assumptions of neoclassical economic theory known as *homo economicus*. Next, I discuss the behavioral assumptions of the neoclassical theory of the firm that evolved from the Chicago school (Jensen and Meckling 1976). These assumptions included an ever-narrowing version of *homo economicus* and the efficient market hypothesis (Fama 1970). Next, I discuss the presence of social norms in Adam Smith's second book, *The Wealth of Nations*. I then present the social norm theory contained in Smith's first book, *The Theory of Moral Sentiments*, which brought him worldwide fame as a philosopher of the highest order. I conclude Chapter 5 by presenting recent social norm theory related to the firm that has proven useful to researchers in economics, accounting, and finance.

In Chapter 6, I summarize the emerging evidence of social norm behavior in experimental research related to the firm. I begin by discussing the key benefits of experimental research. By allowing researchers to manipulate variables to test causal theoretical relations, experimental research provides an important bridge between the powerful yet highly simplified world of the theorist and the naturally occurring yet complex world of the archival researcher. Next, I discuss the early classroom market experiments by Edward Chamberlin at Harvard in the 1940s and Vernon Smith at Purdue in the 1950s and 1960s. I discuss the rigorous experimental methodology developed by Smith and his colleagues based on the insights of early experimentalists in psychology and management science (e.g., Simon 1955, Siegel 1959). Next, I describe key findings from experimental studies of neoclassical market theory. I then discuss experimental studies of two-person strategic games such as the investment game and the principal-agent model, and how they have revealed the robust influence of social norms. I also discuss the growing evidence of norm-based behavior in experimental tests of participative budgeting. The emerging evidence in experimental research represents a significant challenge to the culture-free, norm-free core of the neoclassical theory of the firm.

In Chapter 7, I summarize the emerging evidence of social norm behavior in archival research related to the firm. I first describe theory, research paradigms, and paradigm shifts before explaining how the new theory of the firm that emanated from the Chicago school represented a paradigm shift. I then discuss the mounting evidence against fully efficient markets and the new focus on market inefficiency in archival research. This evidence eventually led neoclassical researchers to soften their position on efficient markets and opened the door to market research related to individual decision-making and trading volume. I discuss this literature and how trading volume research is generating new and important insights regarding market behavior. Next, I discuss archival evidence regarding the effectiveness of financial incentives on manager behavior. By discounting the role of culture and social norms, the Chicago school gave financial incentives a central role in controlling opportunistic behavior in the firm. I discuss the lack of archival evidence supporting a link between financial incentives and firm performance, as well as the possibility that such incentives can be dysfunctional by crowding out intrinsic motivations and causing excessive risk-taking. Finally, I discuss direct archival evidence that social norms play an important role in controlling opportunistic behavior in the firm.

In Chapter 8, I conclude by asking, "Where do we go from here?" This chapter includes a frank and open discussion of the challenges that await researchers attempting to incorporate social norms into the theory of the firm and where this exciting research initiative may lead us in the future. This chapter also includes a discussion of the "bread crumbs" that have been left behind by leading economists of the past that may help guide the way. This discussion emphasizes the ability of the neoclassical theory of the firm to fully incorporate social norms, and advocates an incremental approach that builds on the rich insights contained in neoclassical theory.

PART I

THE FOUNDATION

2

A History of the Firm That Incorporates Social Norms

INTRODUCTION

Alfred D. Chandler Jr. wrote an award-winning history of the firm in 1977 entitled, *The Visible Hand: The Managerial Revolution in American Business*. At the time, economists and historians had begun to turn their attention to the role of large commercial firms in the economy and in society. However, most theorists still viewed the firm as a unit of production, and the most popular economic rationale for the formation of firms was market failure or the accumulation of monopoly power (Coase 1937). Chandler's history of the firm provided a theoretical rationale for the formation and development of firms based on advances in technology, accounting, and financial control. According to his narrative, these advances made it more efficient for independent contractors, who had formerly sold raw materials and labor in simple exchange markets, to come together under the umbrella of the firm to conduct commerce. Chandler concluded that Adam Smith's "invisible hand" of the market had been supplanted by the "visible hand" of managerial control. Similarly, Johnson and Kaplan (1987) provided an insightful history of the firm that emphasized the importance of innovations in management accounting for the formation and development of firms.

More recently, institutional economists and historians have incorporated culture and social norms in narratives explaining the development of free-market economies and capitalist institutions (North 1991, Soll 2014). These narratives emphasize advances in accounting and financial control as a catalyst for such development, as in prior narratives, but they also suggest that a merchant culture that promoted social norms such as transparency and accountability played an important role. To expand the narrative of the firm and lay the foundation for future chapters, therefore,

I provide a history of the firm that incorporates social norms. I begin my history of the firm by describing the birth of free-market capitalism in medieval Italy and the Netherlands. The creation of double-entry accounting in Italy around 1300 helped generate a culture of transparency and accountability, which allowed merchants to invest capital in the pursuit of trading opportunities. This culture led to large merchant cities with capitalist institutions that supported national and international trade. When French and Spanish armies invaded Italy in the late 1400s, however, this merchant culture faded in favor of a monarchy culture. At about this same time, a merchant culture developed in the Netherlands that also led to large cities with capitalist institutions in support of international trade. Again, French and Spanish monarchies posed a continual threat to this culture. I then describe how free-market capitalism spread to Great Britain and the United States. In the late 1600s, England chose the Dutch merchant culture over the French monarchy culture and invited William of Orange to assume the English throne. While the two cultures continued to fight for dominance in what became Great Britain, the merchant culture found its ultimate expression in the English colonies in America.

I next describe how the merchant cultures in Britain and the United States generated two industrial revolutions that led to further developments in the size and complexity of the firm. From textiles and steel factories to railroads and large manufacturers, the expanding firm relied increasingly on the visible hand of managerial control. This generated a demand for advanced systems of accounting and financial control as well as increased transparency and accountability. However, the increasing complexity of big business in nineteenth-century US industries led to the development of another culture. Opportunistic entrepreneurs in the railroad industry made huge fortunes based on a culture of opaque financial reporting, stock manipulation, and insider trading. This opportunism culture required increased regulation and oversight, which was provided by both government and private institutions such as accounting firms and bond rating agencies. The full threat of the opportunism culture became apparent in the twentieth century when a lack of transparency enabled excessive speculation leading to stock market crashes after the Roaring Twenties (1929) and the dot-com bubble (2000). In each case, further regulation and oversight were imposed by Congress. However, the opportunism culture would eventually infect the regulators, including accounting firms and bond rating agencies. This led to another stock market bubble based on mortgage-backed securities that almost took down the entire financial system in 2008.

THE BIRTH OF FREE-MARKET CAPITALISM IN ITALY AND THE NETHERLANDS

Economic historians have applied economic theory and quantitative methods to explain economic development and institutional change. Douglass North (1991, 97) defines institutions as "humanly devised constraints that structure political, economic and social interactions." Such institutions consist of both formal rules (e.g., property rights, laws, and constitutions) and informal rules and norms (e.g., customs, traditions, and codes of conduct).[1] North describes economic development as occurring in stages. First, local trade occurs within small villages and is facilitated largely by informal rules. As trade expands and occurs between villages, terms of exchange must be made more explicit by formal rules. As trade expands further and occurs over greater physical distances, the risk of fraud and unfair practices increases the importance of formal rules. Thus, trade relies increasingly on formal contracting and record-keeping as it expands from intravillage, to intervillage, to international trade. The final stage of economic development is the urbanization of society as more resources and people become involved in the activities of international trade. While formal rules increase in importance as economic development progresses, however, informal rules and norms continue to play an important role.

In his book, *The Reckoning: Financial Accountability and the Rise and Fall of Nations*, Jacob Soll (2014) argues that the advent of double-entry accounting in northern Italy around 1300 marks the beginning of the history of free-market capitalism. Without Arabic numerals, ancient Greek and Roman Empires struggled to develop financial management systems for commerce and government. Such systems had to await new numbers with decimal points and a new method of financial accounting. The new numerical system, which originated in India, was introduced to Europe by Arab mathematicians around the twelfth century. Soon a new double-entry accounting system appeared in northern Italy. By the turn of the fourteenth century, city republics emerged in Florence, Genoa, and Venice that were run by patrician merchants whose wealth came from international trade. These merchants used the new accounting system to coordinate long-distance trade and banking. According to Soll, double-entry accounting and a merchant culture of transparency and accountability allowed free-market capitalism to arise first in northern Italy.

---

[1] In sociology, Richard Scott (1995, 33) defines institutions as "cognitive, normative, and regulative structures and activities that provide stability and meaning to social behavior."

The advanced method of accounting that developed in northern Italy was described by Luca Pacioli in his 1494 treatise on arithmetic, geometry, and proportion (*Summa de Arithmetica, Geometria, Proportioni, et Proportionalita*). In his chapter on accounting, Pacioli explained how double-entry accounting systems allowed merchants to develop profit and loss statements to measure performance and encourage accountability. In contrast to single-entry systems, which also tracked periodic profit and loss, double-entry accounting systems allowed merchants to develop balance sheets that tracked changes in asset values and net worth over time. Called the "Venetian System" by Pacioli, double-entry accounting offered merchants the essential tool of capitalism: the capacity to keep a running total of asset and liability accounts along with contributed capital and retained earnings (Soll 2014). As all students of accounting know, the double-entry system of debits and credits allows managers to track changes in these accounts over time that are due to the operating and investing activities of the firm.

Pacioli's *Treatise* not only set out the fundamentals of double-entry accounting, which has changed very little in over 500 years, it also disclosed the values and norms that were essential to good financial management and good government. Quoting passages and characters from the Bible, Pacioli argued that hard work and profits were virtues and that God would take care of those who worked hard and knew how to count. He also argued that faithfully keeping a timely and truthful account of financial transactions would put merchants in good standing with God. Well before the Protestant Reformation and its strong work ethic, therefore, a Roman Catholic monk emphasized the virtues of hard work, transparency, and accountability (Soll 2014). Raised within the merchant culture of medieval Italy, Pacioli understood that commerce required good accounting and a strong set of social norms. The merchant culture that emerged in northern Italy generated great wealth that financed unparalleled advances in art, architecture, music, science, and literature. Coming as it did after the stagnation of the Middle Ages, this period of renewed prosperity and discovery became known as the Italian Renaissance.

A popular myth is that Pacioli invented double-entry accounting at the time of his treatise in 1494. As is commonly the case, the truth is much more interesting than the myth. Rather than invent double-entry accounting, Pacioli's treatise simply presented the system of accounting taught in accounting and abacus schools throughout northern Italy after about 1300 (Soll 2014). Pacioli's treatise did not achieve either critical or popular acclaim at the time of its publication. This is attributable in part to forces that weakened the merchant culture in Italy. The same year his treatise was published, France and Spain separately invaded the Italian peninsula and turned it into a battlefield for sixty years. Rather than use religion to argue for transparency and accountability, the French and Spanish monarchies used religion to argue for privileged information and the divine rights of kings. The aristocratic humanism that appealed to the new elites of the Italian Renaissance scorned merchant knowledge, and the Roman Catholic Church increasingly associated financial management and banking with immorality. Given these forces, the merchant culture that made northern Italy the center of international trade and banking in Europe began to fade.

The Netherlands soon became the new center of banking and international trade in Europe. Similar to Italy, accounting schools sprang up in Antwerp and throughout the Netherlands to teach double-entry accounting and financial control. These schools helped nurture a culture of transparency and accountability in both commerce and government. In contrast to Italy, the merchant culture that evolved in the Netherlands was supported by the spread of the Protestant Reformation. To the Dutch Calvinists, wealth and success in commerce became signs of one's membership into God's elect. All work was a special calling, which supported a high view of work, commerce, and banking. By 1567, Antwerp was the richest city in the world, with plentiful shops, grand houses, forty-two churches, and a stock exchange. As the strong merchant culture of the Netherlands penetrated society and politics, the seventeen northern provinces eventually threw off the rule of their Habsburg overlords in 1581. In response, King Phillip sent the Spanish Imperial Army to lay siege on the southern city of Antwerp, reducing its population from 100,000 to 40,000 as its artisans and merchants fled to the free north. Soon, Amsterdam became the new center of banking and international trade in Europe. With their accounting schools and well-developed stock exchange, Dutch knowledge of finance and markets soon surpassed that of their Italian predecessors (Soll 2014). It is no coincidence, therefore, that the first publicly traded limited liability company was formed and traded in Amsterdam.

In 1602, the Dutch East India Company issued bonds and shares of stock to the public. Dutch citizens had faith in the value of the publicly traded shares because of their strong merchant culture and its social norms of transparency and accountability. The story of the Dutch East India Company, however, is a case study in the difficulty of maintaining transparency and accountability in capital markets (Soll 2014). The company's managers maintained closed books throughout its nearly 200-year history. Although promised by the company's board, by 1620 no dividends had been paid and no external audits of the company's books had been conducted. This lack of transparency caused investors to suspect that managers and large investors were embezzling funds, and stocks were bought and sold on the basis of marketplace rumors rather than public financial information. As a result, stock prices experienced large fluctuations. Facing a shareholder revolt in 1622, the company's seventeen directors finally agreed to an internal audit conducted by the state in private. Thus, transparency and accountability were never achieved at the first publicly traded corporation.

In 1662, Pieter de la Court published a book explaining the merchant culture that had evolved in the Netherlands entitled, *True Interest and Political Maxims of the Republic of Holland*. His book was an instant best seller throughout the Netherlands and was translated and read in other countries as an explanation for the Dutch economic miracle that was unfolding as a result of free-market capitalism and republican government. De la Court argued that republican government generated greater economic prosperity for its citizens than absolute monarchy. Further, he claimed that successful industry and commerce were not possible without political and economic freedom, accountability, and religious tolerance (Soll 2014). His views were in direct opposition to the power and ambition of the Habsburg overlords. Despite growing hostilities with France and Spain, as well as new hostilities with Sweden and England, the Netherlands entered a Dutch golden age. Similar to the Italian Renaissance, this golden age yielded great advances in art, architecture, music, science, and literature. The merchant culture of the Netherlands, however, also began to fade in 1672 when Louis XIV's troops invaded Holland and William of Orange was made the Dutch stadtholder (ruler).

FREE-MARKET CAPITALISM SPREADS TO BRITAIN AND THE UNITED STATES

Free-market capitalism eventually spread to Great Britain and the United States. Estimates of per capita gross domestic product (GDP) (Maddison 1995, 2001) suggest that the average person experienced zero income growth from 1 to 1000 AD. In contrast, there was meager but steady growth in per capita GDP from 1000 to 1800. As expected, this growth in income was concentrated primarily in Europe and was driven by the merchant economy in Italy, followed by the Netherlands. In the early 1800s, however, worldwide growth in per capita GDP exploded to more than two percent per year and continued at that rate for the following two centuries. This explosion in wealth and prosperity was driven primarily by the free-market economies in Britain and the United States. The dramatic economic growth that occurred in these two countries far surpassed that of Italy and the Netherlands, and had significant implications for the development of the firm.

As with Italy and the Netherlands before them, Britain and the United States developed merchant cultures that generated capitalist institutions that supported international trade. These institutions included both formal rules of law and informal behavioral rules and norms. In contrast to the two previous free-market economies, however, Britain and the United States benefitted from a new theory of natural law that controlled the power of government and provided its citizens with unparalleled civil liberties. The economic, political, and religious freedoms afforded its citizens generated an explosion of innovation in science and technology, and led to two industrial revolutions. The economic growth experienced by Britain and the United States was further fueled by advances in communication and transportation (Bernstein 2004). Early on, for example, the economy in Britain benefitted from a vastly expanded post office, a nationwide network of coffeehouses, an improved system of roads, an expanding system of navigable rivers, and a growing industry in shipbuilding and international travel (Pincus 2009).

The first half of the seventeenth century found England locked in a violent conflict between Parliament and two Stuart Kings, James I and Charles I. This conflict led to a bloody civil war and the eventual beheading of Charles in 1649. The Stuart Monarchy was replaced by the Commonwealth of England (1649–1653) followed by the Protectorate under the rule of Oliver Cromwell (1653–1658) and his son (1658–1659). During the years of the Commonwealth and the Protectorate, England was increasingly influenced by the merchant culture of the Netherlands. Over this time period, unquestioned loyalty to the nobility faded, and public policy became increasingly influenced by Parliament, the courts, and public opinion. Further, public opinion became increasingly shaped by a populace that made its living by buying and selling. By the time the Stuart monarchy was restored with the reign of Charles II in 1660, England had become a trading nation with a vibrant merchant culture (Pincus 2009).

Charles II was king of England, Scotland, and Ireland from the restoration of the monarchy in 1660 until his death in 1685. Charles initially sided with France and his first cousin Louis XIV against the rising economic and military power of the Netherlands. This led to two Anglo-Dutch wars during Charles's reign (1652–1654 and 1665–1667). Although Charles attempted to introduce religious freedom for Catholics in Anglican England, an exclusion controversy arose when it was discovered that Charles's brother and heir James II was a Catholic. This controversy gave birth to two dominant political parties in England: the pro-exclusion Whig party and the anti-exclusion Tory party. While unsuccessful in excluding James II from becoming king upon Charles's death, the Whigs repeatedly blocked attempts by James to impose a French-style monarchy on the English people. The commonality of James's cultural vision with that of the French monarchy is explained by Steve Pincus (2009, 484):

While merchants yearned for a world in which economic, political, and social information was freely available, James saw informational transparency as politically dangerous. His cultural vision, not surprisingly, had much more in common with that of Louis XIV and Jean-Baptiste Colbert than it shared with that of James's father.

Under the reign of James II, both Whigs and Tories grew increasingly suspicious of France's intensions. Jean-Baptiste Colbert's system of accounting and financial control had made Louis XIV the richest prince in Christendom, and Louis was intent on using his great wealth to spread his influence across Europe. The increasing French influence was devastating for England, who soon ran up a large trade deficit with France. In contrast to the Whigs, however, the Tories felt that the Dutch were a greater threat to England than were the French. The Whigs praised the Dutch as defenders of liberty and industrious self-improvement, while the Tories criticized the Dutch as overly individualistic, ambitious, and economically Machiavellian (Pincus 2009). It soon became clear to both political parties, however, that England had to resist the influence of the French monarchy upon their nation. After consolidating political and financial support, and under the invitation of Parliament, William III, Prince of Orange invaded England in 1688. In 1689, he took the English throne jointly with his wife Mary II, the daughter of James II.

Upon returning to England from his self-imposed exile to the Netherlands in 1689, the Whig philosopher John Locke published his classic work on natural law and government, *Two Treatises of Government*. In his first treatise, Locke challenged the divine right of kings by referencing Biblical texts and historical examples. In his second treatise, he established a foundation for law and government based on the concept of natural law.

According to Locke, humans were entirely free and equal in their natural state. The law of nature, therefore, required that they be free, equal, and subject only to the will of the "infinitely wise maker." The purpose of civil government, according to Locke, was to enforce the law of nature and thereby protect the freedom and property of its citizens. Locke's views regarding natural law were so radical at the time that he originally published his Treatises anonymously. Yet, his views became the dominant perspective in Whig England and heavily influenced the English colonists in America. Locke's views on civil government largely paralleled the views of de la Court in the Netherlands over two decades earlier. Locke's views on natural law, however, were instrumental in establishing a new system of common law that supported free-market capitalism in Britain and the United States.

North and Weingast (1989) argue that the Glorious Revolution of 1688–1689 brought in institutions that put Britain on the path toward free-market capitalism and the first Industrial Revolution. In contrast, Pincus (2009) argues that the Glorious Revolution continued the process of modernization that had begun at the beginning of the seventeenth century with debates over the power of the English Church and continued with the English Commonwealth and Protectorate in the 1650s. Thus, formal and informal institutions in support of free-market capitalism were already in place by 1688. Rather than emerge rapidly in the wake of the Glorious Revolution, therefore, capitalist institutions emerged over the seventeenth century as a merchant culture slowly emerged. As in Italy and the Netherlands before it, this culture generated large cities with a populace dedicated to commerce and trade. By the end of the seventeenth century, for example, London had a population of around 575,000 people, which was 65,000 greater than Paris and more than twice the size of Amsterdam. The growing city of London soon became the new center for banking and international trade in Europe (Pincus 2009).

Similar to Italy and the Netherlands before them, Britain's merchant culture was supported by an education system that taught double-entry accounting and financial management. Accounting schools became common in English society, and by the end of the eighteenth century, they had increased to more than 200 (Soll 2014). Heavily influenced by the Protestant Reformation, these schools advanced the ideals of self-discipline, industry, scientific progress, and professional norms. The social norms taught in these schools provided a disciplined and hard-working populace, which further supported free-market capitalism. For example, by most accounts the average Englishman worked three times as many hours in a year as any other European (Burk 2007). The result was the wealth of England, which was the foundation for its imperial power and influence around the world. The strong merchant culture that evolved in Britain fueled great advances in science and technology, and led to the first Industrial Revolution from 1760 to 1840.

The influence of the monarchy culture in Britain, however, had not completely vanished. By the publication of Adam Smith's *Wealth of Nations* in 1776, Britain needed to be reminded of the aspects of the merchant culture that created the country's great wealth. In fact, Adam Smith used the British colonies in America rather than his own home country for his prime examples of free-market capitalism (Phillipson 2010). The establishment of the new nation also reflected the global struggle between the merchant culture and the monarchy culture. By the middle of the eighteenth century, there were approximately 1.5 million British colonists on the continent to only 70,000 French colonists (Burk 2007). Due to continuous fighting over territory and trading rights, England declared war on France in 1756. The French and Indian War lasted seven years, and the victory of the British solidified the influence of the merchant culture in the eyes of what were increasingly becoming American colonists. American leaders such as Benjamin Franklin, John Adams, and Thomas Jefferson were heavily influenced by John Locke and Scottish Enlightenment philosophers such as David Hume and Adam Smith. American colonists were also heavily influenced by the Protestant Reformation and a series of religious revivals on the continent called the "Great Awakening" and led by British Protestants such as Jonathan Edwards, John Wesley, and George Whitfield.

Kathleen Burk (2007) describes how the New World of the American colonies became increasingly similar to the Old World in Britain. In addition to sharing a common language and religion (predominantly Protestant), the two countries shared a common culture tied to Lockean principles of equality before the law, private property, and representative government. By the end of the French and Indian War in 1763, George III was king over Great Britain, and the influence of the Whig party in the Parliament was on the wane. By that time, however, the merchant culture of the Whigs had crossed the Atlantic and was firmly planted in American soil. Thus, it is not surprising that American colonists would seek their independence when King George and the Tory-dominated British Parliament began to infringe on their civil liberties. It is also not surprising that Americans who sought independence from Britain associated themselves with the Whig party while Loyalists associated themselves primarily with the Tory party. Some prominent British Whigs, including Adam

Smith, opposed the heavy hand of Parliament and supported the American colonists' quest for greater liberties and economic freedom (Phillipson 2010).

After the American War of Independence (1775–1783), however, the new nation formed a strong bond with the mother country (Burk 2007). By 1790, Britain received almost one-half of America's exports and supplied more than four-fifths of her imports. In addition to trade, Britain contributed considerable financial resources to help build the new nation, accounting for more than one-half of US bonds held abroad. British investors could be confident in US bonds because of the culture of transparency and accountability that had been planted in American soil. This culture was not always beneficial to the mother country, as when the United States kept a careful accounting of losses and claims relating to a warship named the *Alabama*, which Britain had built for the Confederate side during the US Civil War. Relations between the two countries were not fully normalized until Britain settled these claims in 1872, paying the United States $15.5 million in gold (Burk 2007). At first, the United States exported primarily raw materials and foodstuffs to Britain, including raw cotton, wheat, and tobacco. The second industrial revolution (1870–1914), which involved primarily US industries, allowed the new country to export manufactured goods to the mother country.

German sociologist and political economist Max Weber visited the United States in 1904 and provided a description of the merchant culture that had evolved in the new nation in his classic work, *The Protestant Ethic and the Spirit of Capitalism*, translated into English in 1930 (Scaff 2011). Weber associated the spirit of capitalism with the Protestant Reformation's view that secular work and profit were morally good, and used Benjamin Franklin and the American colonists as his prime examples. As with Britain, free-market capitalism was cultivated in the United States by a merchant culture that valued transparency and accountability. For example, Franklin learned double-entry accounting as a printer's apprentice and kept meticulous books throughout his life. He used his accounting training in his position as Postmaster General of the American colonies and later in his diplomatic missions representing the fledgling republic. This training helped Franklin manage America's international finances and loans. It is not surprising, therefore, that he viewed accounting as essential to good government and recommended that families teach it to their children (Soll 2014). George Washington also kept meticulous records of his spending during the Revolutionary War and promptly produced them when his enemies accused him of profiting from the war.

INDUSTRIAL REVOLUTIONS IN BRITAIN
AND THE UNITED STATES

A number of factors came together in Britain between the late middle ages and the mid-eighteenth century to fuel the first industrial revolution in 1760–1840. Cultural factors included the replacement of medieval Catholicism with enlightenment Protestantism, the adoption by the upper classes of a mechanical worldview inspired by Isaac Newton and the Scientific Revolution, and the spread of that worldview to the working classes through an expansion of literacy in reading and mathematics (Allen 2009). Noncultural factors included the emergence of plentiful coal supplies, a continuous supply of productive labor, an unmatched banking system, manufacturing industries, and the strongest navy in the world to keep international trade routes open and safe. Britain had also built a strong transportation infrastructure of roads, canals, railroads, and naval shipping. These factors gave Britain a large advantage in manufacturing and shipping, and helped the small island nation maintain a comfortable lead of about a century over other European countries in being the first industrial nation (Burk 2007).

Soll (2014) emphasizes the role of Britain's merchant culture in fueling the first industrial revolution. Supported by representative government, the Protestant Reformation, and an education system that taught double-entry accounting and financial management, Britain's merchant culture was unique up until that time. Almost two centuries after Francis Bacon had invented the scientific method, and nearly a century after Isaac Newton had discovered the laws of the heavens, English merchants married scientific rationalism with good accounting to generate great advances in technology and commerce. For example, Josiah Wedgwood used advanced accounting and financial control to increase productivity and profitability in his china company, and James Watt used advanced accounting methods to gain a competitive advantage in his industrial production of the steam engine. Watt's innovations in accounting and steam engine technology at the University of Glasgow were well known by Adam Smith, whose own knowledge of accounting and finance served him well in his role as administrator at the university and later as Commissioner of Customs in Scotland (Phillipson 2010).

At the beginning of the first industrial revolution, the United States was a developing country in need of both capital and labor. The first of Britain's new industries to migrate to the United States was the textile industry. The first water-powered cotton mill was constructed in Lancashire,

England in 1764. By 1812, managers and workers from Lancashire, Yorkshire, and Scotland had crossed the Atlantic to establish textile mills and factories in Massachusetts (Burk 2007). During this time, the firm underwent significant change (Chandler 1977, Johnson and Kaplan 1987). Before the first industrial revolution, raw materials and intermediate inputs going into the production of clothing were priced by markets formed by independent contractors. For example, spinners were paid per pound for yarn, weavers were paid per yard for cloth, and assemblers were paid per unit of clothing. During the first industrial revolution, spinners, weavers, and assemblers were hired by the firm and brought into the factory. Internalizing these former market transactions required advances in managerial accounting and control, as the firm now had to determine prices for all the factors of production. In particular, the accounting system now needed to keep track of the efficiency with which a textile factory used cotton and labor time.

With the end of the US Civil War in 1865, the young country could now dedicate its energy and resources to the development of its own industrial power. This led to a second industrial revolution in the United States from 1870 to 1920. The completion of the transcontinental railways meant that the entire country was open for economic development. As her population grew, so did the demand for new products and means of shipping those products. As a result, hundreds of new industries were established. Further, developing markets in New York provided capital to support the expanding economy. In 1871, America's manufacturing output was one-quarter that of Britain's, US coal production was one-eleventh that of the mother country, and US steel production was almost nonexistent. By the end of the century, however, America's manufacturing output had increased to seventy percent of Britain's, US coal production had almost pulled even, and US steel production was twice that of Britain's. Thereafter, the automobile industry, advances in manufacturing techniques such as the assembly line, and the industrial buildup to World War I created the conditions for further industrial growth. The result of the second industrial revolution is that the United States surpassed Britain as the strongest economic power in the world, and New York surpassed London as the world's center of banking and international trade (Burke 2007).

Industries in the United States at the beginning of the second industrial revolution included iron and steel, foodstuffs, petroleum, chemicals, and machinery. These industries required bigger and more complex organizations, requiring further developments in the firm. The story of the US steel industry is illustrative. Andrew Carnegie migrated with his family to the United States from Scotland in 1848. Beginning as a laborer changing spools of thread in a cotton mill in Pittsburgh, he eventually worked his way up in the Pittsburgh Railroad Company as a telegraph operator and manager and was instrumental in helping the Union transport troops and supplies during the US Civil War. After the war, Carnegie amassed a huge fortune investing in steel mills before donating almost ninety percent of it to charity. Similar to Josiah Wedgwood in his British china factories, Carnegie used accounting and financial control as a competitive advantage. In particular, he used detailed cost information to push his direct costs below that of his competitors so that he could ensure sufficient demand to keep his plants running at full capacity, even during economic recessions. Weekly data on direct material and conversion costs for each process in his mills was sufficient information for Carnegie to invest more capital and earn higher returns than any other steelmaker in the nineteenth century (Johnson and Kaplan 1987).

Another US industry that expanded rapidly during the second industrial revolution is the railroad industry. Fueled by new iron and steam-power technologies, railroad mileage tripled from 1849 to 1856 (Burk 2007). This rapid expansion required a massive influx of capital, and led to $350 million of railroad stock listed on the New York Stock Exchange by 1869 (Soll 2014). By the 1870s, the United States had 51,000 miles of track, which was as much as Britain, Europe, and the rest of the world had at the time. To manage the large volume of transactions over an increasing expanse of miles, railroad companies had to develop advanced accounting systems and financial controls. Tracks, landholdings, coal supplies, stations, ticket sales, freight, and personnel costs had to be carefully recorded and tracked. Teams of accountants from each division of the railroad were required to record transactions and then send the results to the central office. Importantly, advanced accounting procedures were needed to record and control cash at hundreds of locations throughout the country. Thus, the rapid growth of the railroad industry required advances not only in accounting and control, but also in communication technologies such as the telegraph.

A NEW OPPORTUNISM CULTURE EMERGES

The massive scale of railroads in America marked the advent of "big business" (Johnson and Kaplan 1987). It also laid bare, however, the difficulty of maintaining transparency and accountability with large, complex firms (Soll 2014). As capital poured into US railroads from around the globe, vast fortunes were made by "robber barons" who created their wealth through opaque public reporting, insider trading, and stock price manipulation. Jay Gould, for example, used secrecy and stock manipulation to gain control of both the Atlantic and Great Western Railroad and the Erie Railroad. While great fortunes were being made by opaque public reporting and stock manipulation, fortunes were also being lost. The US government soon took steps to correct these and other potential weaknesses that the second industrial revolution had uncovered in the US capitalist system. First, Congress created the Interstate Commerce Commission in 1887 to regulate the railroad industry. Next, Congress passed the Sherman Antitrust Act in 1890 to break up the great monopolies and trusts that had put too much power into too few hands. Private institutions also took an active role in protecting investors. New York began requiring financial audits for publicly traded firms in 1849, and the American Association of Public Accountants was established in 1887. Motivated by the lack of financial information on railroad securities, John Moody began publishing his *Manual of Industrial Statistics* in 1900, which eventually led to the largest bond rating agency in the world.

The industrial revolutions in Britain and the United States increased the size and complexity of the firm, and some entrepreneurs used this complexity to profit at the expense of less informed investors. This spawned a new culture of opportunism based on a lack of transparency and accountability. The opportunism culture of this era is epitomized by J. P. Morgan's quip in 1901, "I owe the public nothing" (Marchand 1998). As the influence of large firms in society grew, this culture of social and moral indifference imposed itself on the whole nation (Khurana 2007). The consequences of the new opportunism culture would soon become apparent. In 1926, William Ripley, a Harvard economics professor, wrote a prophetic article in the *Atlantic Monthly* entitled, "Stop, Look, Listen! The Shareholder's Right to Adequate Information." In the article, Ripley predicted that the current lack of financial transparency would undermine the US economy. At the time, there were no rules to govern corporate financial reporting or public disclosures. Publicly traded companies frequently did not report their earnings or provide balance sheets with accrued liabilities. As a result, the public did not have the information needed to make sound financial investments. Similar to the Dutch East India Company three centuries before, stock prices were based primarily on speculation and marketplace rumors.

Despite Ripley's warning, trading on the New York Stock Exchange (NYSE) continued unabated through the end of the Roaring Twenties.

On October 24, 1929, however, the NYSE experienced a large sell-off that quickly spread across all world markets. Over the next five days, the NYSE lost more than thirty percent of its value, which contributed to the onset of the Great Depression. By 1933, stock prices had dropped eighty-nine percent, wiping out millions of investors. The lack of financial transparency in the stock market did end up undermining the US economy, which did not fully recover until 1940. Despite Franklin Roosevelt's New Deal programs, unemployment remained in double digits throughout the 1930s. At its lowest point, gross domestic product had dropped thirty percent, 9,000 banks had failed, and unemployment had reached twenty-five percent. As Soll (2014, 192) explains:

Never had an economy so rich and so sophisticated, based largely on publicly traded stock, been allowed to remain so opaque.

The US government went into action to increase regulation and oversight. In 1933, Congress enacted the Glass-Steagall Act, which separated the activities of investment and commercial banking to prevent investment banks from putting depositors' funds at risk. In 1934, the Roosevelt administration established the Securities and Exchange Commission (SEC) to standardize accounting and reporting for publicly traded companies. The SEC was charged with increasing financial transparency, limiting insider trading, and banning preferred stock lists that had given some investors special privileges over other, less-connected investors. The task of standardizing accounting and reporting for publicly traded companies, however, was largely delegated to members of the accounting profession. Thus, while the SEC required all publicly held companies to provide financial reports that were audited for their conformance to Generally Accepted Accounting Principles (GAAP), the responsibility for creating and updating those accounting principles was left to independent boards made up primarily of Certified Public Accountants.

The beginning of the US accounting profession can be traced to British accountants in the early nineteenth century. By the 1840s, accounting firms had appeared throughout Britain in response to the growth of large-scale organizations and the introduction of income taxation (Parker 1986). Deloitte, Price Waterhouse, Whinney Smith & Whinney (now Ernst & Young), Touche, and many other accounting firms appeared in London, the Midlands, and Edinburgh. British accountants first migrated to the United States to protect British investments that had been made in the young nation. Sometime after the 1870s, these accounting firms established offices in the United States to handle the emergence of large corporations during the second industrial revolution. In 1900, Arthur Dickinson moved from his home in London to head the New York office of Price Waterhouse. He found US business fast-paced, unpredictable, and largely unregulated. In particular, he discovered that annual audits – always the backbone of business in England – were few in number and dubious in quality (Soll 2014).

In 1913, Arthur Andersen began a uniquely American accounting firm in Chicago. The son of Norwegian immigrants and trained by Price Waterhouse & Company, Andersen was meticulous about audit quality and independence, insisting that auditors answer first and foremost to investors. To teach auditors his high standards of accuracy, discipline, and moral rectitude, Andersen created his own accounting university on a 55,000-acre campus in St. Charles, Illinois. His firm, however, had a more modern view of the role of the accounting profession in the economy. In contrast to British-based accounting firms, Andersen believed that accountants could also act as consultants for their audit clients (Soll 2014). By 1970, with competition growing between the Big Eight accounting firms (Price Waterhouse; Deloitte, Haskins & Sells; Peat Marwick Mitchell; Arthur Andersen; Touche Ross; Coopers & Lybrand; Ernst & Whinney; and Arthur Young), other firms joined Andersen in pursuing lucrative consulting contracts with their audit clients.

The accounting profession soon came under the influence of the opportunism culture. Rather than serving as impartial referees with the highest standards of audit quality and independence, audit firms became ineffective in exposing misleading financial statements and even acted as skilled enablers of financial fraud (Soll 2014). Under a hail of lawsuits against Big Eight accounting firms in 1976, Congress finally stepped in with an investigative committee led by Democratic senator Lee Metcalf. The Metcalf Committee Report criticized the practice of accounting firms providing consulting services for their audit clients, calling it incompatible with the responsibility of auditors to be independent. Given that consulting yielded fees ranging in the tens of millions of dollars, however, accounting firms used their influence to continue the practice. The pursuit of consulting contracts on audit engagements continued unabated, with consulting fees growing in relation to audit fees. In 1989, a consolidation frenzy hit the US accounting profession as Deloitte, Haskins & Sells merged with Touche Ross to form Deloitte & Touche, and Ernst & Whinney merged with Arthur Young to form Ernst & Young.

At about this same time, advances in technology generated the longest bull market in US history, lasting from the end of 1987 to the beginning of

2000. In what would later be called the "dot-com" bubble, this stock market boom fueled an explosion in mergers and acquisitions and created a new generation of high-tech mega-firms. Because of the strong reputation of their consulting arm, Andersen provided both audit and consulting services to many of these large firms, including Enron and WorldCom. As a result, Andersen's consulting fees soon eclipsed its auditing fees. The old, staid culture of transparency and accountability was soon replaced by a high-flying, performance-oriented culture as consulting partners began to assert their influence on the firm. Andersen Consulting required plush, well-furnished offices and lucrative pay packages based on financial incentives for sales performance. Increasingly, Andersen's corporate culture reflected the opportunism culture of the early railroad industry rather than the merchant culture of the accounting profession (Squires, Smith, McDougall, and Yeack 2003; Toffler 2003).

The consequences of this opportunism culture soon became apparent. Under the Energy Policy Act of 1992, Congress allowed states to deregulate their electricity utilities, opening them up to greater competition. Enron quickly took advantage of the new deregulatory environment, purchasing utility and energy firms based on its rising stock price. In 1997, Jeffrey Skilling was promoted to chief operating officer, second only to CEO Kenneth Lay. Skilling set out to hire the best talent, recruiting only from top MBA programs and investment banks, and rewarded his new talent with merit-based bonuses that had no cap (Thomas 2002). As stock prices fell in 2000, however, it became increasingly difficult for Enron to meet analysts' earnings projections and the required leverage ratios of rating agencies. In response, Enron began to inflate its income and keep liabilities off of its balance sheet through the use of special purpose entities (SPEs), which essentially were divisions of the firm reported as independent companies. As predicted in an e-mail to Lay by whistle-blower Sherron Watkins, Enron soon imploded in a wave of accounting scandals (Morse and Bower 2002). Named by Fortune as "America's Most Innovative Company" for six years in a row, Enron filed for bankruptcy in December 2001. The fall of Enron cost investors $11 billion. Skilling's disdain for accounting and accountability was conveyed by his testimony before congress in February 2002. He stated multiple times that he was not an accountant, and was therefore unaware of the accounting scandals perpetuated under his watch. This defense was ineffective, however, as Skilling was convicted of federal felony charges and sentenced to 24 years in prison.

Enron's bankruptcy was the largest in US history until WorldCom's bankruptcy in July 2002, with assets of $63 billion compared to WorldCom's $104 billion. WorldCom's accounting scandal, however, was much simpler. Rather than expense monthly costs of cell phone service, WorldCom capitalized and depreciated the costs over future periods, in violation of GAAP. In effect, the company treated monthly utility expenses like long-term investments. An internal auditor, Cynthia Cooper, uncovered the creative accounting and approached Andersen, but was told matter-of-factly that it was not a problem (Ripley 2002). Both Enron and WorldCom were audited by Andersen, and both firms had lucrative consulting contracts with the accounting firm. The accounting scandals and related audit failures at these large corporations quickly took down Andersen. After the Justice Department secured an obstruction of justice confession from the lead partner on the Enron audit in 2002, Andersen told the SEC that it would no longer audit the books of public companies. Once an accounting and consulting giant with 85,000 staff worldwide, Andersen currently employs only a skeleton staff to manage its continuing litigation (Squires et al. 2003, Toffler 2003).

Similar to the stock market crash that ended the Roaring Twenties, the stock market crash that ended the dot-com bubble led to increased government regulation and oversight. In 2002, Congress passed the Sarbanes-Oxley Act (SOX) to strengthen corporate governance and enact sweeping reforms in the accounting industry. SOX requires all CEOs and CFOs of US-registered companies to certify the honesty of their financial reports. Congress clearly remembered Jeffrey Skilling's attempts to deny knowledge of Enron's accounting manipulations. SOX also makes it unlawful for accounting firms to provide nonaudit services, including tax services, unless the activities are preapproved by the audit committee of the client company's board, and totally bans the provision of eight other categories of nonaudit services. The new legislation also requires the rotation of the lead audit partner and any reviewing partner from a client account after five years. SOX also requires auditors to audit and provide assurance of the effectiveness of the internal controls of the client. The centerpiece of the Act, however, is the creation of the Public Company Accounting Oversight Board (PCAOB). Although the SEC retains oversight and enforcement authority, the new regulatory body is empowered to oversee the quality of audits and initiate its own audits of the audit firms (Squires et al. 2003).

THE OPPORTUNISM CULTURE NEARLY TAKES DOWN THE FINANCIAL SYSTEM

Another Act of Congress, however, made investors increasingly vulnerable by removing an important safeguard that had been in place since the Great Depression. In 1999, Congress repealed the Glass-Steagall Act and replaced it with the Gramm-Leach-Bliley Act. The new Act consolidated the activities of investment and commercial banking, allowing commercial banks to not only take deposits and make loans, but also underwrite and sell securities. This included the underwriting and selling of mortgage-backed securities. As part of the New Deal in 1938, Congress established the Federal National Mortgage Association (Fannie Mae) to purchase certain mortgages from originators and securitize them for resale. Fannie Mae went public in 1970, the same year that the federal government allowed it to purchase conventional mortgages, and issued its first mortgage-backed security in 1981. The Gramm-Leach-Bliley Act, along with mounting pressure from Congress to expand mortgage lending to low- and moderate-income borrowers, increased the mortgage-backed security activities of Fannie Mae and the more recently formed Federal Home Loan Mortgage Corporation (Freddie Mac). These policy changes also increased the mortgage lending activities of banks and loan originators, who were also encouraged to make loans that had a higher risk of default. This gave birth to the "subprime" mortgage with teaser rates and low underwriting standards.

The repeal of Glass-Steagall, combined with other economic and political factors, created a perfect storm of opportunism that nearly took down the world financial system (Financial Crisis Inquiry Commission 2011, FCIC hereafter). At the turn of the new century, the Federal Reserve had cut interest rates to stimulate economic growth after the dot-com crash. Low interest rates and the highly liquid market in mortgage-backed securities, combined with an influx in foreign capital, caused money to wash through the economy "like water rushing through a broken dam" (FCIC 2011, 5). Mortgage lenders such as New Century Financial, Ameriquest, and American Home Mortgage paid their loan originators huge bonuses for loan volume that included subprime mortgages. Meanwhile, bond brokers on Wall Street earned huge bonuses packaging and selling new kinds of mortgage loans in new kinds of investment products that were deemed to be safe but possessed complex and hidden risks. While Fannie and Freddie initially focused on securitizing prime mortgages, Wall Street focused on the higher-yield loans that were either "subprime" or "Alt-A" (between prime and subprime). By 2005 and 2006, Wall Street was secur-itizing one-third more loans than Fannie and Freddie, and more than seventy percent of them were subprime or Alt-A loans (FCIC 2011). Losing market share to Wall Street, Fannie and Freddie soon loosened their underwriting standards, purchasing and guaranteeing riskier loans. From 2005 to 2008, Fannie and Freddie also began to purchase subprime and Alt-A mortgage-backed securities from Wall Street.

The torrent of liquidity now rushing into the mortgage market gener-ated a moral hazard all along the mortgage securitization chain. Mortgage brokers were compensated based on the volume of loans generated rather than on the performance and quality of the loans made. Meanwhile, mortgage securitizers were compensated on the basis of the number of new mortgage-backed securities created and sold to investors. Thus, agents all along the mortgage chain were paid enormous sums for making risky investments, even if these same investments could result in signifi-cant losses for investors and taxpayers. For the long-term health of the financial system, every participant along the securitization chain should have been motivated to maintain transparency and accountability. Instead, they were motivated to hide their private information from participants further down the chain. Normal safeguards proved ineffec-tive at protecting investors from this moral hazard, as government policy at the time promoted market deregulation and mortgage lending to previously disadvantaged groups. Accounting firms were unable to stem the tide of subprime mortgage lending and securitization. The bond rating agencies not only failed to conduct diligent reviews of the quality of the mortgages in the mortgage-backed securities, they also frequently failed to check to see that the mortgages were what the securitizers said that they were (FCIC 2011).

Why didn't Wall Street investment firms step in to protect the interests of investors and taxpayers against this moral hazard? The answer lies, at least in part, on the aggressive actions of the Federal Reserve in bailing out Long Term Capital Management (LTCM) in 1998. LTCM was founded in 1994 by John Meriwether, a University of Chicago MBA and former vice chair and head of bond trading at Solomon Brothers (Lowenstein 2000). Well trained in the modern finance theory emanating from the Chicago school, Meriwether recruited leading scholars in finance to help guide his hedge fund, including Robert Merton of Harvard University and Myron Scholes of Stanford University. Merton and Scholes shared the 1997 Nobel Prize in Economic Science for creating a new method of determining the value of derivatives. Implementing leveraged bond strategies, LTCM earned spectacular returns in the first four years of 19.9 percent, 42.8 percent, 40.8 percent, and 17.1 percent, respectively. In 1998, however, LTCM lost $4.6 billion in less than four months following the Russian bond crisis. This loss represented more than eighty percent of its nearly $5 billion in capital, but the firm had further leveraged itself by entering into $1 trillion in derivatives contracts with many of the largest commercial and investment banks. To avoid a market collapse, the Federal Reserve negotiated an orderly liquidation of LTCM's securities and derivatives with many of the same banks and securities firms. The clear message from LTCM was that even modern finance theory could not avoid the downside of bond market risk. The message that Wall Street received, however, was that financial firms deemed "too big to fail" could expect a bailout from the Fed (FCIC 2011).

Wall Street firms either failed to understand or chose to ignore how dangerously exposed the banking system had become to contagion effects of risky mortgage-backed securities. By the third quarter of 2006, home prices were falling and mortgage delinquencies were on the rise. Despite these warning signs, Wall Street kept ordering up mortgage loans, packaging them into securities, taking profits, and earning bonuses. By the end of 2007, however, most of the subprime mortgage lenders had failed or been acquired. In January 2008, Bank of America announced that it would be acquiring the ailing subprime lender Countrywide. Bear Stearns was bought by J.P. Morgan with government assistance in the spring. By the end of the summer, Fannie and Freddie were in conservatorship. Instead of getting better, the financial system continued to deteriorate. In September, Lehman Brothers failed, and the remaining investment banks, Merrill Lynch, Goldman Sachs, and Morgan Stanley, struggled to survive. AIG, with its massive credit default swap portfolio, was bailed out by the federal government. Large commercial banks were not spared the carnage. Washington Mutual became the largest bank failure in US history in September, and Wachovia struck a deal to be acquired by Wells Fargo in October while Citigroup and Bank of America fought to stay afloat. Before it was over, the federal government was on the hook for trillions of dollars through more than two dozen programs aimed at stabilizing the financial system and propping up the nation's largest financial institutions (FCIC 2011, 23).

As with former stock market crashes after the Roaring Twenties and the dot-com bubble, the market crash of 2008 was fueled by an opportunism culture that did not value transparency and accountability. In addition to the opportunism of actors up and down the mortgage securitization chain, important players who were supposed to protect investors and taxpayers were corrupted by the culture. For example, the bond rating agencies could have stopped the disaster in its tracks. Bond rating agencies evolved from the lack of transparency in the railroad industry during the second industrial revolution. In the late nineteenth century, John Moody saw that there was a lack of useful information on the emerging railroad giants, and that a high percentage of the securities of such corporations "had to be bought on faith rather than knowledge" (Moody 1946, 90). He first began publishing his *Manual of Industrial Statistics* in 1900. The 1907 financial crisis was so severe that it forced Moody to sell the company that published his manual, John Moody & Company. In 1909, however, Moody founded a new company that issued independent credit ratings for bonds. Poor's issued their first credit rating in 1916 followed by Standard Statistics Company in 1922. Following the merger of the last two companies, there are now only two major bond rating agencies – Moody's Investor Services (Moody's) and its competitor, Standard & Poor's (S&P). Smaller bond rating agencies include Fitch Ratings (Fitch) and a multitude of minor domestic rating agencies around the globe.

Similar to the accounting profession, bond rating agencies are paid by the very institutions whose bonds they rate. The purpose of bond rating agencies is to provide surveillance to see who is violating the prevailing norm of creditworthiness. This is based on the institutionalized belief that "repaying debt is morally right and obligatory" (Sinclair 2005, 66). Auditors and bond raters serve the same function in that they support and preserve the social norm of creditworthiness through their reputation for neutrality, objectivity, and expertise. Both auditors and bond raters, however, are subject to corruption and failure to uphold normal standards of professional conduct. For example, similar to Andersen, rating agencies were held liable for their role in enabling the Enron accounting scandal. The rating agencies were central to enabling Enron's scandal for two reasons: (1) maintaining an investment-grade rating allowed Enron to go on raising new funds, and (2) maintaining an investment-grade rating allowed Enron to avoid loan covenant "triggers" that would have caused its loans to come due (Partnoy 2003). When Moody's, Standard & Poor's, and Fitch continued to rate Enron's bonds investment grade until four days before it declared bankruptcy, therefore, they played as significant a role as did Andersen in enabling Enron's accounting scandal.

Similar to their role in keeping Enron afloat, the rating agencies played a central role in enabling the opportunism up and down the mortgage securitization chain. High bond ratings allowed bond issuers to receive approval for their creatively structured mortgage-backed securities, allowed banks and other financial institutions to hold less capital for the bonds, and expanded the type of investors who could hold the bonds in their portfolio. Rather than support the norm of creditworthiness, serving as impartial referees with the highest standards of quality and independence, the bond rating agencies became enablers of the opportunistic players along the mortgage securitization chain (FCIC 2011). First, the rating agencies used antiquated models based, in part, on periods of relatively strong credit performance. Second, the rating agencies did not adequately account for the deterioration of underwriting standards or the possibility of housing prices going down. Third, the rating agencies did not adequately adjust their models to take into account the layered risks of the subprime mortgage securities. Thus, the high credit ratings of mortgage-backed securities by Moody's, Standard & Poor's, and Fitch perpetuated the stock market bubble, and their downgrades through 2007 and 2008 magnified the subsequent market crash.

This history of the firm provides the following insights. First, the social norms of transparency and accountability from the merchant culture are essential to free-market economies in that they assure the flow of investment capital and the proper functioning of organizations and capital markets. This merchant culture of transparency and accountability, however, is difficult to maintain and has frequently been abandoned in favor of an opportunism culture of opaqueness and opportunistic self-interest. When this opportunism culture of greed and corruption becomes apparent and threatens the economy, government regulation and oversight reduce flexibility and freedom, which is consistent with a monarchy culture. Private capitalist institutions, such as external auditing and the bond rating industry, play an important role in maintaining transparency and accountability in free-market economies, but they too are subject to corruption by the opportunism culture. Thus, government regulation plays an important role in maintaining the merchant culture. The appropriate size of that role, given the temptation of opportunism on the one hand and the threat of monarchy on the other, is a constant challenge to policy makers in free-market economies. Unfortunately, the theory of the firm that emanated from the Chicago school provides little support for the merchant culture and few insights regarding the proper role of government in maintaining that culture. The following chapter addresses this theory of the firm, including its history and emerging characteristics.

3

The Theory of the Firm

INTRODUCTION

Why firms form, why they take the forms that they do, and how they can best be managed and controlled are questions of particular interest to theorists. Theory related to the firm spans multiple disciplines, including accounting, business law, economics, finance, management science, moral philosophy, and psychology. In this chapter, I introduce the theory of the firm as it has developed in the academic disciplines of economics, accounting, and finance. I begin by discussing the forces that led to the founding and shaping of the university-based business school. The story of the university-based business school is, in many respects, the story of the theory of the firm. The development of large, multi-divisional firms required advanced systems of accounting and financial control as well as a new army of trained managers. In response to this demand, business schools were established first at the University of Pennsylvania in 1881 followed by the University of Chicago and the University of California at Berkeley in 1898. The university-based business school was founded on the idea that business management could be made into a profession similar to the traditional professions of law and medicine. In the first forty years of the new institution, prominent business school deans voiced this founding ideal by emphasizing professional norms as well as technical business skills.

Next, I discuss the decay and abandonment of professional norms in the university-based business school. In its own quest for legitimacy, the discipline of economics moved increasingly away from the historical method of institutional economics toward the analytical method of neoclassical economics. During World War II and the Cold War, neoclassical theory proved its value in helping defeat fascism and Soviet communism.

This caused institutional economists to lose stature and influence relative to neoclassical economists. The growing influence of neoclassical economic theory eventually impacted the university-based business school, which had been founded largely by institutional economists. In 1959, the Carnegie Foundation and the Ford Foundation issued book-length reports that were highly critical of business school education within the university. The effect of these reports was the continued embrace of neoclassical theory by the university-based business school. Other developments, including the failure of science and the research university to provide a unifying basis for moral instruction and character development, led to the abandonment of the professionalism project. I then describe the growing influence of neoclassical theory and the Chicago school in economics, accounting, and finance.

I conclude this chapter by describing neoclassical economic theories of the firm. The Chicago school used Adam Smith as the poster child for their view of efficient markets and limited government. Thus, I present key insights regarding markets and the firm from his classic work on political economy, *The Wealth of Nations*. To provide an economic explanation for the formation of firms, neoclassical theorists first relied on market failure and the opportunity for monopoly power. Next, neoclassical theorists developed comprehensive theories of the firm that seriously considered the behavioral implications of the visible hand of managerialism, including transaction-cost theory and agency theory. Combined with new developments in finance theory, including the efficient market hypothesis, agency theory reduced the responsibility of management to the maximization of stock price. Given the poor performance of the US economy and the growth of large conglomerates in the 1970s and early 1980s, this powerful theory of the firm made increasing sense whereas other theories emphasizing management's responsibility to multiple stakeholders seemed outdated and inefficient.

THE FOUNDING OF THE UNIVERSITY-BASED BUSINESS SCHOOL

The university has played an important role in generating and communicating new knowledge in Western society, especially in the modern era. Yet, many see the current state of the university as one of crisis and ruin (Readings 1996). Similarly, the ability of the university-based business school to fulfill its founding ideals has been brought into question (Khurana 2007, Miles 2016). Recent criticisms leveled against the university-based business school include that it produces research that is largely ignored by the business community as irrelevant (Pfeffer and Fong 2002), that few innovations in business have been developed within its walls (Skapinker 2008), and that it has created a new class of business faculty with narrowly focused research specializations, little business experience, and little interest in the critical problems facing business (Crowther and Carter 2002, Bennis and O'Toole 2005). Last but not least, the university-based business school has been blamed for much of the irresponsible decision-making and unethical behavior of its graduates (Ghoshal 2005, Podolny 2009).

The modern-day university traces its roots to the medieval universities of Europe, including those in Bologna, Paris, Oxford, Vicenza, and Cambridge. The oldest continually operating university is the University of Bologna in northern Italy, which is believed to have been founded in 1088. It is also the first institution of higher learning to use the term *universitas* to describe the corporations of students and masters whose existence had been recognized by the civil authorities. Early colleges and universities in Europe were funded either by the church or the state. In the former case, the main purpose of the institution was the training of clergy through the teaching of theology and the liberal arts. In the latter case, the main purpose of the institution was the training of civil servants through the teaching of professions such as law, medicine, and later, accounting (Soll 2014). In medieval times, the notion of a complete university was a Faculty of Arts and three "superior faculties" of Theology, Law, and Medicine. In contrast to the view that they are quasi-academic late-comers to the institution, therefore, the professions played a significant role in the formation and development of the university (Miles 2016).

Similar to the first English universities at Oxford and Cambridge, the first US universities were founded as sectarian institutions designed to train students in theology and the liberal arts (e.g., Harvard 1636, William and Mary 1693, Yale 1701). In contrast, Benjamin Franklin sought to found an institution of higher learning that stimulated knowledge in the natural sciences and business professions. In 1749, Franklin wrote a fundraising pamphlet describing the kind of academy he envisioned in his home state of Pennsylvania (Isaacson 2003, 146–147). He argued that the prospective academy should focus not just on theology and the classics, but also on practical instruction such as grammar, arithmetic, accounting, and business skills, with "regard being had to the several professions for which they are intended." Franklin envisioned an academy that served the interests of society, giving students "an inclination joined with an ability to serve mankind, one's country, friends, and family." The new academy opened in January 1751 and became known as the University of Pennsylvania by 1791. While founded on the Protestant religion, the new academy was unique at the time in that it was nonsectarian and based on the broad multidisciplinary model of the medieval university. Franklin remained a trustee of the institution for the rest of his life and considered it one of his proudest achievements.

Early Acts of Congress supported Franklin's conviction that institutions of higher learning should provide practical benefits for both students and the state. As part of the Northwest Ordinance of 1787, the Second Continental Congress encouraged the establishment of state colleges and universities based on the needs of civil government. Later, the Morrill Act of 1862 established state land-grant colleges with a particular focus on agriculture and the "mechanical arts." Radical new ideas regarding the role of the university in society, however, would soon impact the US university. Under the visionary guidance of Wilhelm von Humboldt, the University of Berlin was founded in 1810 on the belief that the university should be free of religious or political influence. The purpose of the new institution was the development of knowledge through independent, academic research conducted across multiple disciplines. Americans soon sought graduate degrees in Germany and returned as trained academic researchers. This trend led to the founding of the first US research university at Johns Hopkins in 1876 followed by other research-focused universities at Clark University in 1887 and the University of Chicago in 1892.

Understanding why the research university failed to live up to its founding ideals helps explain the current state of the university-based business school. Humboldt's bold vision was to form an independent, enlightened community of scholars where "all that concerns the moral culture of the nation comes together" (Wittrock, 1993, 328). Instead, the new institution formed a growing collection of increasingly narrow academic disciplines that were incapable of communicating with each other (Miles 2016). In the face of declining religious belief due to Darwinian evolution and German higher criticism of Scripture, the research university turned to science as a basis for moral instruction and character formation. When the natural and social sciences turned out to be an insufficient source for unifying truth, however, modernism gave way to postmodernism, and the university became the multiversity (Reuben 1996). Another reason the research university has failed to live up to its founding ideals is its organizational structure. The student-master corporations at the University of Bologna were essentially craft guilds, and they petitioned the authorities to be recognized as such (Pedersen 1997). The medieval craft guilds were monopolies, typically granted by a civil authority, that gave its members the power to set all standards for membership and practice within a licensed domain (Lambert 1891). Similarly, the modern university is made up of academic guilds or disciplines that have the power to determine the standards for membership and practice.

While medieval craft guilds died out centuries ago, academic guilds are alive and well in the modern university (Miles 2016). Similar to craft guilds, academic guilds specialize to a greater degree over time (Khurana and Spender 2012). For example, the university has presided over the separation of business disciplines from economics departments and the increasing specialization of theory and methods within the business disciplines. In addition to the separation of finance from accounting, for example, the discipline of accounting has split into multiple specialties. Academic journals have evolved for economics-based accounting research, psychology-based accounting research, and topical research related to auditing, tax, systems, financial accounting, and managerial accounting. In *The Wealth of Nations*, Adam Smith (*WN* I.x.c.27) identified the formation of craft guilds as "a conspiracy against the public" because of the emphasis of such guilds on their own self-interest rather than the interest of the general public. Thus, it is not surprising that the university-based business school has insulated itself from the broader interests of business and society.

Similar to prior capitalist economies in the Netherlands and Great Britain, private business colleges sprang up in the United States well before the first university-based business school. As the firm grew in size and complexity, increasing numbers of accountants, clerical workers, and managers were needed. In response to this growing demand, private business colleges sprang up in the 1820s in large commercial cities such as Boston and New York. By 1893, more than 500 such schools existed across the country, including one in almost every small city. Thus, the incorporation of business schools within the US research university was neither obvious nor inevitable. By the end of the century, however, Humboldt's vision for the research university had captured the American imagination. The aspirations for the research university included the molding of students into a force for civic virtue, the training of new political leaders who would clean up the body politic, and the provision of rational substitutes for religious or political views subject to personal influence (Veysey 1965). Thus, the public's attitude toward the emerging research university took on a "quasi-sacred" character (Shils and Altbach 1997). At the same time, the public's view of business began to crumble due to irresponsible acts committed during the second industrial revolution. Entrepreneurs who had prospered during this period began looking for ways to legitimize their wealth and repair their seedy reputations (Khurana 2007). Salaried business managers also lacked social status and moral legitimacy, and sought to shape their image as trustworthy stewards of economic resources. Within this environment, a consortium of supporters leveraged their social and economic resources to establish business education within the three institutions that had already achieved high status and legitimacy in society: the professions, science, and the research university.

Rakesh Khurana (2007) provides an insightful history of the university-based business school in his book, *From Higher Aims to Hired Hands: The Social Transformation of American Business Schools and the Unfulfilled Promise of Management as a Profession*. Khurana describes the great difficulty that its founders had in establishing the university-based business school. The research university had already forged new alliances with the traditional professions of theology, medicine, and law by the end of the nineteenth century, and the founders desired to put the business profession on the same high moral footing. The challenge was not financial resources, as the founders of the new institution included many wealthy benefactors. The challenge was that the business profession lacked the prestige of the traditional professions. When managers first began to appear in large firms, the general public had little understanding of the work they performed or the value they created. Further, managers had no formal training and possessed no educational credentials to demonstrate their worth. Finally, many viewed managers as simply "hired hands" whose only purpose was to generate profits for the owners of the firm.

In 1881, Joseph Wharton donated $100,000 to found the first university-based business school at the institution of higher learning founded by Benjamin Franklin. Wharton, a devout Pennsylvania Quaker, shared the professional values and norms of the merchant culture. An industrialist who had made his fortune in the steel and nickel industries, Wharton was fully convinced of the need for moral training and character formation in business education. Thus, his vision of what would become the Wharton School included the elevation not only of technical competence but also of social consciousness and moral character. The private business schools that had proliferated across the nation, however, were already teaching the professional norms and technical competence of the merchant culture. According to Khurana (2007, 108), "Wharton's framing of the purpose of his new school, along with his personal reputation for integrity, enabled him to gain the support he required for establishing the Wharton School at the University of Pennsylvania, even in the absence of evidence of a compelling need for it to exist." The professionalism project that Wharton articulated for his business school would become the model for all university-based business schools founded over the next forty years.

Khurana (2007, 104) explains why the professionalization project for business education shifted from the private business school to the university-based business school:

The shift from private business education to the university-based business school was related not only to the cultural prestige of science, ideas about formal pedagogy and the development of technical competence, and the striving for status through higher education. The managerial vanguard engaged in the establishment of university-based business education was also vitally concerned with creating an effective acculturation and socialization process through which norms of business conduct could be transmitted from one generation to the next.

And what were the norms of business conduct that the founders of the university-based business school wanted to transmit from one generation to the next? Similar to law and medicine, the founders desired to transmit professional norms for integrity, honesty, and trustworthiness. A particularly important professional norm for business was disinterestedness. Business professionals were expected to place the interest of those whom they advised and worked for above their own. This included avoiding situations in which one's disinterestedness could be questioned and to refrain from activities that yielded personal advantage. Other important professional norms in the eyes of the founders included transparency, competence, and duties of care and loyalty. These professional norms provided a foundation of trust that was needed in the increasingly impersonal, transactional relationships that came to dominate economic life (Khurana 2007).

The professionalism project of the founders was granted greater urgency during the Great Depression. After becoming dean of the Wharton School in 1933, economist Joseph Willits portrayed the Great Depression as a summons to US business schools to direct their gaze beyond the problems of business to the broader needs of the nation (Sass 1982). That same year, Harvard professor Clyde Ruggles emphasized the need for business schools to study and teach social responsibility at a meeting of the American Association of Collegiate Schools of Business (AACSB 1933, 255–256):

*The business schools have a clear challenge to study standards of business conduct,
and to furnish instruction which will give a clear perspective of the social responsibility of business men . . . (U)niversity education in business will be incomplete in
a vital respect if our studies of the field of business do not recognize the obligations of
these schools to aid in raising the standards of business conduct. If the business
schools do not accept this challenge, they will not only fail to justify their existence as
part of modern university education but they will also fail to make the greatest
possible contribution to business itself.*

As the Great Depression dragged on, and the stock manipulation and
financial abuses of many executives came to light, business school deans
became concerned about the possibility of increased government regulation. Because of the importance of self-regulation in all professions, and
the progressive agenda of the Roosevelt administration, the failure of the
business profession to regulate the conduct of its members made government regulation a real possibility. As Willits stated before a meeting of the
AACSB in 1936, "It may not be unfair to say that the chances of obtaining
a wise and rational policy by government . . . are increased in direct
proportion to the extent to which the ethical standards and social mind-
edness of business men are of a kind that society can approve" (AACSB
1936, 12–13).

Economics faculty played a key role in the founding of university-based
business schools. Thus, it is not surprising that business schools initially
rooted their curriculum in economics. What is surprising is that these same
faculty made deliberate decisions early on to establish independence
between the new business schools and economics departments within
their universities. This may be because institutional economists founded
the business schools at a time when economics departments were becoming increasingly dominated by neoclassical economists. Institutional economists emphasized the role of power, values, belief systems, and historical
contingency in economic behavior, while neoclassical economists emphasized the role of markets, contracts, trade, and property rights.
To institutional economists, even these capitalist institutions were the
product of political, cultural, and historical developments, all of which
were in need of attention and analysis (Bernstein 2001). Throughout the
first half of the twentieth century, institutional economists continued to
dominate university-based business schools even as neoclassical economists came to dominate economics departments. When the influence of
neoclassical economists reached the business school, however, the academic environment became increasingly hostile for institutional economists and their professionalism project.

THE DECAY AND ABANDONMENT OF PROFESSIONAL NORMS

Khurana's (2007) main thesis is that the professionalism project of the university-based business school decayed and was eventually abandoned due to developments within the research university, the field of economics, and the neoclassical theory of the firm. Others have written in detail about the failure of modernism to provide unifying truth and the effect of postmodernism on the research university (e.g., Wittrock 1993, Marsden 1994, Reuben 1996). Thus, I focus on the roles played by the field of economics and the neoclassical theory of the firm in the decay and abandonment of professional norms in US business schools. This discussion is important because developments in the field of economics help explain the current state of the theory of the firm, which is the topic of this chapter. Further, recent scholarship suggests that developments in the theory of the firm significantly influenced the mother discipline of economics (Fourcade and Khurana 2013).

Economists founded their professional association in 1885 on the promise of the social norms of the merchant culture to support free-market capitalism. Richard Ely, the first president of the American Economic Association (AEA), was an institutional economist who viewed the new association as an instrument of reform and moral development (Haskell 1977, Bernstein 2001). Institutional economists dominated the AEA over the first three decades of the association and influenced university-based business schools well into the twentieth century. Prior to the 1920s, for example, the Wharton School included institutional economics in the curriculum as part of the school's larger effort to create socially responsible managers. Simon Patten, an institutional economist who held the directorship of Wharton from 1896 to 1912, believed that there could be "no full discussion of economic problems without bringing political moral principles into relation with the economic" (Sass 1982, 100). Yet, by 1920, neoclassical economists had largely taken over the discipline of economics and were abandoning the study of economic phenomena in relation to historical, cultural, and social forces. Institutional economists would ultimately fail to shape the direction of economics in the twentieth century (Bernstein 2001, Khurana 2007).

The founding of institutional economics is typically traced to a distinctive school of economists in Germany around 1840. Early institutional economists such as Wilhelm Roscher (1817–1894) sought to extend neoclassical economic theory to incorporate insights from history and social institutions. Later, however, institutional economists led by Gustav Schmoller (1838–1917) rejected neoclassical theory completely due to "the unrealism of its assumptions, its degree of theoretical abstraction, and its neglect of interrelated and relevant facts" (Ekelund and Hébert 2014, 275). In rejecting neoclassical methods and theory, Schmoller appeared to promote an "antirationalist" view of economic theory. His writings generated a strong response from Carl Menger (1840–1921), a neoclassical economist and founder of the Austrian school of economics. Called the *Methodenstreit*, or "battle of the methods," the published attacks and counterattacks between Schmoller and Menger plagued the field of economics for decades. The final word on the battle may have come from Joseph Schumpeter (1954, 814), who called it all "pointless."

The battle for the methodological soul of economics eventually spilled over to the United States. The most prominent US institutional economists were Thorstein Veblen (1857–1929), John Commons (1862–1945), Edwin Gay (1867–1946), Wesley Mitchell (1874–1948), and John Galbraith (1908–2006). Born in Wisconsin from parents of Norwegian descent, Veblen was a philosopher turned economist who served for a time on the faculty of the University of Chicago, where he became editor of the *Journal of Political Economy*. In numerous journal articles and books, he scathingly criticized neoclassical economics for what he took to be its excessive abstraction and its failure to include important social and cultural factors. As such, Veblen's writings became the clarion call for US institutional economics in the late 1890s and early 1900s (Bernstein 2001). While Veblen and Commons are regarded as the founders of the US school of institutional economics, it was Mitchell most of all, with the support of Gay, who set much of the methodological agenda for the school. Galbraith's writings popularized institutional economics in the United States by garnering interest among both social scientists and the reading public (Ekelund and Hébert 2014).

The conflict between institutional and neoclassical economists was more than a battle for the methodological soul of economics, however. It was also part of the battle for legitimization that had engulfed the economics discipline since the 1880s. During Woodrow Wilson's presidency (1913–1921), the unique resource problems associated with World War I, the creation of a national banking system, the introduction of a federal income tax, and the many other acts of the progressive administration offered a rich set of policy issues that economists could address. Due to their limited status at the time, however, economists were rarely consulted (Bernstein 2001). When Herbert Hoover became the thirty-first president in 1929, he had served as head of the Food Administration under President Wilson and as Secretary of Commerce under President Harding and President Coolidge. In his previous positions, Hoover had organized shipments of food for the Allies during World War I and helped develop detailed economic data to assist economists in the study of business cycles and public policy. Through all of his public service, Hoover cultivated close ties with leading economists of his day, including both institutional and neoclassical economists.

In a cruel irony of fate, the economics profession did not serve Hoover well during his term as president. Rather than demonstrate the usefulness of economic knowledge to the nation, the Great Depression exposed the discipline's lack of unity and understanding of public policy issues. The Smoot-Hawley Act implemented a large across-the-board increase in import duties, and the Revenue Act of 1932 substantially increased the taxation of dividends. Both were major policy disasters that likely prolonged the economic misery of the Great Depression. The progressive policies of the Roosevelt presidency were also relatively ineffective. For all of the cost and effort of New Deal policies, they were not successful in generating an economic recovery (Bernstein 2001). Years spent cultivating an elite scholarly discipline in economics proved ineffective in the fight against the unparalleled hardship of the Great Depression. The economic recovery would have to await the world's greatest armed conflict.

It was under the unrelenting demands posed by World War II that the economics profession proved its worth to the nation. Their wartime work, along with the ever-increasing interest of the US government in the applicability of their discipline, increased the legitimacy and social status of economists. This increase in legitimacy and status, however, accrued largely to the mathematically and analytically rigorous neoclassical economists. This led to a new view of the discipline as "economic science." Similarly, the view of management shifted toward technical expertise (Khurana 2007). Prior to the war, management theory was heavily influenced by the human relation school, a theoretical perspective that emerged from the Harvard Business School studies of Western Electric's Hawthorne factory in the late 1920s and early 1930s. Similar to institutional economics, the human relation school viewed management as requiring the combined insights of social psychology, anthropology, and sociology. Following the war, however, management came to be viewed increasingly as "management science." In the course of World War II, organizational experts had developed new quantitative tools such as linear programming, systems analysis, computer simulations, network analysis, and advanced cost accounting systems. Rather than argue for the inculcation of professional norms, business school leaders in the postwar era increasingly argued for a science-oriented curriculum based on the new quantitative tools.

THE INCREASING INFLUENCE OF NEOCLASSICAL THEORY AND THE CHICAGO SCHOOL

Fourcade and Khurana (2013) examine the coevolution of economic science and business education over the course of the twentieth century. Similar to Khurana (2007), they identify three historical phases in the development of the US business school: (1) an early phase from the founding of the Wharton School through the 1940s where business management was viewed as a profession with a moral dimension, (2) a second phase in the 1950s where business management was viewed primarily as "scientific" with an emphasis on technical training, and (3) a third phase beginning in the 1960s where business management was viewed primarily as the maximization of stock price. The first phase illustrates the professionalism project of institutional economists and other founders of the university-based business school. The second phase illustrates the decay and eventual abandonment of that professionalism project and the emergence of the scientific conception of management. The third phase illustrates the infusion of neoclassical economics within the university-based business school. Fourcade and Khurana (2013, 123) argue that the third phase "helped produce and sustain new understandings of the nature of the firm, with far-reaching consequences for business practices and economic relations in society."

In retrospect, the postwar period brought the intellectual agenda of neoclassical economic theory in harmony with the needs and ambitions of the nation (Bernstein 2001). Neoclassical economists would not squander this rare opportunity. As neoclassical theory proved its worth during World War II and the victory over fascism, it was called upon once again to win the Cold War. Advanced planning and a vigorous national economy were needed to meet the needs of national defense as well as to demonstrate the virtues of American capitalism to the world. Both guns *and* butter were demanded. Unlike the other major industrial nations of the world, the United States entered the postwar period with its economy intact and its organizational and technological assets preserved. While the labor market faced the normal challenges of demobilization, domestic production was buoyed by foreign demand from those regions devastated by the war. Further, the United States stood as the world's creditor, and the dollar, both by default and by the multilateral agreements at Bretton Woods, had become the world's currency. These strong economic tailwinds aided the United States in achieving unparalleled economic growth throughout the 1950s and 1960s.

Postwar America also saw the rise of a new social contract between the manager, the corporation, and society. The top executive of a large corporation was characterized as a statesman who was involved in professional organizations such as the Business Roundtable and the Council on Foreign Relations, yet was able to work closely with outside parties, including government regulators and elected politicians (Khurana 2007). This executive faced a system of managed competition enforced through a mixture of government policy and informal networks that would later be called "relationship capitalism" (Rajan and Zingales 2004). This new form of capitalism included a considerable amount of government regulation to restrain competition and maintain stability. In 1950, for example, Congress passed the Cellar-Kefauver Act prohibiting firms from using vertical or horizontal mergers to dominate a single industry. In the postwar environment of rapid growth, rising stock valuations, and strong cash flows, firms responded by expanding into unrelated product lines. Thus, the diversified conglomerate became the dominant organizational form of choice for large firms. By 1960, more than half of all Fortune 500 firms operated in multiple industries consistent with the new business model (Fligstein 1990, Nohria 2002).

So effective was the new stabilization policy that it became fashionable by the early 1960s for economists to speak of the "end of the business cycle" (Bernstein 2001). In addition to the policy experience derived from the war, the discipline's confidence in its ability to advance effective public policy was increasing due to a revolution in macroeconomic thought brought about by British economist John Maynard Keynes. In the meantime, the economics profession continued to strive for greater status and legitimacy. In 1950, an ad hoc committee of the AEA Executive Committee recommended that all graduate instruction in economics include the important tools of mathematics, accounting, statistics, history, logic, and the scientific method. The pursuit of disciplinary precision and competence during the postwar decades, however, included the sanctioning of ideas and methods that were deemed to be antithetical to the advancement of economic science. By the late 1950s, a rising number of nationally ranked graduate programs in economics emphasized the latest advances in neoclassical theory in their curriculum, and the cultivation of literacy in the classic texts began to wane. As a result, the historical and cultural insights of institutional economics were largely removed from consciousness.

At about the same time, the legitimacy and status of the university-based business school came under increased scrutiny due to two foundation reports. In 1959, the Carnegie Foundation for the Advancement of Teaching and the Ford Foundation issued book-long reports that were highly critical of business school education (Pierson 1959 and Gordon and Howell 1959, respectively). The Carnegie Foundation had five decades of experience reforming graduate education in the major professions of medicine and law, and was convinced that only intense public scrutiny would stimulate recalcitrant business schools to change. In 1910, Carnegie had released a similar report that was highly critical of US medical schools of the day. Within ten years of the report, forty-five percent of those schools had closed, and those that remained open had made significant changes to increase their stature within the university (Miles 2016). In contrast, the Ford Foundation had recently become the largest philanthropic foundation in the world following the deaths of Henry Ford and his son Edsel, and had relatively little experience in education reform. Leaders of both Carnegie and Ford, however, believed that strengthening the management of business organizations was integral to their postwar missions (Khurana 2007).

The recommendations developed by the Carnegie and Ford foundations were shaped by individuals who had both foundation and business school affiliations (Khurana 2007). This was especially true of the Ford Foundation, which followed up its recommendations with nearly fifteen years of financial grants totaling $35 million (Miles 2016). For example, Donald David, the dean of the Harvard Business School, served on the foundation's board, and George (Lee) Bach, the founding dean of the Carnegie Institute of Technology's Graduate School of Industrial Administration (GSIA), served as special advisor to the board through his close association with foundation vice president Thomas Carroll. Bach was especially successful at promoting GSIA's emphasis on discipline-based research as the new model for business education. The Carnegie and Ford reports were generally unanimous in their condemnation of the quality and stature of US business education. Less than half of faculty members in university-based business schools held doctoral degrees, and there was a glaring lack of interest in research and scholarly activities on the part of the faculty. Teaching loads were so heavy that faculty had little time to conduct research, and approximately forty percent of teaching was delivered by part-time instructors.

Both foundation reports emphasized the need for business faculty to conduct academic research worthy of their place in the research university.

The research agenda recommended by the foundations resembled the ideals of the new business school at Carnegie's GSIA. In operation for barely five years at the time, the GSIA recruited students with a background in engineering and quantitative analysis rather than the liberal arts. In many ways, the GSIA organized itself as the anti-Harvard Business School (Fourcade and Khurana 2013). Thus, it was an important signal about the future trajectory of business school research when Carnegie's GSIA received the first large grant issued by the Ford Foundation. The GSIA cultivated a certain intellectual autonomy that made it an incubator of new ideas in the 1950s and 1960s, including behavioral economics, modern finance theory, and the theory of rational expectations. This attracted top talent in the field of economics to the business school. No less than five individuals who taught at the GSIA (Herbert Simon, Franco Modigliani, Merton Miller, Robert Lucas, and Edward Prescott) and two GSIA PhDs (Finn Kydland and Oliver Williamson) would be awarded the Nobel Prize in Economic Science. Aside from the original behavioral group formed by Herbert Simon, GSIA faculty from the 1950s through the 1970s were predominantly neoclassical economists.

As Fourcade and Khurana (2013, 144) argue, it is not surprising that these innovations in business education occurred at the GSIA. A large proportion of the GSIA faculty were economics PhDs from the University of Chicago. During the heyday of Keynesian economics in the postwar period, not many top economics departments were hiring graduates from the increasing center of free-market economics. "Consequently, faculty members sought to boost their academic status by ruthlessly proclaiming their scientific purity." Herbert Simon's attempts to "preach the heresies of bounded rationality" to the neoclassical economists at the GSIA may have pushed them to articulate more forcefully their own contrary views. By 1965, however, these neoclassical economists "were united enough in their views to cause Simon to quit in disgust and find refuge in the psychology department." Thus, the multidisciplinary emphasis of the GSIA, which had been heavily encouraged by the Ford Foundation, quickly unraveled.

The creation of warring factions at Carnegie's GSIA was not a unique occurrence. An unanticipated consequence of the foundation reforms was the intensification of the academic guilds within the business school (Miles 2016). In particular, the orientation toward rigorous research standards fostered an environment in which individual faculty members became more concerned with building a reputation within their respective disciplines than with making contributions to general business knowledge.

As the proportion of research-active faculty increased at prominent business schools such as Wharton, Stanford, and Chicago, factions made increasing claims over methodological purity and superiority (Khurana 2007). A twenty-five-year retrospective commissioned by the AACSB (Porter and McKibbin 1988) found that the 1959 reports had successfully moved the business school in the direction of Humboldt's ideals for the research university. But just as the Humboldtian model resulted in a university that Humboldt himself would not recognize, the reforms instituted by the foundation reports resulted in a business school that the authors of the foundation reports did not intend (Miles 2016). Whereas the authors envisioned a continuation of the professionalism project through rigorous, multidisciplinary research, the end result was the complete abandonment of the professionalism project and the dominance of an increasingly narrow neoclassical theory of the firm.

The neoclassical economists at the University of Chicago were less successful initially at achieving a similar coup at Chicago's Graduate School of Business (GSB). The University of Chicago was founded in 1892 on Humboldt's ideals of the research university, and Chicago's business school was the first in the country to offer a PhD program in 1920.[1] The early founders of Chicago's business school, however, were institutional economists who saw the study of business as requiring a broad, multidisciplinary approach that emphasized professional norms. Leon Marshall, who became the first dean of Chicago's GSB in 1909, shared Wharton's vision of business education as a professionalism project. Marshall was so committed to Wharton's ideals, that in 1916 he joined Edwin Gay of Harvard in founding the AACSB, an association founded by business school deans to further the professionalism project (Khurana 2007).

Following its experience at Carnegie's GSIA, the Ford Foundation had earmarked future business school grants for the development of "behavioral science" (Fourcade and Khurana 2013). When the new dean of Chicago's GSB, Allen Wallis, applied for a Ford Foundation grant in 1957, therefore, foundation officials were initially suspicious of his intentions. The GSB had already strayed from the liberal arts foundation built by Marshall and was focusing on disciplines closely related to business, including statistics, accounting, law, and especially, economics. Wallis himself was a Columbia-trained statistician who had spent time in the Chicago economics department during the influential 1930s. It was during

---

[1] Chicago's Graduate School of Business was initially named the College of Commerce and Administration and was renamed the Booth School of Business in 2008.

this period that he developed a life-long friendship with fellow Chicago students Milton Friedman and George Stigler. Through Friedman's influence, Chicago recruited Wallis after the war to found a department of statistics. Upon receiving the second largest grant from the Ford Foundation after the GSIA, Wallis hired George Stigler at the GSB. The suspicions of Ford Foundation officials came true as the GSB soon abandoned the behavioral sciences and became a major promoter of the increasingly narrow view of economic man known as *homo economicus* (see Chapter 4).

The increasing number and influence of neoclassical economists at Chicago's GSB and economics department would generate a new school of thought in business and economics known as "the Chicago school." The dominance of economists at the Chicago school can be seen in the extraordinary wave of Nobel Prize–winning Chicago economists, including Friedrich Hayek (1974), Milton Friedman (1976), Theodore Schultz (1979), George Stigler (1982), Merton Miller (1990), Ronald Coase (1991), Gary Becker (1992), Robert Fogel (1993), Robert Lucas (1995), James Heckman (2000), and Eugene Fama (2013). The Chicago school completely transformed the disciplines of economics, accounting, and finance. In particular, research in finance and financial accounting became synonymous with financial economics. Two other institutional developments aided in Chicago's ascendancy as the center for the new financial economics. The first development was the movement of the Cowles Commission for Research in Economics to the University of Chicago in 1939, which made the university a mecca for mathematical economics.[2] The second development was the creation of a unique financial database through a gift from Merrill Lynch. After the mid-1960s, the Center for Research in Security Prices (CRSP) gave researchers easy access to massive amounts of market data in a format that facilitated analysis.

The Chicago school, personified by Milton Friedman and George Stigler in their increasing discourse with the general public (Leeson 2000), was strongly free-market and heavily influenced by neoclassical economic theory. Its neoclassical views and methods, along with the rich market data provided by CRSP, allowed the Chicago school to claim the status of value-free "positive" science. One of the most significant contributions of the Chicago school was the development by Eugene Fama and his colleagues of the efficient market hypothesis (Fama 1970). A student of Merton

---

[2] This was only temporary, however, as the Cowles Commission was moved to Yale University in 1955.

Miller, Fama's contributions in financial economics helped him win the Nobel Prize in Economic Science in 2013. In its strong form, the efficient market hypothesis (EMH) asserts that the price of a firm's securities perfectly reflects all public and private information regarding that firm's value (i.e., expected future cash flows). Hence, a firm's stock price is a valid measure of that firm's fundamental value. Although it did not go over well with many practitioners, who rightly saw it as a threat to traditional investment analysis, the new theory eventually became the foundation for market research in economics, accounting, and finance (MacKenzie 2006). In particular, price reaction studies based on the new finance theory soon became the gold standard for empirical market research and the ticket for faculty positions and tenure at top business schools.

Economic trends would soon infuse the new neoclassical theory coming out of Chicago with important public policy implications. The strong economic tailwinds that fueled the postwar prosperity of the 1950s and 1960s became strong headwinds during the 1970s and 1980s. The Bretton Woods international monetary agreements were abandoned as recovering industrial nations began to meet their own industrial needs. These same industrial nations now began to compete with US companies in international markets. When combined with economic shocks, including the 1973 oil embargo by the Organization of the Petroleum Exporting Countries (OPEC), these trends led to an extended period of economic distress. Once again, neoclassical economists found their intellectual agenda in harmony with the needs and ambitions of the nation (Bernstein 2001). The previous confidence in Keynesian economics was severely shaken as the accelerated inflation of the late 1960s and 1970s was blamed on fiscal interventionism and big government. The combination of economic stagnation and high inflation gave birth to a new economic malady called "stagflation," and the sum of the rates of inflation and unemployment became a new measure called the "misery index." A growing chorus of voices from across the political spectrum began to call for the dismantling of the relationship capitalism that now seemed to have hobbled the economy (Khurana 2007).

The economic distress of the 1970s and early 1980s also had important consequences for the way managers were viewed (Fourcade and Khurana 2013). Some researchers in management and operations placed the blame for the nation's economic troubles squarely on the shoulders of US managers and the uncritical application of scientific management techniques made popular in the postwar era (Hayes and Wheelwright 1984). These criticisms included the increasing reliance on analytical and methodological elegance over insight into the subtleties and complexities of strategic decisions. These criticisms also included the overemphasis on short-term financial returns and the decision by many to diversify into multiple industries (Abernathy and Hayes 1980). Rather than run their companies by the numbers, managers were now advised to get back to the basics. Other management researchers argued that the solution to America's economic woes lay in implementing aspects of the Japanese corporate system, including more cooperative labor-manager relations, quality circles, lean manufacturing techniques such as just-in-time, and progressive human resource policies such as lifelong employment (Ouchi 1981).

The Chicago school also blamed US managers for many of the nation's economic woes, but it did so in a stinging rebuke of the entire system of relationship capitalism (Khurana 2007). From their neoclassical perspective, the diversification strategies of the Fortune 500 were proof of self-interested behavior on the part of managers at large firms. Not only did the Chicago school doubt the ability of managers to voluntarily reform, they openly ridiculed the industrial planning and industrial welfare policies of Japan and Germany. Given their confidence in the EMH, the solution was to subject these self-interested managers to the discipline of the financial markets. In an article in the *New York Times Magazine*, Friedman (1970) argued that "the only social responsibility of business is to increase its profits." Regarding public policy, the Chicago school viewed the government as another special interest group focused on expanding its reach through increased taxes and regulation. From this view, "most government policies (even those prohibiting insider trading, as some of the more extreme members of this group argued) typically destroyed incentives for sound economic and social behavior. Thus, the solution to the problems of American competitiveness entailed minimizing the government's role in the national economy" (Khurana 2007, 301).

The influence of the Chicago school spread when Allen Wallis left Chicago's GSB in 1963 to assume the presidency of the University of Rochester. During his twenty years at the helm, he turned the private university in upstate New York into an eastern outpost of Chicago economists (Fourcade and Khurana 2013). Wallis established a business school at Rochester and staffed it with Chicago PhD graduates. Given the newness of the school, Wallis and his neoclassical economists had great flexibility in shaping the curriculum. While Rochester's business school lacked the backing of the Ford Foundation, the University of Rochester had a large endowment behind only Harvard and Yale. Further, the presence of local

industrial giants such as Eastman Kodak and Xerox provided a constant
source of funds and MBA students. Because the views of the Chicago
school were still an oddity at most academic journals, Rochester founded
new academic journals that promoted the new "positive science," including
the *Journal of Financial Economics*, the *Journal of Accounting and
Economics*, and the *Journal of Monetary Economics*. These journals soon
became leading academic journals, further spreading the influence of the
Chicago school in economics, accounting, and finance.

INSIGHTS ON THE FIRM FROM ADAM SMITH

Milton Friedman, George Stigler, and other prominent members of the
Chicago school used Adam Smith as the "poster child" for their view of
efficient markets and limited government based on his second book,
The Wealth of Nations (Smith 1776/1791). Adam Smith's classic work on
political economy contains important insights that are contained in all
classical and neoclassical theories of the firm. While he is typically characterized as a classical economist, in the following chapter I argue that
Smith's emphasis on history, culture, and institutions makes him more
similar to institutional economists than to current day neoclassical economists. Further, in his first book, *The Theory of Moral Sentiments* (Smith
1759/1790), Smith articulates a rich theory of social norms. The latest
scholarship on Adam Smith suggests that his first book forms the foundation for his second book, and that his book on political economy contains
important extensions of the system of thought in his book on moral
sentiments. These extensions, however, are often implicitly stated or
implied in *The Wealth of Nations*. For my purposes here, I stick to the
common view of Adam Smith held by the Chicago school and expand
upon that view in future chapters.

Adam Smith was born in 1723 in Kirkcaldy, Scotland, situated on the
northern bank of the Firth of Forth across the river from Edinburgh.
Kirkcaldy was unique for its day in that it had a long history as an
international port of trade. By the end of the eighteenth century, the port
town had become the home for a leather making industry, a brick and tile
works, spinning cotton mills and linen factories, and a small shipbuilding
industry. Smith's father, who died just before his son's birth, was
a Presbyterian Whig who served in the Scottish customs office in
Kirkcaldy. This background helps explain why Smith attended the thoroughly Presbyterian University of Glasgow for his initial higher education
in 1737, and why he found himself an outcast at Anglican and Tory Oxford

during his six years of schooling there from 1740 to 1746. This background also helps explain why the church leaders of the Glasgow Presbytery supported Smith's appointment as a professor at the University of Glasgow, first as Professor of Logic in 1751 and then as Professor of Moral Philosophy from 1752 to 1764. Finally, this background helps explain why Smith was a practical economist who met regularly with the Glasgow city merchants who were turning Glasgow into a thriving port city due to the tobacco trade with the American colonies (Stevens 2011).

The breadth and influence of Adam Smith's book on political economy has earned him the title of "father of economics" (Ekelund and Hébert 2014). Regarding its breadth, *The Wealth of Nations* reflects the writings of Locke, Steuart, Mandeville, Petty, Cantillon, Turgot, and especially Quesnay and Hume. Smith mentions more than a hundred authors by name in his book (Heilbroner 1999). In addition to his schooling at Glasgow and Oxford, Smith had traveled to London, Toulouse, Geneva, and Paris discussing the affairs of the day with world scholars and dignitaries such as Quesnay, Voltaire, and Benjamin Franklin (Phillipson 2010). As a result, his perspective was broad, worldly, and contemporary for his day. Regarding its influence, *The Wealth of Nations* became an instant best seller due in large part to the reputation of its author and the timeliness of its message. Within Smith's lifetime, he would see his book on political economy go into its fifth edition in English (a sixth after his death) and be translated into French, German, Danish, and Italian (Campbell and Skinner 1981). The monarchy culture was losing its grip across Europe, even in France, and citizens were increasingly favoring the merchant culture, or what Smith frequently called "the system of perfect liberty." Capitalist institutions had developed sufficiently so that some markets could be characterized as competitive, and the first industrial revolution was awakening in England. As such, Smith's major work on political economy represents an important transition from monarchy rule to the rule of the market, and marks the beginning of the classical period for economics (1776–1870).

As with most economic theorists during this time period, Smith focused on macroeconomic issues involving the relation of the individual to the state and the proper functions of the state in relation to its citizens. Smith focused much of his macroeconomic theory on dismantling the Mercantilist philosophy with its emphasis on gold, agriculture, guilds, and monopolies. Smith rejected both Mercantilism and the Physiocratic economic system promoted by French court physician François Quesnay (1694–1774). The meshing of the public interests of the monarchy with the private interests of the monopolist was a natural part of the English monarchy up through the 1600s and remained a part of the French monarchy much later. In particular, craft guilds and feudal privileges were not abolished in France until 1790 (Heilbroner 1999). Smith rejected Mercantilism due to its emphasis on government control over the economy, including production, imports and exports, and the balance of gold in the treasury. While the Physiocrats in France shared many of Smith's radical economic ideas – such as a belief in natural law, private property rights, and the power of free markets – they believed that agriculture was the source of all wealth and that the government should maintain high agricultural prices. The Physiocrats, who formed the first school of economic thought, were also limited in their ability to criticize the French economic system as part of the French court. Thus, Smith rejected much of their theory of political economy (Ekelund and Hébert 2014).

Although Adam Smith's main focus in *The Wealth of Nations* is on macroeconomic issues related to political economy, he also provides many useful insights related to the firm. Some of these insights have been incorporated into subsequent theories of the firm by neoclassical theorists. Some of them, as discussed in the next chapter, have largely been overlooked. What makes Smith's book on political economy particularly useful for theorists in the theory of the firm, however, is his thoroughly scientific approach based on observation. As with his other writings, he demonstrates a system of thought that leaves no stone unturned and reveals a great capacity for model-building (Campbell and Skinner 1981). While many readers of his day did not understand or appreciate his complete system of thought, Smith's attention to everyday observations and facts gave the book practical relevance. In modern economic language, Smith's positive theory based on history and observation gave his normative prescriptions for economic growth great weight to readers in the eighteenth century as well as today.

In contrast to the Physiocrats, who limited productive labor only to agriculture, Smith's economic system featured productive labor in agriculture, manufacturing, and commerce. In the first three chapters of *The Wealth of Nations* (*WN* I.i, I.ii, and I.iii), Smith introduces the topic of the division of labor, describes its natural source in self-interest, and explains how it is limited by the extent of the market. Smith begins in Chapter 1 with observations from a small pin factory. Without the benefit of machinery or advanced training, Smith estimates that a workman could produce only one to twenty pins in a day. In a small factory employing ten persons with minimal machinery and eighteen distinct operations, however, Smith estimates that production could reach upwards of 48,000 pins in a day. He uses this example to explain the power of the division of labor to drive economic growth and to help explain why "the separation of different trades and employments" has taken place and "is generally carried furthest in those countries which enjoy the highest degree of industry and improvement" (*WN* I.i.4).

But what is the natural source behind this division of labor from which so many advantages are derived? Smith makes clear in Chapter 2 that the principal that gives occasion to the division of labor is not human wisdom or government intervention. Instead, he credits a self-interested propensity unique to human nature, "the propensity to truck, barter, and exchange one thing for another" (*WN* I.ii.1). To emphasize this point, he makes the following well-quoted statement (*WN* I.ii.2):

It is not from the benevolence of the butcher, the brewer, or the baker, that we expect our dinner, but from their regard to their own interest. We address ourselves, not to their humanity but to their self-love, and never talk to them of our own necessities but of their advantages.

In Chapter 3 Smith expresses in what way the division of labor is limited by the extent of the market. He explains how the many advantages of the separation of different trades and employments are limited when the market for such trades is very small. For this reason, some sorts of industries and employments are only possible in great cities and towns. He uses sparsely populated portions of Scotland to illustrate that where the market is very small, "every farmer must be butcher, baker, and brewer for his own family" (*WN* I.iii.2). Thus, Smith's discussion in this chapter explains why free-market capitalism creates large urban areas and cities.

Smith attributes economic growth and wealth creation in nations to this division of labor. As Campbell and Skinner (1981, 43) state, "Even when Smith recognized the theoretical possibility of the operation of other factors – an increased labour force or mechanization – the division of labour remained in practice the fundamental cause of economic growth." The propensity for individuals to improve their station in life through trade generates markets and opportunities to gain from the division of labor, which generate advances in innovation, which generate further opportunities to gain from the division of labor. The constant desire to better one's condition also contributes to economic growth by encouraging the flow of savings into the economy. Smith refines his treatment of the division of labor by developing a macroeconomic theory of the circulating capital of society. He identifies the circulating capital of society as including the supply of money necessary to carry out circulation, the stocks of materials and goods in process held by manufacturers, and the stocks of finished goods available for sale in the hands of producers or merchants. His macroeconomic theory appears to owe a great deal to the Physiocrats and his close friend David Hume (Campbell and Skinner 1981).

The Wealth of Nations also contains microeconomic theory related to the firm. Because the firm brings together the necessary labor, plant, and machinery for production, everything Smith writes regarding prices, markets, and the division of labor applies to the firm. Smith breaks new ground when he formally isolates the three main factors of production: rent, wages, and profit. To Smith, the "natural price" of a product covers its cost of production reflected in the "natural rates" of these three factors. In contrast, the "market price" of the product is determined by the natural forces of supply and demand and is always gravitating toward the natural price (*WN* I.vii.15). Smith also breaks new ground by discussing forces that determine the natural rates of each of the three factors of production.

Of particular relevance to the theory of the firm is Smith's discussion of forces determining the natural rates of wages (*WN* I.viii). Wages depend upon the contract made between laborers and the providers of materials, plant, and machinery (*WN* I.viii.8–11). Smith devotes an entire chapter to wages and profit in the different employments of labor and capital stock (*WN* I.x). He points out that pecuniary wages and profit "are every-where in Europe extremely different accounting to the different employments of labour and stock. But this difference arises partly from certain circumstances in the employment themselves . . . and partly from the policy of Europe, which no-where leaves things at perfect liberty" (*WN* I.x.a.2). The wages of labor vary with the ease, cleanliness, and honorableness of the employment (*WN* I.x.b.2), the easiness, difficulty, and expense of learning the business (*WN* I.x.b.5), the consistency of employment (*WN* I.x.b.11), the level of trust that must be reposed (placed, rested) in the worker (*WN* I.x.b.17), and the probability of success in the employment (*WN* I.x.b.20).

Smith attributes wage inequalities to the nature of the employment rather than to shortcomings in the markets for labor or production per se. Smith's theory of wage rates, however, was based on the small manufacturing setting of eighteenth-century Britain. John Stuart Mill (1806–1873) expanded Smith's theory to include economies of scale observed during the industrial revolution. Mill recognized another cause of firm growth, which is the introduction of processes requiring expensive machinery. By growing its production capability through such machinery, and thereby increasing the productivity of its labor, a firm is able to reduce its prices compared to its smaller competitors and thereby increase market share. Mill's major economic work, *Principles of Political Economy* (Mill 1848), was another watershed in classical economics because it expanded the economic paradigm begun by Smith and successively refined insights provided by other classical economists such as David Ricardo and Thomas Malthus (Ekelund and Hébert 2014). Until replaced by Alfred Marshall's major economic treatise almost sixty years later, Mill's *Principles* represented the latest economic theory related to the firm.

NEOCLASSICAL THEORIES OF THE FIRM

Whereas classical economic theory was largely a British invention, neoclassical economic theory was an international invention nurtured by contributors from multiple nations and fields (Ekelund and Hébert 2014). These contributors included engineers and mathematicians from France, Germany, and Austria. Antoine-Augustin Cournot (1801–1877), a French mathematician and economist, criticized the simplistic use of arithmetics and algebra by the classical theorists. He championed the use of differential and integral calculus to find and express relations between important economic variables. Through the use of differential calculus and geometry, Cournot developed the "marginal principle," which became the organizing principle of microeconomic theory. Given a certain set of simplifying assumptions, economists could now provide a straightforward solution to some of the firm's most fundamental questions, such as what quantity to produce and what price to charge. Cournot developed monopoly and duopoly models of the firm based on the principle of profit maximization. The French engineer Jules Dupuit (1804–1866) expanded the growing list of microeconomic tools by developing a theory of utility, which he used to develop the concept of marginal utility and relate it to a demand curve.

In Germany, Johann Heinrich von Thünen (1783–1850) is credited with developing such concepts as economic rent, diminishing returns, opportunity costs, and the marginal-productivity theory of wages. Hermann Heinrich Gossen (1810–1858) was the first theorist to develop a full-fledged theory of consumption grounded in the marginal principle. He viewed economics as the theory of how people as individuals and as groups realize the maximum of pleasure with the minimum of pain. Thus, he attempted to mathematize Jeremy Bentham's (1748–1832) hedonic utility function. As institutional economists gained the upper hand in Germany in the late nineteenth century, however, the seat of neoclassical economics shifted to Austria. Carl Menger (1840–1921), who is best known for his spirited defense of neoclassical theory against the criticisms of Gustav Schmoller, founded the Viennese school of economics. Similar to Gossen, Menger pushed the envelope of the utility function to include subjective valuation for noneconomic goods, such as air or water, whose supply exceeds requirements. Friedrich von Wieser (1851–1926) was the first to coin the term "marginal utility" (*grenznutzen*), although the idea of marginal utility was at the center of Menger's analysis. Wieser was also the first economist to show the generality of the theory of utility valuation and to make explicit the usefulness of the market system in allocating resources.

By the 1870s, the pace of neoclassical theory work quickened and formed a synthesis in economics. Historians typically characterize neoclassical economics as a tripartite development launched in Great Britain by William Stanley Jevons (1835–1882), in Austria by Carl Menger (1840–1921), and in France by Léon Walras (1834–1910). Under this neoclassical synthesis, the focus of analysis became the individual whose preferences and calculations symbolized the workings of the market system and the economy (Heilbroner 1999). Whereas prior theorists provided the microeconomic focus and many of its analytical tools, British economist Alfred Marshall (1842–1924) provided the systematic development that the new paradigm required. In his *Principles of Economics*, first published in 1890, Marshall brought the current insights in neoclassical economics together to advance the understanding of firm and market behavior. He viewed the expanding science of economics as an extension of the basic ideas espoused by Adam Smith (Ekelund and Hébert 2014). Marshall's original contribution was a new emphasis on time in the working-out of the equilibrium process. In particular, he focused on the self-adjusting, self-correcting nature of the economic world. Similar to most neoclassical theorists, Marshall used the partial equilibrium method that relied on *ceteris paribus* assumptions that held nonessential features of the market constant to focus on the phenomena of interest.

Marshall devoted his attention primarily to models of perfect competition on the one hand and pure monopoly on the other. In the first case, a large number of sellers produce a homogeneous product so that no one firm can affect the price and output decisions of other firms. In the second case, a single firm has exclusive control over the price and output of the good in question. In the first case, which typically includes the assumption of costless entry and exit, there is no possibility of long-run economic profits or economic rents. In the second case, economic power is greater and more concentrated than under any market structure that includes more than one seller. One of the most significant extensions of the neo-classical synthesis under Marshall (1890/1920) was the search for more descriptive models of markets (Ekelund and Hébert 2014). American economist Edward Chamberlin (1899–1967) and British economist Joan Robinson (1903–1983) published important works in 1933 providing market theories that incorporated some aspect of pricing and output power for the firm without the assumption of pure monopoly. Chamberlin called his market theory "monopolistic competition," whereas Robinson called her market theory "imperfect competition."

One of the most important insights of Chamberlin's monopolistic competition theory was that firms engage in nonprice competition in addition to price competition. This was an important advance in the theory of the firm as products often achieve some degree of "uniqueness" due to copyrights, trademarks, brand names, location, etc. Chamberlin's new theory also helped explain the use of advertising as a means of product differentiation. This led to a great deal of interest in monopolistic competition in the 1930s, 1940s, and 1950s (Ekelund and Hébert 2014). Robinson's comparative analysis of monopolistic and competitive markets contributed little to the roles of product differentiation and advertising as elements of monopolistic markets, but her theory introduced a set of tools that has become invaluable in the partial-equilibrium setting of Marshall. These tools included the geometry of marginal revenue, marginal cost, average revenue, and average costs, establishing the theory of the firm found in modern introductory economics textbooks (Backhouse 2009). Because Robinson's tool kit was more like Marshall's, her approach was both more traditional and more general than Chamberlin's approach.

The economic function of a firm is to combine economic resources (plant, machinery, labor) in order to produce goods and services demanded by consumers. Up to this point, I have discussed neoclassical theories of the firm that rely on the invisible hand of market coordination. These theories combine cost curves based on resource productivity with demand and revenue curves to model firms categorized by market structure (i.e., perfect competition, pure monopoly, monopolistic competition, imperfect competition, etc.). Next, I discuss neoclassical theories that seriously consider the behavioral implications of the visible hand of managerialism (Chandler 1977). Such theories build on prior classical theory, such as economic self-interest, as well as the neoclassical tools and synthesis of Marshall (1890/1920). Instead of having firm decisions determined by signals of supply and demand provided by the market, however, firm coordination is directed by the judgments and decisions of managers. Furthermore, resources within the firm are not bought and sold but instead are transferred through managerial directives (Ekelund and Hébert 2014).

The first task of such a theory is to explain why firm coordination is superior to market coordination. In other words, why do firms exist at all? In a seminal paper published in 1937 entitled, "The Nature of the Firm," Ronald Coase (1910–2013) argued that firms emerge as a least-cost means of economic coordination. In other words, firms emerge when the cost of firm coordination is lower than the cost of market coordination. According to Coase, therefore, entrepreneurs use market coordination unless market imperfections such as transaction costs, search costs, and negotiation costs make it more efficient to use firm (managerial) coordination. The second task of such a theory is to explain firm size. In other words, when do firms stop growing in size? Coase argued that firms face rising marginal costs of organization and direction, and so they will eventually stop growing when the marginal costs rise to meet the marginal benefits. As a practical matter, however, many firms use both firm coordination and market coordination simultaneously for different resource inputs. An example is automakers who use outside suppliers for tires (Ekelund and Hébert 2014).

Coase (1937) moves beyond neoclassical theories of the firm based on market supply and demand and gets into the profit-maximizing black box of the organization (Williamson 2009). The evolution of large firms with diffuse ownership, however, posed a new challenge to economists. Berle and Means (1932, 121) asked if it is reasonable to assume that managers of the modern corporation will "choose to operate it in the interests of the owners." Initially, theorists simply restated the objective function of the firm to include alternative goals of the manager besides profit maximization. For example, William Baumol (1959) postulated that large firms maximize revenues subject to a minimum profit constraint, Robin Marris (1964) advanced a growth maximization constraint, and Oliver Williamson (1964) added managerial staff and emoluments to the objective function of the firm. All three of these models maintained the previous neoclassical tools and the view of the firm as a production function but incorporated the possibility for conflicting goals between owners and managers of the firm.

A new class of neoclassical theories took a different approach to the separation of ownership from management in the modern corporation. John Commons (1932, 4) reformulated the problem of economic organization as follows: "the ultimate unit of activity . . . must contain in itself the three principles of conflict, mutuality, and order." This reformulation introduced the concept of corporate governance in that the organization "is the means by which to infuse order, thereby to mitigate conflict and realize mutual gain" (Williamson 2009, 249). This conceptualization of the firm as conflict, mutuality, and order eventually led to the "nexus of contracts" view of the firm. Alchian and Demsetz (1972) advanced this view of the firm by emphasizing the importance of monitoring within the firm. They argued that the manager acts as a team monitor to ensure efficiency in production settings where individuals or groups must work together to accomplish a task. Thus, firms emerge when teams can produce goods and services at a lower cost than individuals can, despite the higher costs of monitoring team performance.

Jensen and Meckling (1976, 310) took the nexus of contracts view of the firm to its ultimate conclusion by arguing that contractual relations "are the essence of the firm, not only with employees but with suppliers, customers, creditors, etc." They concluded that all of these contracts involve the problem of agency costs and monitoring. Their neoclassical theory of the firm, called agency theory, became the dominant theory of the firm in economics, accounting, and finance. I explain this theory of the firm in more detail in Chapter 5, including its basic assumptions, characteristics, and predictions. In the following chapter, I complete the foundation laid in the front part of this book by presenting social norm theory related to the firm.

4

Social Norm Theory Related to the Firm

INTRODUCTION

As stated by Jon Elster (1989, 101), "The workplace is a hotbed for norm-guided action." Only recently, however, have researchers begun to incorporate social norms into the theory of the firm. This new research initiative is driven by three factors. First, evidence continues to build that social norms are important from both a positive (descriptive) and normative (prescriptive) perspective. Second, experimental economists have documented consistent norm-based behavior in laboratory tests of game theory and agency theory. Third, social norm theory has developed to the point where it is useful to explain organizational and managerial behavior. I summarize the latest theoretical, experimental, and archival research in the following three chapters. In this chapter, I complete the foundation laid in the past two chapters by presenting social norm theory related to the firm.

I begin this chapter by analyzing the behavioral assumptions of neoclassical economic theory known as *homo economicus*. This analysis includes the source and purpose of these behavioral assumptions as well as their realism. Next, I discuss the behavioral assumptions and implications of the neoclassical theory of the firm that evolved from the Chicago school – agency theory. These assumptions included an ever-narrowing version of *homo economicus* and a highly efficient capital market (Fama 1970). Despite a strong emphasis on positive economic theory related to "what is," agency theory had a strong influence on normative theory related to "what should be." Next, I discuss the presence of social norms in *The Wealth of Nations*. While the Chicago school attributed their narrow view of economic man to Adam Smith, a deeper analysis of Smith's classic work of political economy reveals a fuller, social science view of man with an emphasis on culture, institutions, and social norms. Rather than built on the "granite of self interest" (Stigler 1971a, 265), therefore, this analysis suggests that Smith built his economic system on the foundation provided in his first great work, *The Theory of Moral Sentiments*. Consistent with recent scholarship, I argue that Smith had a complete system or opus in mind when he wrote both works, and that his economic system can best be described as institutional individualism (Song 1995). I then present the social norm theory contained in Smith's work of moral philosophy, which brought him worldwide fame as a philosopher of the highest order.

I conclude this chapter by presenting recent social norm theory related to the firm that has proven useful to researchers in economics, accounting, and finance. This includes Eric Posner's (2000) theory of law and social norms, Vernon Smith's (2003, 2008) theory of ecological rationality, and Cristina Bicchieri's (2006) theory of social norm activation. Posner defines social norms as behavioral regularities that emerge as a consequence of people acting in their rational self-interest and their desire to reap the financial rewards of such behavior. Thus, individuals do not have preferences for social norms per se but only for the signaling benefits of social norm behavior. Posner's signaling model, however, is unable to explain recent evidence of norm-based behavior in single-period tests of game theory and agency theory. Nobel Laureate Vernon Smith attributes this evidence to "ecological rationality" or the emergent order of home-grown norms, traditions, and morality. Consistent with this extended notion of rationality, Bicchieri argues that individuals have conditional preferences for social norms from past social experience, and that such social norms may be activated in an economic setting by information and situational cues that generate behavioral expectations. Her model of social norm activation is able to explain the norm-based behavior arising in experimental tests of neoclassical theory.

THE BEHAVIORAL ASSUMPTIONS OF *HOMO ECONOMICUS*

In his paper, *Social Norms and Economic Theory*, Jon Elster (1989, 99) identifies two main views of man and states that they represent "one of the most persistent cleavages in the social sciences." One he associates with Adam Smith called *homo economicus*; the other he associates with Emile Durkheim called *homo sociologicus*. In the former, the behavior of man is assumed to be guided by instrumental rationality and narrow self-interest. In the latter, the behavior of man is assumed to be guided by culture, institutions, and social norms. The association of Adam Smith with the narrow view of man called *homo economicus* is a common misconception that has been perpetuated by many economists in the neoclassical tradition. More recently, however, researchers have associated the father of classical economics with a fuller, social science view of man that is more consistent with *homo sociologicus* (Song 1995; Barbalet 2005, 2007). As a moral philosopher who published a detailed theory of social and moral norms before his work on political economy, Adam Smith would likely not recognize the narrow view of man that has been credited to him by the Chicago school.[1]

Mary Morgan (2006) provides an insightful account of the development of economic models of man beginning with Adam Smith. She argues that Smith's portrait of the factory worker in *The Wealth of Nations* does not fit the narrow model of man called *homo economicus*. In particular, the worker who provides the potential for specialization and division of labor is "a complex mixture of instincts, talents, motivations, and preferences" (Morgan 2006, 2). Smith paints a portrait of man as having a natural propensity to "truck, barter and exchange" and possessing talents that can be further developed to form specialization and efficiency gains. Self-interest is certainly present, but "it is a mistake to think that self-interest is all there is to Smith's central economic character." Smith does include passages attributing specialization and the division of labor to self-interest rather than to government planning, but these passages do not support a model of man based exclusively on narrow self-interest. As is true of classical economists, Smith focused primarily on macroeconomic theory related to political economy, which did not require a detailed model of man. Recent research shows that Smith built his political economy on the foundation provided by his model of man in *The Theory of Moral Sentiments*. In fact, he considered his first book "a much superior work" to his political economy (Phillipson 2010, 274) and was continually updating it up to the time of his death (Raphael and Macfie 1982).[2]

The narrow view of economic man called *homo economicus* is more accurately attributable to another classical economist, John Stuart Mill

---

[1] I was heavily influenced by the Chicago school view of Adam Smith early in my career. It took a semester at the Adam Smith Research Foundation at the University of Glasgow for me to fully appreciate the richness of Adam Smith's system or opus in his life and writings. I also thank Vernon Smith and experimental economists at Florida State University for helping me discover the real Adam Smith.

[2] Smith's sixth and final edition of *The Theory of Moral Sentiments* was published shortly before his death in 1790, and it contained very extensive additions based on his lifelong reflections on economics and society.

(1806–1873).[3] In an essay on research method, Mill (1836, 323) defined political economy as "The science which traces the laws of such of the phenomena of society as arise from the combined operations of mankind for the production of wealth, in so far as those phenomena are not modified by the pursuit of any other object." Influenced by his famous economist father James Mill (1773–1836) and by David Ricardo (1772–1823), he developed a model of man that incorporated those aspects of man's behavior that came under the realm of his newly defined science of political economy. For this purpose, he limited the motivations of mankind to a desire for wealth and a dislike of work. He also endowed his model of man with full rationality to obtain his desired ends. Mill's portrait of economic man, however, was only offered as a useful portrait for the study of political economy. He emphasized that no "political economist was ever so absurd as to suppose that mankind are really thus constituted" (Mill 1836, 322). As Morgan (2006, 7) describes it, Mill's narrow view of man was a "fiction in the service of science."

Interestingly, Mill's (1836) methodological essay contains many of the same points as Milton Friedman's (1953) methodological essay (see Chapter 1). Mill (1836, 325) characterizes the science of political economy "as essentially an *abstract* science" that uses deductive logic to make predictions from underlying assumptions. "It reasons, and, as we contend, must necessarily reason, from assumptions, not from facts." Mill (1836, 335) emphasizes, however, that the deductive logic of the political economist "must at least enable him to explain and account for what *is*, or he is an insufficient judge of what ought to be." As with Friedman, this places positive theory before normative theory. Mill also does not conceive of the possibility of experimental tests in political economy, and labels this as a significant weakness of the social science of political economy compared to the physical sciences. Finally, Mill (1836, 334) emphasizes that the political economist is not immune to bias. "In these complex matters, men see with their preconceived opinions, not with their eyes: an interested or a passionate man's statistics are of little worth; and a year seldom passes without examples of the astounding falsehoods which large bodies of respectable men will back each other in publishing to the world as facts within their personal knowledge."

---

[3] Mill did not use the label *homo economicus* in describing his narrow view of economic man. This label came to be used many years later, often by his detractors. Mill appeared to support aspects of socialism later in life, which may be why the Chicago school never attributed their narrow view of *homo economicus* to him.

Similar to Friedman, Mill (1836, 323) promoted a cost/benefit approach to expanding the underlying behavioral assumptions of political economy:

So far as it is known, or may be presumed, that the conduct of mankind in the pursuit of wealth is under the collateral influence of any other of the properties of our nature than the desire of obtaining the greatest quantity of wealth with the least labour and self-denial, the conclusion of Political Economy will so far fail of being applicable to the explanation or prediction of real events, until they are modified by a correct allowance for the degree of influence exercised by the other cause.

Neoclassical economists, however, found little occasion to extend Mill's simplified behavioral assumptions. In fact, until very recently they have gone further than Mill in maintaining that *homo economicus* is a realistic model of man in economic settings related to the firm and markets.

Morgan (2006, 9) describes the process of developing an economic model of man as involving "definitional work, theoretical speculation, and observing activity." She further depicts this process as involving four general types of analyses: generalizing, simplifying (also called isolating), abstracting, and idealizing. *Generalizing* involves picking out the general characteristics found in all cases while leaving out the particularities that differ between cases, and *simplifying (isolating)* involves stripping away most of the elements of a complex reality to focus on certain characteristics of that reality. *Abstracting* and *idealizing*, in contrast, are more invasive in that the former involves extracting the most important elements for study, and the latter involves focusing on the most perfect version of the object of study. Morgan argues that these four types of analyses in economic modeling are not always easy to distinguish. For example, she describes Mill's narrow model of economic man as a simplification whereas Mill himself described it as an abstraction (Mill 1836, 326–327).

Early neoclassical economists such as William S. Jevons (1835–1882) took for granted that the laws of economics were mathematical and required formal models. As Morgan (2006, 13) points out, Jevons's formalizing required an increasingly "idealized" model of economic man:

This is why Jevons is so often lauded as one of the founders of "modern" economics . . . By his kind of work, methods of theorizing ideal types became inextricably linked with "formalizing," that is with changing the language of economics from the informal and hugely nuanced possibilities of expression in our verbal languages to the more constrained forms but more powerful reasoning we associated with mathematics.

Although the individual had greater causal power under the new neoclassical economics, because the laws of economics operated at the level of the individual, the mathematical nature of the analyses required an increasingly idealized characterization of economic man. For example, Jevons (1871) assumed that man's desires or needs were primary and they dictated his economic valuations and choices. By the mid-twentieth century, however, neoclassical economists had made valuations and choices the dominant focus, and assumed that desires could only be maximized by "rational" choices. Thus, neoclassical economists assumed less and less about individuals' desires or motivations and focused instead on rational choice (Morgan 2006). This focus on rational choice is well described by Paul Samuelson (1947, 97–98):

The utility analysis rests on the fundamental assumption that the individual confronted with given prices and confined to a given total expenditure selects that combination of goods which is highest on his preference scale. This does not require (a) that the individual behave rationally in any other sense; (b) that he be deliberate and self-conscious in his purchasing; (c) that there exist any intensive magnitude which he feels or consults.

This narrow view of rational choice only requires complete, consistent, and transitive preferences over a range of options. This is an "instrumental rationality," in that nothing is really claimed about economic man's underlying preferences, valuations, or feelings. In particular, the focus is entirely on consequences or outcomes, not causes of behavior. This idealized view of economic man, while useful for formal modeling and powerful theorizing, has made the central character of neoclassical economic theory a mere calculator. This stands in sharp contrast with institutional economic theory, which characterizes economic man as influenced by culture, institutions, and social norms. Only recently, when economic man has become the subject of laboratory investigation, have the true causal capacities of economic man become visible and worthy of theorizing by neoclassical economists (Morgan 2006).[4]

THE ASSUMPTIONS AND IMPLICATIONS OF AGENCY THEORY

Fourcade and Khurana (2013, 151) attribute the development of agency theory to a newly revitalized neoclassical economic theory:

(A)gency theory created a unified approach to organizations that would have repercussions in corporate finance, organizational behavior, accounting, and

---

[4] By ignoring preferences for social norms, economists have also ignored whether such preferences are "rational" in the traditional sense. Until very recently, neoclassical economists have simply assumed that any preferences outside of *homo economicus* were irrational and unworthy of theorizing.

corporate governance. Unlike much of the earlier scholarship in business schools, the core ideas of agency theory were derived not from inductive observation and practical experience but, instead, from the theoretical musings of a newly revitalized neoclassical economic theory.

As discussed in Chapter 3, this rigorous and powerful theory of the firm reflected the increasing influence of neoclassical economists over institutional economists, first in economics and later in the business school. By emphasizing neoclassical theory, researchers in economics, accounting, and finance addressed calls from the Ford and Carnegie Foundations to increase the scientific rigor of the university-based business school. Thus, it is not surprising that agency theory emanated from the Chicago school, which was itself a product of the reform movement launched by the foundations (Khurana 2007).

The influence of agency theory as a fully developed theory of the firm can be traced to the seminal work of Michael Jensen and William Meckling (Jensen and Meckling 1976), two University of Chicago graduates who came together at the University of Rochester from 1964 to 1983. From its beginnings in information economics (Spence and Zeckhauser 1971, Ross 1973), agency theory has developed into two aligned but mostly separate literatures: positive agency theory and principal-agent theory. Both literatures address the contracting problem between self-interested, utility-maximizing parties and both share the same general organizational goal of minimizing agency costs due to information asymmetry and opportunistic self-interest. The positive agency literature, however, is nonmathematical and empirically oriented while the principal-agent literature is highly mathematical and generally not empirically oriented (Jensen 1983). For my purposes here, I merge the two literatures and discuss a single theory of the firm called agency theory.[5]

In contrast to earlier neoclassical theory, which attributed firm coordination primarily to signals of supply and demand provided by the market, agency theory got inside the "black box" of the organization to examine the judgments and decisions of managers. In the hands of economists associated with the Chicago school, however, agency theory took on a decidedly analytical focus that de-emphasized the legitimacy of management and public policy. In particular, agency theory utilized an

---

[5] I discuss principal-agent theory in length in Chapter 5, including its assumptions, characteristics, and predictions. As part of that discussion, I present a principal-agent model that includes a social norm for promise-keeping to demonstrate how researchers can incorporate social norms into the most formal neoclassical theory of the firm.

increasingly narrow view of *homo economicus*, which I label "opportunistic self-interest."[6] When combined with the efficient market hypothesis (Fama 1970), this theory of the firm reduced both managers and regulators to self-interested opportunists and reduced managerial responsibilities to maximizing share price. This generated a "managerial revolution in reverse" whereby Chandler's (1977) visible hand of management was replaced by the invisible hand of the market (Fourcade and Khurana 2013, 151). Michael Jensen played a significant role in this revolution by promoting the policy implications of agency theory through academic journals and practitioner-oriented outlets such as the *Harvard Business Review* and the *Wall Street Journal*.

Despite its focus on positive economic theory related to "what is," agency theory reshaped normative theory related to "what should be." Regarding the firm, agency theory was used to encourage some forms of organizational control and discourage others. For example, Jensen's writings helped legitimize the takeover movement in the 1980s by presenting it as an important aspect of corporate governance (Dobbin and Zorn 2005), and encouraged the proliferation of lucrative stock options and incentive pay to align incentives between management and shareholders (Bebchuk and Fried 2004). Jensen also used agency theory to discourage commonly used organizational controls such as participative budgeting and the balanced scorecard. In the *Harvard Business Review*, Jensen discouraged the use of participative budgeting because "it encourages managers to lie and cheat" (Jensen 2001, 96). In the *Business Ethics Quarterly*, he discouraged the use of the balanced scorecard because "maximizing the total market value of the firm" is the only objective function needed by management to efficiently run an organization (Jensen 2002, 239). This latter argument, of course, also discouraged corporate social responsibility (CSR) and any expansion of management responsibilities to other stakeholders of the firm besides shareholders.

The new theory of the firm out of the Chicago school was promoted in the field of accounting by University of Rochester accounting faculty. Ross Watts and Jerold Zimmerman published an influential paper in 1978 entitled, "Towards a positive theory of the determination of accounting standards," where they characterized the standard-setting process as a conflict between self-interested parties (Watts and Zimmerman 1978). They also launched the *Journal of Accounting and Economics* in 1979 and in

---

[6] Oliver Williamson (1993, 97) has labeled this narrow view of *homo economicus* "self-interest seeking with guile."

1986 published a book entitled, *Positive Accounting Theory*. In their book, Watts and Zimmerman (1986, 5) described how the new theory and methodology was initially met with resistance among researchers in accounting. "However, over time the approach gained popularity, and papers based on it now constitute a large fraction of papers published by the leading academic journals." Watts and Zimmerman (1986, 6) promoted a particularly narrow view of financial regulation in their view of positive accounting theory:

Another basis for the emerging accounting theory was the ongoing debate over the desirability of government regulation of financial disclosure. The early empirical studies had questioned the existing rationales for regulation, but researchers found new rationales in economic theory. The debate over those new rationales, in turn, led to the recognition that the (old) rationales relied on simplistic models of the behavior of politicians and bureaucrats that were inconsistent with the evidence emerging in economics. This realization caused accounting researchers to adopt the assumption that politicians and bureaucrats, like managers and accountants, act to maximize their own welfare and to use that assumption to model the effect of regulation on accounting practice.

Rather than support the importance of financial regulation in promoting transparency and accountability, this view of positive accounting theory reduced such regulation to narrow self-interest on the part of regulators. For example, Watts and Zimmerman (1986, 3) argued that a regulator at the SEC "is concerned with the effect of an accounting standard on the attitude of members of Congress toward the SEC because that affects the SEC's budget and the resources under that individual's control."

The policy implications of agency theory identified by the Chicago school followed naturally from a narrow view of Mill's *homo economicus*, a strong belief in the efficient market hypothesis, and a rigid adherence to Friedman's (1953) research methodology. These policy implications did little to promote a merchant culture of transparency and accountability, but instead focused on financial incentives to control opportunistic behavior in the firm. For example, Jensen and Murphy (1990) used agency theory to argue that executive compensation schemes were not sufficiently "high-powered" or incentive-based. To better align the interests of managers with owners of the firm, they argued that the pay and personal wealth of top executives should be tied substantially to stock price or accounting-based measures associated with stock price. In response, corporate boards throughout the 1990s steadily increased the financial incentives of executives by incorporating large bonuses based on stock price and earnings targets. Between 1992 and 2000, the average inflation-adjusted pay of CEOs at S&P 500 firms climbed from $3.5 million to $14.7 million (Bebchuk and Fried 2004). This increase in CEO pay, which included shares of stock granted as part of stock options, far outpaced the growth in average employee pay. As a result, the ratio of average CEO pay to average worker pay at the largest public companies grew from 140:1 to 500:1 (Revell 2003). Outside consultants frequently used the new theory of the firm to develop and justify high-powered financial incentives (Bebchuk and Fried 2003).

The actions of top executives at Fannie Mae and Freddie Mac leading up to the market meltdown of 2008 (see Chapter 2) demonstrate the unintended consequences of agency theory's focus on financial incentives. When Franklin Raines accepted the CEO position of Fannie Mae in 1999, he had an impressive resume as a partner at investment bank Lazard Freres, vice chairman at Fannie Mae, and budget director under President Bill Clinton. Based on modern finance theory, Congress had mandated in 1992 that "pay for performance" be a substantial component of top executives' total compensation at the government-sponsored enterprise (Emmons and Sierra 2004). In an effort to turbocharge Raines's financial incentives, therefore, Fannie Mae's board tied his yearly cash and stock bonuses to meeting annual earnings goals. During the four-year period from 2000 to 2003, Fannie Mae reported increased earnings each year, which surpassed the annual earnings goal. During this period, Raines amassed $13 million in annual cash bonuses and almost $30 million worth of Fannie Mae shares under his generous compensation package (Bebchuk and Fried 2005).

In December 2004, however, the same board that doled out Raines's lucrative compensation package demanded his resignation. This action followed the determination by the SEC that Fannie Mae had used accounting manipulations to inflate its earnings over the previous four years by at least $10 billion, wiping out a large portion of the company's total reported profits during those years (Bebchuk and Fried 2005). Fannie's regulator, the Office of Federal Housing Oversight (Ofheo), determined that the company's hedging activities and derivative transactions violated Generally Accepted Accounting Principles (GAAP). Also in violation of GAAP, Fannie had used a "cookie jar" reserve for its portfolio of mortgage-backed securities to smooth its quarterly earnings. Ofheo concluded that the leaders of the company had developed a corporate culture that tolerated lax internal controls, deferred expenses to achieve bonus compensation targets, and emphasized stable earnings at the expense of accurate financial disclosure (Fannie Uncovered 2004).

The accounting scandal at Fannie Mae and a similar accounting scandal at Freddie Mac generated widespread calls for increased government regulation. However, the opportunistic culture at the two government-sponsored enterprises (GSEs) continued up to the mortgage market meltdown in 2008. As discussed in Chapter 2, Fannie and Freddie loosened their underwriting standards over this time period, purchasing and guaranteeing riskier loans. From 2005 to 2008, in particular, Fannie and Freddie began to purchase subprime and Alt-A mortgage-backed securities from Wall Street. The results of these actions would be disastrous for investors and taxpayers. Fannie and Freddie were completely wiped out by the mortgage market meltdown in 2008 and were among the first large financial institutions to receive massive federal bailouts. From January 1, 2008 through the third quarter of 2010 the two GSEs lost $229 billion, requiring a bailout from the US Treasury of $151 billion (FCIC 2011).

As discussed in Chapter 2, the stock market crash of 2008 was fueled by an opportunism culture that had forgotten the merchant culture values of transparency and accountability. In addition to the opportunism of actors up and down the mortgage securitization chain, important players who were supposed to protect investors and taxpayers were corrupted by the culture. I now add Fannie Mae and Freddie Mac to that list of players. But what role did agency theory play in this opportunistic culture? Did the high-powered financial incentives promoted by the theory encourage opportunistic behavior and excessive risk-taking? Did the lack of financial regulation promoted by the theory leave financial markets particularly vulnerable to such behavior? These are difficult questions, and satisfactory answers will be difficult to come by. Yet, the inability of agency theory to support a merchant culture of transparency and accountability argues for enhancing the behavioral assumptions of the neoclassical theory of the firm. Fortunately, researchers have begun to expand the boundaries of the theory to include the effects of institutions, culture, and social norms. This research initiative has been aided recently by the rediscovery of the importance of social norms in Adam Smith's writings.

THE PRESENCE OF SOCIAL NORMS IN *THE WEALTH OF NATIONS*

The legacy of Adam Smith has been expanded by economists and historians examining his full system of thought, or "opus." This integrative view of Smith's writings yields a striking resemblance to the writings of German sociologist Max Weber (Haakonssen and Winch 2006). Considered one of the most influential thinkers of the Scottish Enlightenment (Broadie 2003), Smith was a product of the merchant culture that had evolved in northern Italy, spread to the Netherlands, and then was firmly planted in Great Britain (see Chapter 2). In addition to spreading Locke's view of natural law and civil liberty, eighteenth century Scottish Presbyterians spread the Protestant Reformation to all aspects of society, including commerce and government. Thus, it is not surprising that Britain's merchant culture would manifest itself most fully in Scotland and, similar to the Italian Renaissance and the Dutch Enlightenment, lead to an explosion of wealth, learning, and literature. The Scottish Enlightenment would play an important role in the export of the merchant culture to the United States, as students educated in the ancient universities of Scotland (Glasgow, Edinburgh, and Aberdeen) migrated to the new nation in large numbers (Broadie 2003).

The Chicago school's interpretation of Adam Smith's classic work of political economy supported their narrow view of economic man as motivated solely by opportunistic self-interest. George Stigler (1911–1991), who joined Milton Friedman at the University of Chicago in 1958 and received a Nobel Prize in Economic Science in 1982, stated that "*The Wealth of Nations* is a stupendous palace erected upon the granite of self interest" (Stigler 1971a, 265). While Stigler is best known for his economic theory of information (Stigler 1961), he also developed an economic theory attributing all government regulation to self-interested behavior on the part of regulators and other special interest groups (Stigler 1971b). Watts and Zimmerman's (1978, 1986) view of financial regulation in their positive accounting theory appears to have been heavily influenced by Stigler's economic theory of government regulation. Later in his career, Stigler (1982) even attributed the behavior of economists and the development of all economic theory to narrow self-interest. Thus, it is not surprising that Stigler would focus on those passages in *The Wealth of Nations* that supported his narrow view of economic man.

The notion that Adam Smith attributed all of human motivation to narrow self-interest can be traced to Henry Thomas Buckle's (1864) clumsy attempt to reconcile Smith's two classic works (Haakonssen and Winch 2006). Buckle maintained that Smith attributed human motivation to "altruism" in *The Theory of Moral Sentiments* and "self-interest" in *The Wealth of Nations*. This simplistic and misguided interpretation of Smith's two works led to the accusation of a conceptual inconsistency in Smith's thinking and fueled a major debate in Germany called "Das Adam Smith Problem." In the 1870s, this debate in the German-speaking world reduced the significance of Smith's first major work in the eyes of many economists (Reeder 1997). The conceptual inconsistency view of Smith's writings, however, was always highly problematic. Smith continuously revised his two major works up to the year of his death in 1790 and never hinted at any discrepancy or recanted any of his views as other great philosophers did in their lifetimes (e.g., Mill, Kant, and Heidegger). In fact, the sections that he revised demonstrate a growing concern over the importance of institutions and social norms in commerce and society.

With the help of newly discovered student notes from his lectures at Glasgow, new details regarding his career, and a comprehensive view of his writings, scholars have assembled a more complete system of thought in Adam Smith's writings. This research demonstrates that Smith viewed *The Wealth of Nations* as part of a comprehensive system or opus that had as its foundation *The Theory of Moral Sentiments* (Griswold 1999; Haakonssen and Winch 2006). Even before taking his first position at Glasgow in 1751 as Professor of Logic, Smith included material in political economy in his Edinburgh lectures (1748–1750). Further, Smith included this material in his early lectures as Professor of Moral Philosophy in 1752 (Raphael and Macfie 1982). Thus, content from both books was part of Smith's opus from the very beginning. In the Glasgow Edition of Adam Smith's works and correspondence, Campbell and Skinner (1981, 18) state,

In terms of Smith's teaching, his work on economics was designed to follow on his treatment of ethics and jurisprudence, and therefore to add something to the sum total of our knowledge of the activities of man in society. To this extent, each of the three subjects can be seen to be interconnected, although it is also true to say that each component of the system contains material which distinguishes it from the others. One part of Smith's achievement was in fact to see all these different subjects as parts of a single whole, while at the same time differentiating economics from them.

In *The Wealth of Nations*, Smith offers a theory of political economy that incorporates institutions and social norms and claims to better the lot of ordinary people. He bases his political economy on the ideals of "perfect liberty" and recommends extending this liberty to all of mankind, including slaves and American colonists. Smith asserts that it can never be the interest of the upper class to oppress the middle and lower classes. "The establishment of perfect justice, of perfect liberty, and of perfect equality, is the very simple secret which most effectually secures the highest degree of prosperity to all the three classes" (*WN* IV.ix.17). Campbell and Skinner (1981, 47) attribute the great success of Smith's classic work of political economy to its "institutional emphasis" and this "plea for liberty," which was in accord with the intellectual presuppositions of the eighteenth century. More recently, researchers have labeled Smith's social science view of man "institutional individualism" (Song 1995).

In *The Wealth of Nations*, Smith grants commerce, religion, education, and government important roles in maintaining high moral character and advancing the common good (Griswold 1999). It may appear surprising that Smith includes commerce among the properly structured social institutions that maintain high moral character among a nation's citizens. This aspect of his political economy has received little attention. Smith states, "Honour makes a great part of the reward of all honourable professions" (*WN* I.x.b.2). Further, he argues that those professions that require the most trust and trustworthiness receive the highest pay (*WN* I.x.b.19). This grants business professionals both a financial and a nonfinancial incentive to be honorable and prove themselves trustworthy. Smith also argues that individuals are naturally motivated to "excel in any profession" because of the nonfinancial reward of "(t)he publick admiration which attends upon such distinguished abilities . . ." (*WN* I.x.b.24). This grants all workers a financial and nonfinancial incentive to develop their skills and abilities, which supports Smith's underlying economic engine of specialization and the division of labor (see Chapter 3).

Charles Griswold Jr. (1999, 296) identifies two mechanisms by which free commerce helps maintain high moral character in Smith's political economy: (1) the opportunity to sell one's own labor, and (2) the civilizing role of persuasion. To Smith, the liberty to sell one's labor is not only just, but it is also conducive to the formation of moral character. Consistent with Weber's Protestant Work Ethic, Smith views this liberty as essential to fostering virtues such as independence and self-reliance. Smith promotes the virtue of self-reliance by encouraging higher wages for common laborers so that they can "bring up a family" (*WN* I.viii.15). He also promotes the virtue of self-reliance by encouraging the unencumbered activity of independent workers, who are more highly motivated to work hard and be industrious than are dependent workers. "The one, in his separate independent state, is less liable to the temptations of bad company, which in large manufactories so frequently ruin the morals of the other" (*WN* I.viii.48). Finally, Smith promotes the virtue of self-reliance by encouraging the free workings of the market to create "universal opulence which extends itself to the lowest ranks of the people" (*WN* I.i.10). A large weakness of the guilds and monopolies of the mercantile system, in contrast to Smith's ideal political economy of perfect liberty, is that they create one-way dependencies that corrupt the character of all involved.

This concern over the corrupting influence of dependency spans all of Smith's writings (Perelman 1989, Özler 2012). The strongest expression of this concern appears in Smith's lectures on jurisprudence at Glasgow University (Smith 1762–63, vi.6):

Nothing tends so much to corrupt and enervate and debase the mind as dependency, and nothing gives such noble and generous notions of probity as freedom and independency.

The civilizing role of persuasion is another mechanism by which free commerce maintains high moral character in Smith's political economy. Smith identifies the propensity in human nature "to truck, barter, and exchange one thing for another" (*WN* I.ii.1), and attributes this propensity to "one of those original principles in human nature" or "the necessary consequence of the faculties of reason and speech" (*WN* I.ii.2). "In civilized society (man) stands at all times in need of the co-operation and assistance of great multitudes, while his whole life is scarce sufficient to gain the friendship of a few persons" (*WN* I.ii.2). Thus, man's survival in modern society is dependent upon his ability to persuade perfect strangers to provide what he needs or wants. On what basis, however, do we persuade strangers to provide our needs or wants? This leads to the famous passage quoted by some economists to attribute all human motivation in Smith's political economy to narrow self-interest: "It is not from the benevolence of the butcher, the brewer, or the baker, that we expect our dinner, but from their regard to their own interest" (*WN* I.ii.2). Rather than attribute all human motivation to narrow self-interest, however, this passage demonstrates another mechanism by which free commerce helps maintain high moral character. As Griswold (1999, 297) explains, "(P)recisely in appealing to each other's self-interest, precisely in enacting what seems to be our fundamental separateness and indifference to one another, we 'civilize' ourselves and each other by binding ourselves to one another."[7] The civilizing role of persuasion promotes a number of important virtues and social norms in society, including honesty, fairness, trustworthiness, and reciprocity.

---

[7] Raphael and Macfie (1982, 20) are particularly damning in their condemnation of the traditional interpretation in economics of Smith's statement attributing specialization and the division of labor to self-interest: "There is nothing surprising in Adam Smith's well known statement (*WN* I.ii.2) . . . Who would suppose this to imply that Adam Smith had come to disbelieve in the very existence or the moral value of benevolence? Nobody with any sense."

In Book V of *The Wealth of Nations*, Smith grants religion and education important roles in maintaining high moral character and promoting social order. In contrast to Karl Marx, Smith never characterizes religion as an opium of the people. He introduces his analysis of institutionalized religion with a discussion of education, however, and thereby avoids direct questions of theology and religious dogma (*WN* V.i.f.25):

> *In every age and country of the world men must have attended to the characters, designs, and actions of one another, and many reputable rules and maxims for the conduct of human life, must have been laid down and approved of by common consent. As soon as writing came into fashion, wise men, or those who fancied themselves such, would naturally endeavor to increase the number of those established and respected maxims, and to express their own sense of what was either proper or improper conduct.*

Smith acknowledges that society "necessarily places the greater part of individuals in such situations as naturally form in them, without any attention of government, almost all the abilities and virtues which that state requires" (*WN* V.i.f.49). Examples of virtue-building institutions in society include the civilizing influence of family, religion, and educational institutions. Smith spends the rest of Book V explaining how parochial and public schools teach the maxims of prudence and morality to the general populous. In addition to moral education, these schools teach the common people "the most essential parts of education...to read, write, and account" (*WN* V.i.f.54). Thus, we see in Adam Smith's work of political economy the merchant culture emphasis on practical skills as well as the social norms of transparency and accountability.

Finally, Smith includes government among the properly structured social institutions that maintain high moral character and advance the common good (Griswold 1999). In his introduction to Book IV of *The Wealth of Nations*, Smith states that the role of the state is "to provide a plentiful revenue or subsistence for the people, or more properly to enable them to provide such a revenue or subsistence for themselves" (*WN* IV.Intro.I). Consistent with his emphasis on self-reliance as a virtue, Smith warns the state to avoid dependency, even in its role of providing "a plentiful revenue or subsistence for the people." In particular, he provides the most direct statement in Book IV of the ability of self-interest to motivate specialization and the division of labor: "(H)e is in this, as in many other cases, led by an invisible hand to promote an end which was no part of his intention. Nor is it always the worse for the society that it was no part of it. By pursuing his own interest he frequently promotes that of the society more effectually than when he really intends to promote it" (*WN* IV.ii.9). Again, the best way for government to provide a plentiful revenue or subsistence for its people is to promote Smith's ideal system of perfect liberty. Thus, much of Book IV is also spent criticizing the mercantile system, which used the power of the state to favor certain trades and industries and tightly control international trade.

In Book V of *The Wealth of Nations*, Smith grants the state three legitimate functions: (1) the defense of the society, (2) the administration of justice, and (3) the facilitation of commerce. Smith states that the first duty of the state is to defend "the society from the violence and injustice of other independent societies," and that this duty "grows gradually more and more expensive, as the society advances in civilization" (*WN* V.i.a.42). The second duty of the state is "that of protecting, as far as possible, every member of the society from the injustice or oppression of every other member of it, or the duty of establishing an exact administration of justice" (*WN* V.i.b.1). A large part of this duty of justice, according to Smith, involves the protection of a member's private property or the defense "of those who have some property against those who have none at all" (*WN* V.i.b.12). The third and final duty of the state is that of erecting and maintaining public works and institutions "which, though they may be in the highest degree advantageous to a great society, are, however, of such a nature, that the profit could never repay the expense to any individual or small number of individuals." Among the public works that benefit commerce, Smith includes good roads, bridges, navigable canals, harbors, etc. (*WN* V.i.d.1).

Smith does not ignore the burdens of the working poor who must labor under the boring and tedious jobs created by the division of labor. First, he expresses concern that the progress of the division of labor will confine common laborers to one or two simple operations of production, and will thus corrupt the laborer's "intellectual, social, and martial virtues" (*WN* V. i.f.50). Second, he expresses concern regarding the tendency for the uneducated and disenfranchised to develop a "mutilated and deformed" character and become liable to "the delusions of enthusiasm and superstition, which, among ignorant nations, frequently occasion the most dreadful disorders" (*WN* V.i.f.61). "An instructed and intelligent people besides are always more decent and orderly . . . (and) feel themselves, each individually, more respectable, and more likely to obtain the respect of their lawful superiors, and they are therefore more disposed to respect those superiors" (*WN* V.i.f.61). Because of these concerns, Smith urges the state to educate its citizens in the requisite abilities and virtues required of both commerce and a free society. The broad education that Smith has in mind includes science, philosophy, and the arts (Griswold 1999).

This short review of the latest scholarship regarding *The Wealth of Nations* suggests that, rather than building on the "granite of self interest" (Stigler 1971a), Adam Smith built his work of political economy on the foundation provided by his work of moral philosophy (Raphael and Macfie 1982). This analysis rejects the common interpretation "that Smith's whole enterprise was to liberate economics from the reign of virtue or ethical concerns" (Mehta 2006, 247). This analysis also rejects the common interpretation that Smith's purpose was to liberate economics from all state interference. As Griswold (1999, 295) concludes, Adam Smith knew well that "competition and liberty, protected by a spectating 'night-watchman state,' are in themselves insufficient to sustain a peaceful and just society, for they cannot be counted upon always to generate the requisite civic virtue." In particular, Smith knew well that "(w)ithout a modicum of habituated virtue (moral and intellectual) in the citizens, the invisible hand behaves like an iron first." Rather than promoting narrow self-interest, therefore, Smith's classic work of political economy promotes the proper structuring of social institutions to establish and maintain proper virtues and social norms.

SOCIAL NORM THEORY IN *THE THEORY OF MORAL SENTIMENTS*

Adam Smith published the first edition of *The Theory of Moral Sentiments* in 1759 during his tenure as Chair of Moral Philosophy at the University of Glasgow. He published a second edition of the book in 1761 in response to comments received after his first edition. This was followed by editions 3 (1767), 4 (1774), and 5 (1781), which differed little from edition 2. Edition 6, however, which he published in the final year of his life (1790), contained extensive additions, including a whole new section devoted to the topic of moral virtue (Part VI). Coming as it did at the end of his life, this new material reflects Smith's lifelong reflections on commerce and society (Raphael and Macfie 1982). Thus, rather than reflecting a model of man that he would abandon in his later years, *The Theory of Moral Sentiments* reflects Smith's final and most developed view of man in society. The latest research on Adam Smith suggests that there was no significant change in his views over time and that, in fact, "Smith had become 'alarmed' at the falling stock of moral capital in commercial society" (Alvey 2007, 79).

The latest research suggests the following regarding Adam Smith's two major works. First, Smith's moral philosophy in *The Theory of Moral Sentiment* is widely consistent with the Christian Stoicism of the Scottish Enlightenment. Although he adopts many of the modernizing views of his close friend, David Hume, his moral philosophy follows closely that of his teacher and mentor, Francis Hutcheson. In particular, rather than support the secularism movement of Hume, Smith's writings support Hutcheson's moderating movement that sought to rescue religion and society from the dead weight of clerical authority on the one hand and excessive enthusiasm on the other (Cockfield, Firth, and Laurent 2007).[8] Second, Smith's political economy in *The Wealth of Nations* is part of a larger system or corpus that is itself a branch of moral philosophy (Griswold 1999). Student notes and correspondence regarding Smith's days at Glasgow confirm that political economy was included from the start in his lectures on moral philosophy. Furthermore, Smith viewed narrow self-interest as a vice or a corruption of our moral sentiments. Each edition of *The Theory of Moral Sentiments* begins with the following passage (*TMS* I.i.1.1):

How selfish soever man may be supposed, there are evidently some principles in his nature, which interest him in the fortune of others, and render their happiness necessary to him, though he derives nothing from it except the pleasure of seeing it.

Thus, Smith begins his corpus by refuting the very position for which he has been credited by the Chicago school. This statement rejects the view among some modern economists that "we empathize with others only when we think it to our advantage to do so – that is, that we treat others as means to our self-interest, narrowly understood" (Griswold 1999, 78). Not only does Smith grant mankind the ability to empathize with others, which he calls *sympathy*, he makes it *the* major force behind all moral behavior. All of Smith's system or corpus, therefore, is based on the inherent tension between sympathy and the vice of selfishness. In particular, this tension is fundamental to both *The Theory of Moral Sentiments* and *The Wealth of Nations*.

---

[8] The removal of explicitly Christian passages and the preservation of references to "the author of nature" in subsequent editions of *The Theory of Moral Sentiments* suggests that Smith may have become a deist over time. The "new view" of Adam Smith, however, is that there was no fundamental shift in his underlying theology over time (Alvey 2007). In particular, recent research views Smith's moral philosophy less as a rejection of a religious worldview than a rejection of the repressive and dogmatic practices of the eighteenth century Scottish Kirk (Clarke 2007).

As if the point needed special emphasis, Smith devotes an entire section of *The Theory of Moral Sentiments* to debunking the view that the whole of mankind's motivations can be attributed to "selfishness" (Part VII). In his day, this view was espoused by Hobbes, Pufendorf, and Mandeville, but it is reflected more recently in the writings of Ayn Rand. Smith attacks this view by confronting the writings of Bernard Mandeville, a Dutch philosopher and political economist living in London. Mandeville had written a political satire on the state of England in 1705 describing a bee community that thrives until the bees are suddenly made honest and virtuous. Republished in 1714 as *The Fable of the Bees: or Private Vices, Public Benefits*, Mandeville's satire glorified the desire for personal gain and attributed all so-called "virtue" to vanity and self-interest. Smith calls out "Dr. Mandeville" by name and directly contradicts his narrow view of virtue (*TMS* VII.ii.4.7):

Dr. Mandeville considers whatever is done from a sense of propriety, from a regard to what is commendable and praise-worthy, as being done from a love of praise and commendation, or as he calls it from vanity. Man, he observes, is naturally much more interested in his own happiness than in that of others, and it is impossible that in his heart he can ever really prefer their prosperity to his own. Whenever he appears to do so, we may be assured that he imposes upon us, and that he is then acting from the same selfish motives as at all other times.

Smith condemns Mandeville's self-interested view of virtue by emphasizing two important and commonsense points regarding self-interest. First, he points out that "self-love may frequently be a virtuous motive of action" (*TMS* VII.ii.4.8). Smith calls this form of self-interest *prudence* and identifies it as one of the three main categories of virtues discussed in Part VI. Second, he calls the dishonorable form of self-interest *selfishness*, and identifies it as a vice that he strongly condemns. Thus, Smith fully rejects Mandeville's glorification of narrow self-interest as good for commerce and society. Ironically, many economists and politicians who have associated Smith's political economy with Chicago's self-interested view of economic man have also associated his moral philosophy with Ayn Rand's radical individualism. The latest research on Smith's total system of thought, however, reveals an institutional individualism view that emphasizes culture, institutions, and social norms. Throughout his writings, Smith rejects Hume's religious skepticism, Mandeville's cynicism, and Rousseau's despair (Phillipson 2010). In particular, Smith's writings do not support Rand's controversial views on religion or morality (Burns 2009).

Smith's moral philosophy reflects three major influences in his life: Stoicism, Hutcheson, and Hume. The influence of stoic philosophy can be seen in Smith's emphasis on virtue and duty and in his frequent references to ancient stoic philosophers (Epictetus, Marcus Aurelius, and Cicero). Smith follows the Stoics in holding that self-preservation is the first task committed to us by nature and that self-interested behavior is a virtue so long as it does not injure others (Raphael and Macfie 1982). The influence of stoic philosophy can also be seen in Smith's pragmatism and his view that life is largely unfair and susceptible to luck (Griswold 1999). Finally, Smith follows the Stoics in his belief that good can come out of evil (Raphael and Macfie 1982). Smith's views reflect the influence of Hutcheson and Hume in three important aspects. He joins his two mentors in rejecting the view that all human behavior is attributable to narrow self-interest or "selfishness." He also joins Hutcheson and Hume in granting a significant role to the passions over reason in moral judgment. Thus, Smith would reject rationalist models of morality including, for example, Kohlberg's (1969, 1976) theory of moral reasoning. Finally, he joins Hutcheson and Hume in maintaining ancient philosophy's emphasis on the spectator in moral judgment. This emphasis promotes the importance of a detached, disinterested perspective in moral judgment.

In *The Theory of Moral Sentiments*, Smith focuses on the relation between the "agent" and the "spectator." In Chapter 1, titled "Of Sympathy," he stresses that as the spectator, we do not have access to the agent's mind but only to his observable circumstances and actions. Thus, moral judgment involves putting one's self in the agent's circumstances and then evaluating the motives behind a given action. If we are able to sympathize with or share in the agent's motives, then we approve of the action. If we cannot sympathize with the agent's motives, then we disapprove of the action. The former causes us great pleasure, but the latter causes us shock or pain.[9] Similar to Hume, therefore, Smith defines sympathy as an emotion of fellow-feeling that is an act of the imagination. The role of sympathy in moral judgment, however, is more developed in Smith's account than in Hume's in that it determines the appropriateness of the motives behind the action rather than simply the utility of the action. Smith strongly rejects Hume's assertion that the appropriateness of an

---

[9] In Chapter 2, titled "Of the Pleasure of mutual Sympathy," Smith emphasizes that nothing pleases us more than to sympathize with another's motivation, and nothing pains us more than the appearance of the contrary. "But both the pleasure and the pain are always felt so instantaneously, and often upon such frivolous occasions, that it seems evident that neither of them can be derived from any such self-interested consideration" (*TMS* I.i.2.1).

action depends upon its overall utility (Griswold 1999). Thus, Smith's moral philosophy rejects both egoism and utilitarianism.

The use of an impartial spectator for moral judgment can be seen in the writings of the ancient Stoics, which Smith learned as Hutcheson's student at Glasgow. Smith's unique contribution is the use of the impartial spectator to explain the moral conscience and how humans become moral beings. Consistent with other writers of the Scottish Enlightenment, Smith holds that humans are social creatures who require extended nurture and are susceptible to habits or norms of behavior (Berry 2003). To Smith, the impartial spectator is the personification of society's standards or social norms, which is developed over time from social experience. Individuals observe what constitutes praiseworthy behavior over time and eventually internalize these behavioral norms so that they feel guilt and remorse when they violate these norms. Thus, the impartial spectator helps humans learn right from wrong and thereby become moral beings (Griswold 1999). In contrast to Kant's moral reasoning or Hutcheson's moral sense, Smith relies on the voice of conscience to maintain moral behavior in society (Firth 2007).

Smith's approach in *The Theory of Moral Sentiments* reflects the Scottish Enlightenment emphasis on science (Berry 2006). Smith believed that there was an underlying order in the natural, social, and moral worlds, and that social systems needed good design and constant management if good ends were to be achieved (Thorpe 2007). Rather than use the abstract language common in contemporary works of moral philosophy, Smith used the language of science and art, and included examples from everyday life, history, drama, and travelers' tales (Barbalet 2007). As Smith explains in a footnote, his moral theory concerns itself primarily with matters of "fact" rather than matters of "right" (*TMS* II.i.5.10). Thus, his moral theory is a positive theory in the sense of Friedman's positive economics (1953).

Rather than Mill's *homo economicus*, Smith's view of man in *The Theory of Moral Sentiments* resembles the *homo sociologicus* view in sociology and social psychology (Campbell 1971, Barbalet 2005). In fact, Smith's notion of the impartial spectator and the internalization of behavioral norms has been credited with providing the seeds of social norm theory (Blay et al. 2017). In support of Smith's emphasis on sympathy or what we today would call empathy, the biological sciences have documented the ever-present influence of empathy in human behavior. Researchers have found two regions of the brain related to moral judgments. The frontal lobes are engaged in moral decision-making that is purely calculative in nature, whereas the ventromedial prefrontal cortex is engaged in moral decision-making that is empathetic in nature. This brain research suggests that empathy is a natural and powerful social mechanism, and it often takes special training or a brain injury to disengage it (Lakoff 2009).

In addition to the importance of sympathy and the impartial spectator, Smith maintains an important role for the virtues in moral judgment. In the sixth and final edition of *The Theory of Moral Sentiments*, Smith adds a new section devoted to the topic of moral virtue (Part VI). Similar to the ancient moral philosophers, Smith emphasizes the four virtues of *courage, temperance, justice,* and *prudence.* He also emphasizes the virtue of *benevolence,* which is analogous to Hutcheson's virtue of love.[10] Smith also distinguishes between the "negative" virtue of justice (the virtue of abstaining from injurious behavior) and the "positive" virtues of courage, temperance, prudence, and benevolence (Haakonssen 2006). Finally, similar to Kant, Smith emphasizes the importance of duty or a solemn regard for general rules of conduct (Firth 2007). According to Smith, the impartial spectator is not immune to self-deceit, and is therefore not sufficient to ensure moral behavior in all occasions. To remedy this deficiency in the impartial spectator, human beings are endowed with a natural respect for general rules of conduct. For example, Smith emphasizes the social norm of honesty in business (*TMS* I.iii.3.5):

In all the middling and inferior professions, real and solid professional abilities, joined to prudent, just, firm, and temperate conduct, can very seldom fail of success ... The good old proverb, therefore, That honesty is the best policy, holds, in such situations, almost always perfectly true. In such situations, therefore, we may generally expect a considerable degree of virtue; and, fortunately for the good morals of society, these are the situations of by far the greater part of mankind.

In summary, Adam Smith's moral philosophy and political economy both address the fundamental conflict between sympathy and the vice of selfishness. Both books reflect Smith's overall system of thought or opus, which aims to improve the lot of the average citizen in society, and neither work can be fully understood in isolation from the other. In particular, the view that Smith based his moral philosophy on sympathy and his political economy on selfishness is erroneous and misguided. In the sixth and final edition of *The Theory of Moral Sentiments*, which contains the final word on his opus, Smith makes moral virtue an important aspect of moral judgment while maintaining the importance of behavioral rules or social

---

[10] Hutcheson included the "Christian" virtues of faith, hope, and love in his list of moral virtues.

norms. This emphasis on virtue, when combined with his conceptualization of sympathy and the impartial spectator, dictates that the individual is
driven not only by the desire for *praise* but also by the desire to be
praiseworthy. This analysis suggests that institutions and social norms
play a central role in Smith's overall system of thought, which includes
both his moral philosophy and his political economy.

RECENT SOCIAL NORM THEORY RELATED TO THE FIRM

Researchers in economics, accounting, and finance have stretched the
boundaries of traditional economic theory. Behavioral economists, for
example, have examined the impact of irrational or "quasi-rational" behavior in the theory of the firm. Some of this research has earned Nobel Prizes
in Economic Science for its contributors, including Herbert Simon (1978),
Daniel Kahneman (2002), and now Richard Thaler (2017). Other economists have earned Nobel Prizes for questioning the historic commitment to
narrow self-interest in neoclassical economic theory, including Gary
Becker (1992) and Amartya Sen (1998). In an article entitled, "Rational
Fools: A Critique of the Behavioral Foundations of Economic Theory," Sen
(1977, 317–318) asks the following question:

*The issue is not why abstractions should be employed in pursuing general economic
questions—the nature of the inquiry makes this inevitable—but why would one
choose an assumption which he himself believed to be not merely inaccurate in detail
but fundamentally mistaken? As we shall see, this question is of continuing interest to
modern economics as well.*

Sen takes on the "revealed preference" notion of rational choice that has
come to dominate neoclassical economics (Samuelson 1947). He argues
that this view of rationality asks far too little, leads to a remarkably mute
economic theory, and is circular in nature. In particular, he criticizes
a world in which behavior is explained in terms of preferences, and
preferences in turn are defined only by behavior. Sen (1977, 323) points
out: "But if you are consistent, then no matter whether you are a single-
minded egoist or a raving altruist or a class conscious militant, you will
appear to be maximizing your own utility in this enchanted world of
definitions." Thus, "if the Arrow-Hahn justification of the assumption of
egoism amounts to an *avoidance* of the issue, the revealed preference
approach looks more like a robust piece of *evasion*." Sen calls for a new
economic world in which there are social preferences derived from sympathy and commitments to behavioral rules. He also argues against

"viewing behavior in terms of the traditional dichotomy between egoism and universalized moral systems (such as utilitarianism)" (Sen 1977, 344).

Sen (1977, 342) argues that allowing commitments to behavioral rules does not require a view of man as an "irrational creature." Regarding the revealed preference notion of rational choice, for example, he states that "there is no reason to think that admitting commitment must imply any departure from rationality." He acknowledges, however, that this is a weak sense of rationality. A stronger notion of rationality, which is also prevalent in economics, is the justification of each act in terms of narrow self-interest. Sen identifies three distinct elements in this approach that limit its usefulness as a standard of rationality. First, it judges acts only by their consequences. Second, it evaluates acts alone and not in relation to potential rules of behavior. Third, it includes only consequences related to one's own interests. Sen argues that "even within a consequentialist act-evaluation framework, the exclusion of any consideration other than self-interest seems to impose a wholly arbitrary limitation on the notion of rationality." He presents arguments against all three elements of this notion of rationality and argues that admitting commitments to behavioral rules implies no denial of reasoned assessment as a basis for action.

Researchers in economics, accounting, and finance have found recent social norm theory useful in extending the theory of the firm to incorporate commitments to social norms. This includes Eric Posner's (2000) theory of law and social norms, Vernon Smith's (2003, 2008) theory of ecological rationality, and Cristina Bicchieri's (2006) theory of social norm activation. I conclude this chapter by briefly discussing each social norm theory.

Eric Posner (2000, 46), a professor of law at the University of Chicago, acknowledges that social behaviors "bubble forth from a cauldron of instincts, passions, and deeply ingrained attitudes." His book, *Law and Social Norms*, is based on the claim "that rational choice theory can shed light on social norms by focusing on the reputational source of behavior regularities to the exclusion of their cognitive and emotional sources." Posner does not claim that cognition and emotion are irrelevant to norm-based behavior, or that rational choice theory can offer a complete explanation of social norms. He argues, however, that such cognition and emotion "are just not well enough understood by psychologists to support a theory of social norms, and repeated but puzzled acknowledgements of their importance would muddy the exposition of the argument without providing any offsetting benefits." Thus, Posner defines social norms narrowly as behavioral regularities that emerge as a consequence of people acting in their rational self-interest and their desire to reap the financial rewards of such norm behavior. He offers a signaling model in which individuals do not have preferences for social norms per se but only for the signaling benefits of social norm behavior.

Posner uses his signaling model to explain why individuals conform to some behavioral regularities and not others. In particular, Posner (2000, 4) focuses his analysis on the relationships between the law and "nonlegal" mechanisms of cooperation within society. He observes, "Most people refrain most of the time from antisocial behavior even when the law is absent or has no force. They conform to social norms. The question left unanswered by law and economics is why people conform to social norms. Without an answer to that question, one cannot understand the effect of laws on people's behavior." To help answer this question, Posner develops a general model of nonlegal cooperation based on a signaling game. In the signaling game, people who care about "future payoffs" not only resist the temptations to cheat in long-term relationships, they signal their ability to resist the temptation to cheat by conforming to various social norms. Posner uses his signaling game, based on traditional notions of rational choice, to explain previously neglected concepts in law and economics such as trust, status, group solidarity, community, and social norms, and the relationship between these concepts and the law.

Posner's signaling model, however, is unable to explain consistent evidence of norm-based behavior in repeating, single-period tests of game theory and agency theory in the laboratory. Participants in these experimental studies frequently follow behavioral standards and social norms in direct violation of narrow self-interest. Thus, these experimental studies support what the great philosophers of the Scottish Enlightenment believed about social and moral norms – that they are a naturally occurring part of human behavior and are thus discoverable within a scientific framework. This growing body of experimental evidence has led economists such as Vernon Smith (2003, 2008) and Larry Samuelson (2005) to ask, "What is the subject's perception of the problem that he or she is trying to solve?" (See Chapter 5.)

In the Nobel lecture for his 2002 Nobel Prize in Economic Science, Vernon Smith referenced Adam Smith and the Scottish Enlightenment philosophers to explain the norm-based behavior emerging in experimental tests of neoclassical economic theory (Smith 2003). Hayek (1988) argued that rather than exhibit the deductive reasoning of economists, which he called *constructivist rationality*, human behavior and institutions reflect home-grown norms and traditions that frequently lie beneath our conscious awareness. Called *ecological rationality*, these norms and traditions emerge out of social, cultural, and biological processes. This second form of rationality resembles Adam Smith's impartial spectator, which is based on the socialization process rather than on philosophical reasoning (Cockfield et al. 2007). Vernon Smith pointed out that while constructivist rationality had been strongly supported in impersonal market exchange settings – market efficiency has been documented in hundreds of market experiments under much less restrictive conditions than neoclassical theory would suggest – constructivist reasoning has not fared well in personal exchange experiments testing the behavioral predictions of game theory (see Chapter 6). In particular, norm-based behavior has arisen consistent with preferences for fairness, reciprocity, and trustworthiness. Smith identified ecological rationality as a likely explanation for this norm-based behavior.

Consistent with this extended notion of rationality, Cristina Bicchieri (2006) argues that individuals have conditional preferences for social norms based upon past social experience and that these norms may be activated by information and situational cues present in an economic setting. After reviewing the experimental evidence, Bicchieri (2006, 57) concludes, "Research by economists, decision scientists, psychologists, and other social scientists seems to agree that context matters. However, a model of just how context matters is absent." To fill this void, Bicchieri develops a formal model that provides the necessary and sufficient conditions for a social norm to be activated in a given social setting. According to Bicchieri's model, the decision to follow a social norm is conditional upon the belief that a norm exists and applies to the current situation (*contingency condition*), the belief that a sufficiently large subset of people conforms to the norm in similar situations (*empirical expectations condition*), and the belief that a sufficiently large subset of people expects conformance to the norm in similar situations (*normative expectations condition*). If all three conditions are present, an individual will exhibit a preference for the norm and thereby experience positive utility for conformance and negative utility for nonconformance (*conditional preference condition*).

Bicchieri (2006, 59) summarizes social norm activation as follows: "To 'activate' a norm means that the subjects involved *recognize* that the norm applies: They infer from some situational cues what the appropriate behavior is, what they should expect others to do, and what they are expected to do themselves, and act upon those cues. It is the cues one focuses on that govern the mapping from context to interpretation and, ultimately, the activation of social norms." Rather than assume consistent preferences, as is commonly assumed in traditional economic theory,

Bicchieri's model assumes that individuals have *conditional preferences* for conforming to social norms and that such preferences are activated by situational cues present in the social setting. As such, Bicchieri's model of social norm activation is consistent with Adam Smith's impartial spectator, Sen's (1977) notion of commitments to relevant behavioral rules, and Vernon Smith's (2003, 2008) notion of ecological rationality.

Bicchieri's model suggests three motivations that may lead an individual to comply with a social norm in a given social setting: (1) fear of the consequences for noncompliance, (2) the desire to please, and (3) acceptance of the social norm as valid (Bicchieri 2006, 23–24). The first motivation may exist because the individual fears potential sanctions or penalties from violating the norm. Bicchieri's model extends traditional economic theory by including *behavioral* penalties, such as resentment, in addition to financial penalties. The second motivation may exist because the individual desires potential rewards from fulfilling the norm, consistent with Posner's (2000) signaling model. Again, Bicchieri's model extends traditional economic theory by including *behavioral* rewards, such as respect and dignity, in addition to financial rewards. The third motivation has no equivalent in traditional economic theory in that it provides a reason for individuals to conform to a social norm even when their norm-based behavior is private. As such, Bicchieri's model of social norm activation extends traditional economic theory by providing behavioral as well as financial motivations for norm-based behavior. Her model is also consistent with Adam Smith's impartial spectator in that it dictates that individuals are driven not only by the desire for *praise* but also by the desire to be *praiseworthy*.

It is important to emphasize, however, that Bicchieri's model does not require that individuals take a *deliberate* route of conscious decision-making to follow a social norm. In particular, her model incorporates evidence that following a social norm often takes a *heuristic* route of simplified or even subconscious processing. Bicchieri (2006, 3) states, "The definition of social norm I am proposing should be taken as a *rational reconstruction* of what a social norm is, not a faithful descriptive account of the real beliefs and preferences people have or of the way in which they in fact deliberate" (italics in the original). Thus, Bicchieri's model allows for the possibility of intuitive or subconscious processing as well as conscious processing, consistent with Hayek's (1988) and Vernon Smith's (2003, 2008) notion of ecological rationality. Conscious processing of situational cues and information, however, may be increasingly important in organizational settings where social norms frequently conflict with self-interest. Furthermore, motivating norm-based behavior by engaging such conscious processing may be of critical importance to the firm. Thus, researchers have recently found Bicchieri's model useful not only to explain prior experimental evidence but also to make predictions regarding the effects of information and situational cues on behavior in the firm (Blay et al. 2017).

Theorists in economics, accounting, and finance have begun to model norm-based behavior using the traditional tools of neoclassical theory. This growing literature has provided valuable new insights and has expanded the boundaries of the theory of the firm. In Chapter 5, I describe formal models incorporating social norms into the theory of the firm along with the key findings of these models.

PART II

THE EVIDENCE

5

Formal Models Incorporating Social Norms into the Theory of the Firm

INTRODUCTION

The past three chapters have laid the foundation for me to present the latest theoretical, experimental, and archival research incorporating social norms into the theory of the firm. In Chapter 2, I presented a history of the firm that incorporates social norms to demonstrate the importance of social norms not only to the firm, but also to capitalist institutions and free-market capitalism as a whole. In Chapter 3, I revealed how the neoclassical theory of the firm has transformed the fields of economics, accounting, and finance, and has had a considerable influence on the university-based business school. In Chapter 4, I discussed how the neoclassical theory of the firm has taken an increasingly narrow view of economic man consistent with Mill's *homo economicus*, and presented social norm theory related to the firm. Neoclassical economics, however, has grown in influence over the past two centuries and is now the dominant framework for economic theory and education (Ekelund and Hébert 2014, 637). Thus, any attempt to incorporate social norms into the theory of the firm will be easily ignored unless it is capable of demonstrating its usefulness using neoclassical economic theory.

In this chapter, I demonstrate the usefulness of incorporating social norms into the theory of the firm using the most formal neoclassical theory of the firm: principal-agent theory. I begin by discussing the benefits of mathematical modeling and why it has been utilized by theorists to develop and communicate economic theory. As classical and neoclassical economists developed advanced mathematical tools and used them to generate important insights regarding the firm, they emphasized the abstract nature of their models and the potential for future theorists to incorporate social constructs such as social and moral norms. The potential for the theory of the firm to be enhanced by social norms can be seen in the writings of leading classical economists such as Adam Smith and John Stuart Mill as well as top neoclassical economists such as Alfred Marshall and Kenneth Arrow. More recently, even prominent members of the Chicago school have challenged theorists to incorporate social norms and values into the theory of the firm (Jensen 2008).

Next, I describe the essential features of principal-agent theory and the challenges to incorporating social norms into the theory. I then present a principal-agent model that incorporates a promise-keeping norm (Stevens and Thevaranjan 2010). The model adds the simple assumption that the agent suffers a disutility if he provides less than a previously agreed-upon standard level of effort. The disutility is increasing in the magnitude of the violation of the standard and the agent's sensitivity to the social norm. We examine the interplay between this sensitivity and firm productivity in determining the optimal salary contract, and contrast our solution with the traditional incentive solution that is required when the agent has zero social norm sensitivity. We find that adding a simple promise-keeping norm increases the descriptive, prescriptive, and peda-gogical usefulness of the principal-agent model. Of particular interest, we show that sensitivity to the social norm allows the agent to earn a return on developing his skill, which fuels specialization and the division of labor. Thus, our model suggests that Adam Smith's engine of economic growth requires the presence of social norm sensitivity. I conclude by presenting other formal models incorporating social norms into the theory of the firm.

BENEFITS OF MATHEMATICAL MODELING

From the inception of economic theorizing, economists have sought effec-tive ways to display their concepts and ideas to facilitate communication (Ekelund and Hébert 2014). While economic theory was initially framed in purely literary prose, economists began to communicate their theory using mathematical equations and geometric graphs as early as the eighteenth century. The French philosopher and mathematician Antoine Augustin Cournot (1801–1877) is typically considered the founder of mathematical economics. Cournot used algebraic formulations as well as Euclidian geometry to facilitate economic intuition regarding how certain economic values (e.g., price and quantity) were related. In his *Researches into the Mathematical Principles of the Theory of Wealth*, Cournot stated that mathematical modeling was useful to "facilitate the exposition of problems, to rend it [sic] more concise, to open the way to more extended developments, and to avoid the digressions of vague argumentation" (Cournot 1838, 4).

A purely literary communication of economic theory is readily intelligible to the largest audience but, as Cournot recognized, it can lead to ambiguities and digressions. Graphs are especially useful to explain relations between economic variables in two dimensions. Such graphs become cumbersome when extended to three dimensions, and they are impossible in more than three. Mathematical modeling, therefore, is arguably the most precise and powerful method of communicating economic theory. However, this precision comes at a cost. Alfred Marshall (1925, 84), one of the most influential neoclassical economists, stated that overreliance on mathematical formalism "might lead us astray in pursuit of intellectual toys, imaginary problems not conforming to the conditions of real life: and, further, might distort our sense of proportion by causing us to neglect factors that could not easily be worked up in the mathematical machine." Nevertheless, mathematical modeling remains a powerful tool for economic theorists because, 1) it makes underlying assumptions and premises explicit, 2) it makes the theory more precise and concise, and 3) it allows the theorist to deal with more complex relations (Ekelund and Hébert 2014).

Classical economists focused on macroeconomics and political economy, and their economic theory was generally less mathematical. Adam Smith was well versed in mathematics, Newtonian physics, and natural philosophy (science) and was a studier of systems and machines (Thorpe 2007). His admiration for mathematics is reflected in a passage of the *Theory of Moral Sentiments* where he states, "It is in the abtruser sciences, particularly in the higher parts of mathematics, that the greatest and most admired exertions of human reason have been displayed" (*TMS* IV.2.6.7). Nevertheless, Smith's political economy was built primarily on empirical observations and systematic reasoning, and he held a broad social science view of economic man that incorporated culture, institutions, and social norms. Even Mill (1836, 323) acknowledged the potential for theorists to incorporate social and moral aspects of human nature to expand the ability of political economy to explain and predict behavior.

Neoclassical economists, in contrast, have focused primarily on microeconomics related to the firm and markets, and their theory has been more mathematically rigorous. Nevertheless, early neoclassical economists were also open to the inclusion of other preferences besides wealth and leisure. As discussed in Chapter 3, Cournot (1801–1877) laid the groundwork for neoclassical theory by using differential calculus and Cartesian geometry to solve some of the firm's most fundamental questions, such as what quantity to produce and what price to charge. Dupuit (1804–1866) expanded the list of neoclassical tools by developing a theory of utility, which he used to develop the concept of marginal utility and relate it to a demand curve. It was British economist William Stanley Jevons (1835–1882), however, who developed a *subjective* maximand and gave it the leading role in neoclassical economic theory. Following the lead of Jeremy Bentham (1748–1832), Jevons identified a person's total utility as the sum total of that person's pleasure and pain. Thus, the utility that an individual sought to maximize could include subjective aspects in addition to objective aspects such as wealth and leisure. Jevons also was one of the first economists to assert that individual behavior revealed a person's utility and preferences (Jevons 1871).

Bentham was a utilitarian who argued that economic policy should seek to maximize the total utility or net pleasure (pleasure minus pain) of individuals across society. To simplify his "moral arithmetic," he chose money as the appropriate measure of pleasure and pain, although he did not incorporate the diminishing marginal utility of money in his calculations of total utility (Ekelund and Hébert 2014). Similar to Bentham, Jevons maintained that the value of pleasure and pain varied along four dimensions: (1) intensity, (2) duration, (3) uncertainty, and (4) nearness. In contrast to Bentham, however, Jevons was more of a marginalist than a utilitarian, and he did not measure all pleasure and pain in monetary terms. In fact, Jevons (1871, 11) warned against measuring nonmonetary utility in monetary terms:

A unit of pleasure or of pain is difficult even to conceive; but it is the amount of these feelings which is continually prompting us to buying and selling, borrowing and lending, labouring and resting, producing and consuming; and it is from the quantitative effects of the feelings that we must estimate their comparative amounts. We can no more know nor measure gravity in its own nature than we can measure a feeling; but, just as we measure gravity by its effects in the motion of a pendulum, so we may estimate the equality or inequality of feelings by the decisions of the human mind.

As neoclassical economists developed more powerful tools for mathematical modeling, they emphasized the abstract nature of their models and the potential to incorporate social constructs such as social and moral norms into an individual's utility function. Alfred Marshall was instrumental in building the neoclassical synthesis at Cambridge University toward the end of the nineteenth century, and was an enthusiastic and capable mathematician. Yet, he largely eschewed the presentation of mathematical equations in his writings, choosing to target a wider audience, including business-people and policymakers. In his *Principles of Economics*, Marshall (1890/1920) confined his use of mathematical equations and notations to foot-notes and appendices so as not to allow the mathematics to detract from the economic intuition. He viewed economic science as a broader social science, consistent with Adam Smith, and was willing to take other social forces into account provided they occurred with sufficient regularity within economic life (Ekelund and Hébert 2014).

More recently, neoclassical economists have emphasized the potential for theorists to incorporate social norms into the theory of the firm. Kenneth J. Arrow (1921–2017), the youngest economist ever to win a Nobel Prize (in 1972, at the age of 51), emphasized the potential for principal-agent models to incorporate social rewards and penalties (Arrow 1985). A graduate of Columbia, Arrow spent his early career (1946–1949) as a research associate at the Cowles Commission at Chicago before taking a faculty position at Stanford. Arrow joined with Gérard Debreu to provide the first rigorous proofs of the existence of a general market-clearing equilibrium, showing that Adam Smith's invisible hand of the market was truly efficient. Arrow went on to include uncertainty and information asymmetry in his analysis of markets and the firm. Arrow's (1962) "learn-ing by doing" model suggested that the more a firm produces, the smarter and more efficient it becomes. This supported Smith's notion that eco-nomic growth is fueled in part by a firm's incentive to continuously innovate. In his review of principal-agent theory, Arrow (1985, 50) identi-fied "socially mediated rewards" as an important element missing from the theory:

Still further extensions are needed to capture some aspects of reality, for there is a whole world of rewards and penalties that take social rather than monetary forms. Professional responsibility is clearly enforced in good measure by systems of ethics, internalized during the education process and enforced in some good measure by formal punishments and more broadly by reputations. Ultimately, of course, these social systems have economic consequences, but they are not the immediate ones of current principal-agent models . . . It may well be one of the greatest accomplish-ments of the principal-agent literature to provide some structure for the much-sought goal of integrating these elements with the impressive structure of economic analysis.

This statement by a leading neoclassical economist harkens back to the professionalism project of the American Economic Association (AEA), the university-based business school, and the American Association of Collegiate Schools of Business (AACSB). This statement also reflects the concerns of institutional economists that economic theory incorporate culture, institutions, and social norms. Finally, Arrow's statement above reflects Adam Smith's broad social science view of economic man. Other neoclassical economists have recently joined Arrow in challenging theorists to incorporate social and moral norms into the theory of the firm. Michael Jensen (2008, ix-x), for example, communicated this challenge in his forward to a book on the role of values in the economy:

Economics, having traditionally focused on the positive analysis of alternative institutional structures, has far too long ignored the normative world. By the term 'positive analysis,' I mean, of course, the analysis of the way the world is, however it behaves, independent of any normative value judgments about its desirability or undesirability ... By 'normative,' I mean establishing, relating to, or deriving from a standard or norm that specifies desirable or undesirable conduct or behavior, that is, what ought to be ... I look forward to seeing the creation of an entirely new field of inquiry in economics, and in its sister social sciences, focused deeply on the positive analysis of the role of values in elevating the possible outcomes of human interaction ...

The potential for principal-agent relationships in the firm to be influenced by social and moral norms appears self-evident. This is why there has always been a movement to incorporate such norms into the theory of the firm. For example, shortly after Watts and Zimmerman (1986) published their book applying the new theory of the firm to the discipline of accounting, Eric Noreen (1988) published a paper challenging accountants to use the new theory to illustrate the adverse consequences of unethical behavior in the firm. Shortly after Pratt and Zeckhauser (1985) published their book making the new theory of the firm accessible to managers, Bowie and Freeman (1992) published a book containing scholarly articles emphasizing the moral implications of the theory. Despite strong statements urging theorists to incorporate social norms into the theory of the firm by neoclassical economists and other researchers in accounting, management, and philosophy, theorists have been slow to do so. This may be due to the social and career costs mentioned in Chapter 1. However, there are also many challenges to modeling social norms using principal-agent theory. Before discussing these challenges, I introduce the essential features of this neoclassical theory of the firm.

ESSENTIAL FEATURES OF PRINCIPAL-AGENT THEORY

The essential features of principal-agent theory have been presented by theorists such as Stephen Ross (1973), Kenneth Arrow (1985), Stanley Baiman (1990), and Richard Lambert (2001). Principal-agent theory is the highly mathematical version of agency theory (Jensen 1983), and is the most formal neoclassical theory of the firm (see Chapter 4). Through its mathematical rigor, it has become one of the most important theoretical frameworks in accounting and finance (Lambert 2001).[1] As is characteristic of all neoclassical theories of the firm, principal-agent theory focuses on the behavior of individuals who are narrowly self-interested and subject to the influences of the market. Rather than focus on market prices driven by forces of supply and demand, however, the theory focuses on the many agency relationships that make up the firm (Arrow 1985). These agency relationships involve opposing incentives, private information, and a temporal sequence of actions, which makes principal-agent theory a form of game theory (Rasmusen 1990).

Principal-agent theory views the firm as a cascade of agency relationships, including the relationship between owners (investors) and upper management, upper management and division managers, division managers and supervisors, and between supervisors and laborers. Because principal-agent theory focuses on contract solutions to agency problems that arise in these agency relationships, the theory is consistent with a "nexus of contracts" view of the firm (Jensen and Meckling 1976).[2] As Arrow (1985, 38) states:

The principal-agent theory is in the standard economic tradition. Both principal and agent are assumed to be making their decisions optimally in view of their constraints; intended transactions are realized. As is usual in economic theory, the theory functions both normatively and descriptively. It offers insights used in the construction of contracts to guide and influence principal-agent relations in the real world; at the same time it represents an attempt to explain observed phenomena in the empirical economic world, particularly exchange relations that are not explained by more standard economic theory.

To explain the essential features of principal-agent theory, I describe the classic principal-agent model in which the principal is a manager and the agent is a worker.[3] In the model, the principal seeks to hire the agent to provide a productive effort, and the agent acquires private information

---

[1] Barry Mitnick (1974) developed a theory of agency in political science at about the same time as Ross (1973) and is frequently given joint credit for developing the initial theory. The form of agency theory that developed in political science, however, was always open to social constructs, such as social norms, in contrast to the form that developed in economics, accounting, and finance (Mitnick 1992).

[2] Jensen and Meckling (1976, 310) state, "It is important to recognize that most organizations are simply *legal fictions which serve as a nexus for a set of contracting relationships among individuals*" (italics in the original).

[3] The principal is often thought of as a "representative shareholder" or board of directors, and the agent is often thought of as the management of the firm (Lambert 2001).

about his skill and/or his effort. That is, the skill and/or effort of the agent are unobservable to the principal. This provides a new purpose for the firm, which is as a means of gathering and training agents and assuring adequate effort (Arrow 1985). There are two principal-agent problems that arise as a result of the private information of the agent: the *hidden action* of effort and the *hidden information* of skill. As both of these principal-agent problems provide an opportunity for the agent to take advantage of the principal, they represent a potential *moral hazard* to the principal. The term *opportunistic* has been used to describe agents who take advantage of their private information to increase their payoff at the expense of the principal (Williamson 1975).

In the most basic principal-agent model, the principal provides capital and determines the compensation contract, whereas the agent provides a productive effort. The agent's productive effort helps determine the firm's production, which requires the agent's effort but is also affected by other factors. Under the traditional economic assumptions of *homo economicus*, the principal's only preference is to earn the highest return on her capital and the agent's only preference is to acquire the highest level of wealth with the lowest amount of effort. That is, the principal's utility is increasing in the return on capital and the agent's utility is increasing in wealth and decreasing in effort. Thus, the principal's problem is to choose the compensation contract that will induce the agent to provide the optimal level of effort at the lowest cost. If the principal knows the agent's skill but not his effort, then the principal's problem is called *moral hazard with hidden action*. If the agent discovers his skill after accepting the contract but it remains hidden to the principal, then the principal's problem is called *moral hazard with hidden information*. If the agent knows his skill from the start but the principal does not, then the principal's problem is called *adverse selection*.

I focus on the single-period principal-agent model incorporating moral hazard with hidden action. This principal-agent model has been called the "Production Game" in game theory (Rasmusen 1990). The first mover is the principal, who offers the agent a compensation contract. The second mover is the agent, who decides whether to accept or reject the contract and, if accepted, the level of effort to provide. At the end of the period, the output of the agent's effort is observed by both parties. The output is stated in monetary terms and represents the end-of-period cash flow or liquidating value of the firm. For simplicity, it is commonly assumed that there are many potential agents in the labor market, so the agent's equilibrium utility under the contract equals the minimum that induces him to provide the desired effort. This minimum utility is called the agent's *reservation utility*, and providing at least this minimum utility represents the first constraint on the compensation contract. This first constraint is commonly called the *individual rationality* constraint. The agent privately provides the productive effort after accepting the contract, and so the second constraint on the principal's contract is that it induce the agent to voluntarily provide the principal's desired effort. This second constraint is commonly called the *incentive compatibility* constraint.

Given this framework and its underlying assumptions, we can state the principal's problem as a constrained maximization problem in which she chooses the compensation contract that maximizes her expected utility subject to the two constraints:

Maximize: the principal's expected utility
  Subject to:
    Individual rationality constraint
    Incentive compatibility constraint

If the principal offers the agent a (nonnegative) flat wage contract, the economic prediction is simple but inefficient. The agent will accept the contract and then provide zero effort. This is because the agent's utility is increasing in wealth but decreasing in effort. Knowing this, the principal's best response is to offer the agent a flat wage of zero. This shows the severity of the principal's moral hazard problem in the traditional principal-agent model. Assuming that the agent is opportunistically self-interested with preference only for wealth and leisure, the principal can never offer the agent a flat wage contract and expect any effort in return. This is the game theoretic outcome of the single-period principal-agent model assuming the traditional view of *homo economicus* (Rasmusen 1990).

To quantify the agency cost of the agency relationship, and create a benchmark for comparison purposes, theorists initially solve the principal's problem assuming away the incentive problems inherent in the relationship (Lambert 2001). This "first-best" solution is derived assuming that the wage and the level of effort are chosen cooperatively with both parties' interests in mind. In particular, the wage and the effort are chosen so as to maximize the principal's expected utility subject to meeting the agent's reservation wage. Thus, the first-best solution maintains the maximization problem stated above minus the incentive compatibility constraint, which is no longer necessary as the agent's effort is chosen cooperatively rather than opportunistically. This solution provides the first-best wage for the first-best level of effort, which pays the agent's reservation wage for the optimal level of effort. As before, the reservation wage motivates the agent to accept the contract, but the first-best solution assumes that the agent will cooperatively provide the optimal level of effort after accepting the contract.

Again, firm production is assumed to be affected by other factors besides the agent's effort. Absent this assumption, the principal would simply learn the agent's effort after observing firm production at the end of the period. This assumption is typically modeled by making production a random variable whose distribution is affected by the agent's effort. With uncertainty in the production process, the principal must select a compensation contract that both shares risk optimally and motivates the agent to provide the optimal effort (Lambert 2001). Thus, the risk preferences of the principal and the agent become an important consideration in the optimal contract. Because the principal can diversify her risk across multiple investments whereas the agent cannot, theorists typically assume that the principal is risk neutral and the agent is risk averse. Given these risk preferences, the first-best solution is a flat salary that pays the agent his reservation wage for the optimal level of effort. In this case, the principal does not mind bearing all of the risk of production because she is risk neutral and she knows that the risk-averse agent will require a premium for bearing any of the risk.

This discussion of the essential features of principal-agent theory explains why the first-best solution is unachievable in the traditional single-period principal-agent model. Given the assumption of opportunistic self-interest on the part of the agent, inducing any effort from the agent after he accepts the contract requires an incentive contract that links the agent's pay to the production outcome. An incentive contract, however, is always less efficient than the first-best contract because it requires the principal to pay the agent a risk premium for carrying some of the risk. Theorists have extended the model to determine the conditions under which the first-best solution is achievable (Lambert 2001). A natural question is whether the first-best solution is achievable when the assumption of opportunistic self-interest is relaxed; that is, when we allow for norm-based behavior on the part of the agent. Because principal-agent theory functions both normatively and descriptively (Arrow 1985), another important question is whether incorporating social norms improves the normative and descriptive power of the theory. These questions are of great importance to the theory of the firm, and yet theorists have just begun to address them. In attempting to address these questions, theorists have found inherent challenges to modeling social norms in principal-agent theory. I discuss these challenges next.

CHALLENGES TO MODELING SOCIAL NORMS IN
PRINCIPAL-AGENT THEORY

Principal-agent theory provides a powerful framework for examining theoretical relations between information, incentives, and behavior within the firm (Lambert 2001). The theory requires clear and disciplined reasoning regarding underlying assumptions, variable definitions, and theoretical relations. The theory also provides a common language that has become familiar to theorists and nontheorists alike. This helps explain why principal-agent theory has become the foundational theory of the firm in economics, accounting, and finance, and why it has been found to be useful in other disciplines such as management, political science, and law. This neoclassical theory of the firm also provides a powerful framework to examine the effects of social norms on agency relationships across the firm. There are many challenges, however, that must be overcome in order to model social norms in principal-agent theory.

In their review of accounting and principal-agent theory, Koford and Penno (1992, 127–128) argue that the assumption of opportunistic self-interest on the part of the agent is rather severe because it assumes that the agent will behave opportunistically even when the personal benefit is very small and the damage done to other individuals is very large. They recommend relaxing the assumption of self-interested behavior for greater normative and descriptive validity:

We suggest that when the assumption of self-interested behavior is relaxed, some results of principal-agent models change. The different results, however, may more accurately reflect accounting institutions and concerns. In particular, detailed control systems that are cost-justified when all agents are self-interested may not be justified when agents display some ethical behavior. Also, informal social control mechanisms may be alternatives to formal accounting mechanisms. Finally, since agents have some underlying ethical standards, accounting control systems will be more effective if they reinforce and utilize those standards.

Koford and Penno use the standard neoclassical tools of mathematical equations and graphs to demonstrate how relaxing the assumption of opportunistic self-interest in principal-agent theory could generate new and useful insights. They analyze two approaches to modeling norm-based behavior: 1) assume that some individuals are motivated by social norms and others are motivated purely by opportunistic self-interest, and 2) assume that all individuals can be motivated by social norms in some situations. The first assumption focuses on social norm "types" across agents, and the second assumption focuses on the "activation" of social norms within agents. Koford and Penno show that either assumption is capable of generating new results that expand the normative and descriptive power of the theory. For example, they demonstrate that the types assumption provides an incentive for principals to test or monitor the behavior of agents to determine their type. The types assumption also suggests that opportunistic agents will self-select into firms or departments where monitoring is low.

Koford and Penno find that both modeling approaches support the importance of cultivating a strong corporate culture. Because the agent's gain from self-interested behavior can never be completely eliminated, norm-based behavior in the firm must be encouraged through recruiting, training, and organizational controls. The types assumption suggests that screening and self-selection can increase the proportion of norm-motivated agents in the firm if a sufficiently strong culture of social norms is present. Furthermore, the activation assumption suggests that a sufficiently strong culture of social norms can encourage agents to follow norm-based behavior on the margin. For example, accounting systems and controls can establish clear rules and norms for agents to follow, as can professional codes of conduct. Thus, as the merchant culture has repeatedly demonstrated down through history (see Chapter 2), good accounting systems can make social norms salient in the firm and encourage norm-based behavior. Koford and Penno (1992, 137) conclude:

The "ethical component" of utility functions may be reinforced by sound accounting practices. Here we suggest some ways in which utilities might be modeled, and how that might affect accounting principal-agent theory. We believe (by introspection and casual observation, along with some careful experimental evidence) that most people have attitudes toward telling the truth and putting out "fair" amounts of effort; these are not currently included in principal-agent models, and so may neglect a significant element of reality. People's attitudes toward the "truth" or "fairness" depend upon whether it is clear to them and to others what is true or false, fair or unfair. Accounting systems can reinforce or dissipate these perceptions.

Why has it taken so long for economists to incorporate social norms into principal-agent theory? One common objection I have heard is that extending the theory to incorporate social norms would be too simplistic and result in truisms or self-evident results. Another common objection is that incorporating social norms would be too complex and would render the original intuition and insights of the theory meaningless. Finally, economists have objected to incorporating social or moral norms into the theory because of the belief that it goes against the literature's emphasis on "positive economics" (Friedman 1953). I agree with Koford and Penno's (1992) assessment that opportunistic self-interest on the part of the agent is an extreme case. As Pratt and Zeckhauser (1985, 4) point out, it is important for theorists not to model an aberrant case. In particular, "The employee who loafs or fabricates an illness or even a disability claim may be one of a very small number who exploit a system that on the whole works fairly well with individuals with representative preferences or values." Persistent evidence of norm-based behavior in real-world organizations and in experimental tests of agency theory (see Chapter 6) suggests that the traditional principal-agent model is indeed an aberrant case.

Incorporating norm-based behavior on the part of the agent requires altering the agent's utility function. In the traditional principal-agent model, the agent's utility function is defined over both the compensation wage, w, and the effort level, a. More effort is assumed to increase the expected firm production, but it causes disutility for the agent. Furthermore, the agent's utility function is assumed to be additively separable in the wage and effort components. Thus, the agent's utility function is commonly expressed in the following form:

$$H(w,\ a) = U(w) - V(a)$$

At a fundamental level, adding a disutility for violating a social norm, s, to the agent's utility function poses no insurmountable challenge to theorists. Neoclassical economists have incorporated other factors in the agent's utility function besides wealth and leisure since Bentham and Jevons in the eighteenth and nineteenth centuries. Furthermore, it is reasonable to assume that the disutility for violating a social norm is nonmonetary and additively separable from both the wage and the effort components. That is, there is no rationale for stating the disutility for social norm violation in monetary terms or to comingle this disutility with the disutility for effort. Thus, the agent's utility function can be extended to the following form:

$$H(w,\ a,\ s) = U(w) - V(a) - W(s)$$

It is also reasonable to assume that the disutility for violating the social norm is increasing in the agent's sensitivity to the social norm and the level of violation. This increases the generalizability of the model by allowing differential sensitivity to the norm and the potential for training and corporate culture to increase such sensitivity. As with the traditional principal-agent model, it is easy to incorporate risk aversion by making the utility for wealth concave. It is also easy to incorporate an increasing cost of effort by making the disutility for effort convex. The above formulation suggests that a social norm can be incorporated into the principal-agent model in a way that preserves all other aspects of the traditional model.

A principal-agent model that incorporates social norms should be judged based on its ability to generate new and useful insights that are capable of increasing the normative and descriptive power of the model. To avoid the criticism that the model is too simplistic or that it yields self-evident results, there must be distance between the social norms incorporated into the model and the model's results. Untrained readers frequently confuse a model's results with its underlying assumptions. Underlying assumptions and manipulated theoretical variables are exogenous to the model and are not the results of the model, which are endogenously determined by the theoretical relations in the model. Ideally, the model should demonstrate how incorporating social norms changes the types of contracts available to the principal and potentially increases the efficiency of the principal-agent relationship in ways that are descriptive of organizational settings. The model should also incorporate social norms in a way that is intuitive and generalizable to principal-agent relations in the firm.

A PRINCIPAL-AGENT MODEL WITH A PROMISE-KEEPING NORM

To demonstrate the usefulness of incorporating social norms into the theory of the firm, I present the results of a principal-agent model that includes a promise-keeping norm. Joel Demski and Gerald Feltham (1978, 346) raised the possibility for social norms to control self-interested behavior in an early paper applying insights from principal-agent theory to the accounting literature:[4]

The pure salary contract can be quickly discarded from our consideration in that it provides no incentives. If such a contract were signed in our model, the worker would

---

[4] I thank Joel Demski and Gerry Feltham for helpful conversations regarding the potential benefit of incorporating social norms in principal-agent theory. I especially thank Joel for emphasizing that this idea is not new and that theorists have been thinking about this possibility since the inception of the theory.

take his salary and select an effort level of zero. (To be sure, this is a rather extreme result, but it would occur to some extent even if we modify the worker's preference function to reflect social norms that induce him to provide some effort for his salary.)

Demski and Feltham's article was so influential that it was awarded a *Seminal Contribution in Accounting Literature Award* in 1994 by the American Accounting Association. The above quote demonstrates several things. First, theorists understood early on how extreme the prediction was for the agent to provide zero effort after agreeing to a salary contract in a single-period principal-agent model. Second, theorists understood that this extreme prediction was due to the neoclassical view of economic man as motivated only by wealth and leisure. Third, theorists understood that social norms could induce the agent to provide some effort for his salary.

I had the privilege of working with an agency theorist at Syracuse University on a principal-agent model that incorporated social norms. It was an enlightening experience that revealed the enormity of the challenge. I had worked with theorists in modeling financial analysts' information environment using characteristics of their earnings forecasts (Barron, Kim, Lim, and Stevens 1998), and my agency theory experiments had demonstrated the power of social norms to control self-interested behavior on the part of the agent. Thus, I thought it would be interesting to attempt to incorporate social norms into the formal principal-agent model. Alex and I spent almost ten years developing our model and presenting it at research workshops at Florida, Florida State, Minnesota, Ohio State, Pittsburgh, Syracuse, SUNY Buffalo, and Washington. I even presented our model at the AAA Annual Ethics Research Symposium. We received valuable feedback from such agency theorists as Joel Demski, Harry Evans, John Fellingham, Gerry Feltham, Paul Fischer, Steve Huddart, Chandra Kanodia, and Barry Mitnick. We also received valuable feedback from experimental economists such as Mark Isaac, Don Moser, Tim Salmon, Brian Shapiro, and Rick Young. After much effort and persistence, our principal-agent model finally appeared in *Accounting, Organizations, and Society* (Stevens and Thevaranjan 2010).

In our principal-agent model, the principal specifies a standard level of effort in addition to the wage at the time of contracting. Any notion of a standard for effort is ignored in the traditional principal-agent model because it would be completely irrelevant with an opportunistically self-interested agent. In our model, however, we assume that the agent suffers a disutility if he chooses to violate the standard for effort after agreeing to the contract. Thus, we extend the traditional model by incorporating a social norm for promise-keeping (Bicchieri 2006). In our model, this promise-keeping norm affects the expectations of both the principal and the agent. In particular, the principal knows that she can induce a certain amount of effort from the agent by communicating the standard for effort. We defend this assumption as follows (Stevens and Thevaranjan 2010, 129):

We find it reasonable to assume that the principal would have a standard for effort in mind when offering the agent a compensation wage. The notion of shirking assumes an expected level of effort and real-world organizations spend significant time explaining job descriptions and performance expectations at the time of employment contracting. We also find it reasonable to assume that the agent would experience some level of disutility for shirking his effort commitment after agreeing to the contract. The literatures in moral philosophy and social norms suggest that individuals experience some level of shame or guilt for violating norms that they believe to be legitimate (Smith, 1759/1790, Brandt 1979, Bicchieri 2006), and the norm of "promise-keeping" is widely viewed as a legitimate norm by practitioners and moral theorists alike (Adams and Maine 1998, Beauchamp and Bowie 2004, Bicchieri 2006).

We model the agent's disutility for violating the agreed-upon standard for effort as increasing in the agent's sensitivity for the social norm (moral sensitivity) and the level of violation of the standard. As suggested above, we also make the disutility for violating the social norm additively separable from the agent's utility for the net wage (wage less the cost of effort). We preserve all other assumptions of the traditional single-period principal-agent model found in the literature (see above). In formal modeling terms, we utilize the popular joint assumptions that have become known as LEN: Linear incentive contracts, Exponential utility functions, and Normal distributions of noise terms (Lambert 2001). We also assume that all information and preferences are common knowledge to the principal and the agent except for the effort provided by the agent. Thus, our principal-agent model captures the traditional principal problem called *moral hazard with hidden action.*

To accentuate our solution to the principal's moral hazard problem and contrast it with the incentive solution required by the traditional principal-agent model, we initially assume that the principal can only offer the agent a fixed salary contract. Again, the principal and the agent could never agree to a fixed salary contract under the assumption of opportunistic self-interest because the agent would provide zero effort after agreeing to the contract. We examine the interplay between the agent's sensitivity to the social norm and firm productivity in determining the optimal salary contract. Later, we allow for the possibility of incentive contracts and contrast our fixed salary solution to the traditional incentive solution that becomes necessary when the agent is assumed to be opportunistically self-interested.

Our single-period principal-agent model with a promise-keeping norm yields six main results:

1) The agent would rather provide the standard level of effort than shirk as long as the standard is below a *critical level* and the principal pays him his reservation utility for the effort. We interpret the critical level of effort as the maximum effort that the agent perceives to be reasonable or "fair" for a wage that covers his reservation utility for the effort (i.e., his cost of effort). Thus, the promise-keeping norm generates a "work ethic" in the agent that deters his opportunism.

2) The principal can induce the agent to provide effort beyond his critical level by paying a salary that includes a premium that more than compensates the agent for the additional effort. In effect, the salary premium increases what the agent considers to be reasonable effort. To receive more than the agent's critical level of effort, therefore, the principal must share the incremental gain from the extra effort with the agent. Thus, the promise-keeping norm generates an "employment ethic" in the principal that deters her opportunism.

3) The first-best contract is attainable under unobservable effort for firms with low productivity relative to the agent's social norm sensitivity. For these firms, the first-best level of effort is below the agent's critical level, so the principal can obtain the first-best effort by communicating it as the standard effort in the contract and setting the wage equal to the agent's reservation utility for the effort. In this special case, the firm can rely on the agent's work ethic to induce the first-best effort.

4) The optimal salary contract for firms with high productivity relative to the agent's social norm sensitivity involves a salary premium. For these firms, the first-best level of effort is significantly above the agent's critical level, so it is optimal for the principal to pay the agent a salary premium that shares the incremental gain from the extra effort with the agent. Because of the additional cost of the salary premium, however, this solution is second-best.

5) The optimal salary contract for firms with medium productivity relative to the agent's social norm sensitivity is an "expectations reduction" contract. For these firms, the marginal cost of the salary

premium to the principal is greater than her marginal benefit from sharing the additional benefit, so it is optimal for the principal to reduce her expectations and settle for the agent's original critical level of effort. In this special case, the cost of the salary premium again constrains the opportunism of the principal in that she cannot make excessive demands of the agent.

6) The agent's social norm sensitivity does not have to be very high for the first-best solution to become attainable for some firms. In particular, the required level of social norm sensitivity to achieve the first-best solution decreases quadratically with decreases in the firm's productivity. Further, a fixed-salary contract only loses the power to induce effort from the agent when the agent has zero social norm sensitivity (i.e., an incentive contract is required to induce any effort from the agent only when social norm sensitivity is zero).

Our principal-agent model with a social norm for promise-keeping (Stevens and Thevaranjan 2010) supports the usefulness of incorporating social norms into the neoclassical theory of the firm. First, our model demonstrates that assuming away such norms is a limiting case of a more general model. Furthermore, our model supports the assertion that assuming away such norms is a severe or aberrant case (Pratt and Zeckhauser 1985, Koford and Penno 1992). When the agent's social norm sensitivity is nonzero, the fixed salary solution is more efficient than the traditional incentive solution for firms with relatively low and high levels of productivity. Moreover, when the agent's social norm sensitivity is sufficiently high, the fixed salary solution dominates the traditional incentive solution across all levels of productivity. Thus, our model suggests that ignoring the potential for norm-based behavior is inefficient for the firm.

Our model supports the assertion by Elster (1989, 101) and others that "The workplace is a hotbed for norm-guided action." In particular, by incorporating a social norm for promise-keeping, the possibility of other forms of norm-based behavior arises endogenously in our model. For example, the agent's sensitivity to a promise-keeping norm gives rise to the potential for a reciprocity norm in addition to a norm for providing reasonable effort (work ethic), and the principal takes both norms into consideration when solving for the optimal contract. For high productivity firms, for example, our model suggests that the principal will invoke both the reciprocity norm and the work ethic in the optimal contract. The agent's sensitivity to a promise-keeping norm, however, also gives rise to the potential for a fairness norm. In particular, the principal must treat the agent fairly and share with him the additional profits when inducing more effort than the agent is willing to provide for the reservation wage.

Our principal-agent model with norm-based behavior has important implications for both classical and neoclassical theory related to the firm. As discussed above, Arrow's (1962) "learning by doing" model suggests that the more a firm produces, the smarter and more efficient it becomes. This supports Adam Smith's notion that economic growth is fueled in part by a firm's incentive to continuously innovate. Prior to Arrow's model, economists had no explanation for why firms innovated and invested in technology improvements.[5] Our model extends Arrow's intuition by showing that social norm sensitivity allows the principal and the agent to benefit from productivity gains due to improvements in the firm's production technology. In particular, our model suggests that the principal will be able to profit from such productivity gains by paying a salary premium that shares the higher profits with the agent. Because the productivity of the agent's effort is affected by his skill, our model also suggests that social norm sensitivity allows the agent to directly benefit from improvements in his skill. Absent social norm sensitivity, however, the principal is forced to utilize an incentive contract that inflicts financial risk on the risk-averse agent and only grants him his reservation utility. This suggests that social norm sensitivity represents a type of human capital that fuels the specialization and division of labor that Adam Smith theorized was the basis for economic growth and the wealth of nations. Finally, the historical ability of the merchant culture to fuel economic growth emerges endogenously in our model with social norm sensitivity.

In summary, our principal-agent model demonstrates that incorporating social norms increases the descriptive, prescriptive, and pedagogical usefulness of the theory of the firm. Incorporating social norms increases the descriptive usefulness of the theory by increasing its ability to explain organizational phenomena (positive theory). In particular, it helps explain the existence of salary contracts and predict when such salaries will include a premium to induce additional effort from the agent. Incorporating social norms increases the prescriptive usefulness of the theory by increasing its ability to make effective recommendations for increasing the efficiency of

---

[5] A literature in endogenous growth theory developed based on Arrow's model and related work by Paul Romer (1986).

agency relations throughout the firm (normative theory). Our model shows that the benefits of social norm sensitivity extend beyond the principal to the agent and to the economy as a whole. This justifies the emphasis that business practitioners, regulators, and educators place on social norms and professional ethics. Finally, incorporating social norms increases the pedagogical usefulness of the theory by increasing its ability to demonstrate the importance of social and moral norms. In particular, our model supports arguments by Noreen (1988), Koford and Penno (1992), and others that principal-agent theory can be used to demonstrate the cost to the firm of opportunistic behavior and the benefits of norm-based behavior.

OTHER FORMAL MODELS INCORPORATING SOCIAL NORMS INTO THE THEORY OF THE FIRM

I conclude this chapter by discussing other principal-agent models incorporating social norms into the theory of the firm. In an interesting study, Daniel Arce (2007, 709) uses a principal-agent model to examine the conditions under which the formal theory of the firm is self-activating/socially causal. He explains the potential influence of the theory on organizational behavior and corporate culture: "The principal-agent model is an example of a widely disseminated theory in which those who are exposed to it are expected both to put it into practice and have it practiced on them. Consequently, the model raises expectations about the usefulness and occurrence of incentive-based compensation schemes through its underlying assumptions about agents' opportunism" (Arce 2007, 709). To support this potential influence, Arce cites empirical studies demonstrating that the norm of opportunistic self-interest is highest among students in business and economics. For example, Frank, Gilovich, and Regan (1993) report that economics students were more likely to frame the objective of the Prisoner's Dilemma in self-interested terms rather than considering issues such as fairness, trust, or social norms. As Brennan (1994, 39) states, "If we go on hammering into our students the mistaken notion that rationality is identical with self-interest, we shall gradually make our models come true."

Arce develops an evolutionary framework of preference formation to explore the effect of introducing the principal-agent framework into an existing situation where agents have a rational concern for autonomy. First, he presents a principal-agent model with monitoring and characterizes the distributions of principals who monitor and agents who either work or shirk. Next, he contrasts this "types" model with a model where agents possess intrinsic preferences for autonomy (disutility for being monitored). Finally, he identifies conditions under which the traditional agency approach is self-activating. Arce finds that the selection of the "virtuous" equilibrium where agents never shirk and principals need not monitor is highly sensitive to the magnitude of the incentive wage. This is consistent with the notion that introducing traditional agency theory solutions may lead to increased opportunism. Arce also finds that the virtuous equilibrium is likely to evolve only if at least half of the agent population exhibits intrinsic preferences. This supports suggestions by theorists that more attention be paid to issues of business ethics and professional norms in the theory of the firm (Noe and Rebello 1994, Arce 2006).

Dirk Sliwka (2007) uses a principal-agent model to examine the surprising finding in economics that paying an incentive for a given productive effort decreases the intrinsic, nonmonetary motivation for that effort. Motivational crowding theory suggests that rewards and punishments may change the social context from one where pro-social behavior is the norm to one where opportunistic behavior is the norm. Persistent evidence of this "crowding-out effect" is considered by some to be one of the most important anomalies in economics (Frey 1994, Frey and Jegen 2001). This crowding-out effect is consistent with management research suggesting that the mere presence of a control system reduces intrinsic motivation for trustworthiness by signaling distrust (Tenbrunsel and Messick 1999). To explain this behavior, Sliwka models a setting where the principal can choose whether to *control* or to *trust* the agent, and afterward the agent chooses the level of effort to provide. The agent is modeled as one of three types: a *selfish* agent who only cares about his own payoff, a trustworthy or *fair* agent who also cares for the principal's payoff, or a *conformist* agent who is influenced by the social norm suggested by the behavior of other agents. Sliwka assumes two forms of information asymmetry: only the agent knows his type, but the principal has superior information regarding the distribution of types in the population.

In Sliwka's principal-agent model, the principal can assure that even selfish agents exert effort by setting financial incentives. When the principal chooses to trust rather than control agents through incentives, however, she makes herself vulnerable to selfish agents but also signals her conviction to conformist agents that most agents are fair. Sliwka finds that paying a fixed wage rather than a financial incentive can be a credible signal of trust, and this signal positively influences the effort of agents even when financial incentive pay would be optimal with symmetric information about the agent's type. Sliwka also examines self-selection effects of trust. His model shows that firms may forego high-powered financial incentives because they attract agents who respond solely to the incentives which, in turn, undermine the behavior of agents who conform to the behavior of others.

Fischer and Huddart (2008) incorporate social norms into the principal-agent model by assuming that an agent's cost of implementing an action depends on the social norm for that action, defined as the average level of that action chosen by the agent's peer group. Thus, Fischer and Huddart incorporate the assumption that individuals have an innate preference to conform to the behavior of their peers, consistent with Sliwka's conformist agents. In their principal-agent model, a principal contracts with a continuum of agents, and each agent influences the performance measure that determines his compensation through two action choices. The desirable action benefits the principal (such as productive effort), and the undesirable action imposes a cost on the principal (such as earnings management).

Fischer and Huddart's model suggests that social norms influence the financial incentives provided to members of the firm, the boundaries of the firm, and the types of agents in the firm. Interestingly, social norms create a multiplier effect in that the effect of an increase in the power of financial incentives on the desirable action is multiplied by the presence of a social norm for the desirable action. In contrast, the effect of an increase in the power of financial incentives on the desirable action is reduced by the presence of a social norm for the undesirable action. Based on these results, Fischer and Huddart conclude that the presence of social norms should be considered when determining the power of financial incentives within the firm. They also find that it can be optimal to split the firm into two separate organizations in order to eliminate externalities of having agents in the firm with both high-powered and low-powered financial incentives. Thus, their model suggests that an organization's boundaries should be chosen in light of the norms those boundaries engender. Finally, they find that when agents differ in their sensitivities to the social norms for desirable or undesirable actions, these differential sensitivities influence the power of financial incentives and the type of agent that is attracted to the firm.

Mark Penno (2017) points out that organizations rely on both formal controls and informal "tone at the top" to assure that objectives are met and resources are safeguarded (organizational control). Thus, he develops a principal-agent model to determine how these two organizational controls relate. Penno assumes that, ceteris paribus, a stronger tone at the top contributes to a higher expectation that agents will not behave opportunistically. He also assumes that this expectation is increasing in the level of formal control. The two forms of organizational control differ, however, in that tone at the top is developed over time and is fixed in the short run while formal control is not fixed in the short run. Formal control, thereby, is the organization's decision variable in the short run. Penno uses his model to examine how the marginal benefit of formal controls is influenced by the level of tone at the top.

Penno finds that tone at the top and optimal formal controls are complements when the former is low, but the two forms of organizational control are substitutes when tone at the top is high. That is, a threshold is identified where the relation between formal control and tone at the top cleanly reverses from being complements to being substitutes. Penno uses his model to explain mixed results reported in empirical studies of the relation between formal controls and tone at the top. His model suggests that a given optimal level of formal control may be consistent with various levels of overall control, creating ambiguity if reporting requirements put undue weight on documentable formal controls. Finally, Penno's model suggests that increases in control aversion may result in more formal control rather than less, and that the above reversals may completely disappear at sufficiently high levels of control aversion.

The above principal-agent models demonstrate how theorists have already incorporated social norms into the formal theory of the firm to develop new insights and advance the descriptive power of the theory. In particular, theorists have used the traditional tools of neoclassical economic theory to incorporate social norms into principal-agent theory and have found that doing so advances the ability of the theory to describe behavior in organizational settings. These advances in theory have been motivated by persistent experimental and archival evidence of social norm behavior in economic settings related to the firm. The following two chapters are dedicated to this experimental and archival evidence. As I discuss in the following chapter, economists have developed a rigorous experimental methodology to test the assumptions and implications of neoclassical economic theory. This experimental economics research has documented persistent evidence of norm-based behavior in both game theory and agency theory settings. This growing body of evidence represents the biggest challenge to the institution-free, norm-free core of neoclassical economic theory. Theorists continue to respond to this experimental evidence by expanding the traditional boundaries of the theory of the firm.

6

Emerging Evidence of Social Norms in Experimental Research

INTRODUCTION

Similar to classical economists such as Adam Smith and John Stuart Mill, Milton Friedman (1953) and other neoclassical economists initially regarded economics as an inherently nonexperimental science. It was not until the 1980s that the experimental work of a prominent group of economists and developments in game theory opened up the "dismal science" to the powerful world of experimental research. Vernon Smith's Nobel Prize in Economic Science in 2002 recognized his role in helping economics become an experimental science capable of testing the assumptions and implications of economic theory. His Nobel lecture and follow-up book (Smith 2003, 2008) gave a personal account of how a neoclassical economist changed his thinking due to experimental tests of market theory and game theory. This growing body of experimental research is changing the thinking of many economists regarding the importance of institutions and social norms in the theory of the firm.

In this chapter, I summarize the emerging evidence of social norm behavior in experimental research related to the firm. I begin by discussing the key benefits of experimental research in economics. By allowing researchers to manipulate variables to test causal theoretical relations, experimental research provides an important bridge between the powerful yet highly simplified world of the theorist (see Chapter 5) and the naturally occurring world of the archival researcher (see Chapter 7). Next, I discuss the early classroom market experiments by Edward Chamberlin at Harvard in the 1940s and Vernon Smith at Purdue in the 1950s and 1960s. Smith participated in one of Chamberlin's classroom markets while at Harvard and was initially dismissive of the usefulness of such markets for research purposes. After using them in his own classes, however, Smith discovered the power of experimental markets for theory building in economics. I discuss the rigorous experimental methodology developed by Smith and his colleagues based on the insights of early experimentalists in psychology and management science (e.g., Simon 1955, Siegel 1959).

Next, I describe key findings from experimental studies of neoclassical market theory. Initially, these experiments documented that capital asset markets were efficient under a less restrictive set of assumptions than theorists had anticipated. This demonstrated the power of the invisible hand of the market to generate efficient outcomes for investors and the economy. Subsequent market studies, however, demonstrated a tendency for experimental asset markets to underreact to readily available public information. As the mathematical field of game theory developed, it became apparent that a deeper understanding of *homo economicus* was needed to select among the many equilibrium solutions that were possible in strategic two-person exchanges. Thus, the importance of experimental research in economics grew in the eyes of many neoclassical economists. I discuss experimental tests of game theory and principal-agent theory and how they have revealed the presence of *homo sociologicus*. These experiments have demonstrated the robust influence of norm-based behavior in strategic game settings related to the theory of the firm. Finally, I discuss the growing evidence of norm-based behavior in experimental studies of participative budgeting.

BENEFITS OF EXPERIMENTAL RESEARCH

Experimental research has become a powerful tool to develop and refine economic theory related to capital markets and the firm. In particular, researchers have found experimental methods useful to test the underlying assumptions and implications of the neoclassical theory of the firm. The theory of the firm promoted by the Chicago school came with a strong set of assumptions, including narrow self-interest, preferences only for wealth and leisure, and highly efficient capital markets. As researchers in economics developed experimental methods relevant to their field and utilized them in their research, these assumptions were submitted to rigorous testing. As reflected in Milton Friedman's (1953) classic methodological essay, mainstream economists were initially uninterested in testing the underlying assumptions of neoclassical theory. As consistent evidence emerged inconsistent with these assumptions, however, even mainstream neoclassical economists began to sit up and take notice.

Daniel Friedman and Shyam Sunder explain the rigorous methodology of experimental economics in their 1994 book entitled, *Experimental Methods: A Primer for Economists.* I have used Friedman and Sunder's book plus Vernon Smith's writings (Smith 1982, 2008) to explain the benefits of experimental research in my PhD seminars at Syracuse, Florida State, and Georgia State (Robinson College of Business). Friedman and Sunder (1994, 1) argue that "a discipline becomes experimental *when innovators develop techniques for conducting relevant experiments*" (italics in the original). Similar to economics, researchers in other sciences such as astronomy, physics, chemistry, and biology were originally deemed unamenable to experimental inquiry. As innovators in these fields developed techniques for conducting relevant experiments, however, these sciences developed a strong experimental tradition. Similarly, innovations in experimental economics research in the 1960s and 1970s gave birth to an experimental literature that, by the 1980s, mainstream economists could no longer ignore.

As I have discussed in previous chapters, early classical economists focused primarily on macroeconomic theory, which precluded the development of controlled experiments due to the sheer size of its topics related to political economy. In contrast, neoclassical economists focused primarily on microeconomic theory related to producers, consumers, and the firm, which was more amenable to experimental methods. Due to their willingness to utilize abstracting, simplifying, and idealizing assumptions (see Chapter 4), neoclassical economists were initially uninterested in testing the realism of their underlying assumptions. In particular, mainstream neoclassical economists were interested primarily in testing the *consequences* of their traditional economic assumptions (e.g., *homo economicus*, rational optimization, and equilibrium behavior), which had been chosen more for their simplicity and tractability than for their realism. Thus, it is not surprising that mainstream economists such as Paul Samuelson and Milton Friedman regarded economics as an inherently nonexperimental science until well into the mid-twentieth century. Given the strong tradition of experimental research in psychology and other social sciences, however, it was inevitable that innovators would develop techniques for conducting relevant experiments in economics.

In assessing the benefits of experimental research in economics, it is important first to address the interactive relation between experimental evidence and economic theory. Some researchers, including those who conduct experiments, have questioned the usefulness of experimental research for testing a given economic theory. For example, what is to be gained from attempting a direct experimental test of principal-agent theory? As discussed in Chapter 5, this formal theory of the firm consists of a set of simplifying assumptions and definitions along with the results that logically flow from them. The theory is formally valid in that it is internally consistent and the results and conclusions are provable from the underlying assumptions. Thus, what can be gained by conducting an experiment designed as a direct test of the theory? If the experiment yields results *consistent* with the theory, then little has been gained beyond the original intuition of the theory. If the experiment yields results *inconsistent* with the theory, on the other hand, then such results can always be questioned by theorists as a failure to replicate the many underlying assumptions of the theory. Thus, a direct test of principal-agent theory in the laboratory represents a lose-lose proposition with few prospects for publication.[1]

Given the above, many researchers regard experimental research as useful primarily for testing the behavioral assumptions of a given economic theory. For example, an experimentalist could examine whether the underlying behavioral assumptions of principal-agent theory are descriptively valid. This more modest approach has much theoretical merit, especially if an alternative behavioral assumption is offered and the experiment allows a powerful test of the two alternative assumptions. Because theorists use behavioral assumptions more for their simplicity and tractability than for their realism, however, a theorist may still find such research of little interest. Thus, some neoclassical economists have argued that it is more accurate and productive to view the purpose of experimental research as that of providing regularities in observed behavior over a broad range of interesting settings that have implications for economic theory (Smith 2008). In this regard, the purpose of an experimental study is not different from that of an empirical study using nonexperimental methods (see Chapter 7). Experimental research is a powerful tool of economic theory building, however, in that it allows researchers to examine nonexisting settings that are useful to examine boundaries or extremes (corner solutions) of existing theory. Experimental research also allows researchers to

---

[1] Another reason that such a direct experimental test of principal-agent theory is ill-advised is the strong prior beliefs of researchers on both sides. Mainstream neoclassical researchers are likely to view the theory as nearly self-evident whereas behavioral researchers are likely to view the theory as irrelevant due to its unrealistic assumptions. Such strong priors suggest little potential belief revision even from a powerful experimental test of the theory (Burgstahler 1987).

uncover empirical regularities in economic settings where existing theory is silent or has little to say.

The interactive relation between experimental evidence and theory has great potential to yield important theoretical breakthroughs. For this potential to be realized, however, the experimental researcher must have a strong understanding of both relevant economic theory and experimental methods. The ideal experimental setting forms a win-win proposition for the researcher with many prospects for publication. In particular, it provides the opportunity to turn up behavioral regularities that spur refinements of economic theory, usually as minor adjustments but sometimes as major revisions. Existing theory is important to experimental research because it tells researchers what data to gather and how the data should be organized and analyzed. Data from well-designed experiments, in turn, are important because they help theorists refine existing theory or develop new theory that is worthy of future refinement. As Friedman and Sunder (1994, 3) state, "The alternation of theory and empirical work, each refining the other, is the engine of progress in every scientific discipline." The emphasis in experimental economics on building upon preexisting neoclassical theory differentiates it from other experimental traditions in the social sciences.

The ideal experimental setting to advance economic theory not only allows for a powerful test of behavioral regularities, but also provides an opportunity to select among alternative assumptions or theories that might account for such regularities. Brown, Evans, and Moser (2009) review the growing experimental literature in accounting related to participative budgeting. As I discuss below, this experimental literature has been a valuable source of data for incorporating social norms into the theory of the firm. Brown et al. argue that experimental studies provide the most useful empirical data to agency theorists when they contain a strong agency prediction and an opposing prediction from an alternative behavioral theory. In agency theory related to participative budgeting, the strong agency prediction is that the agent will maximize his earnings by building the highest amount of available slack in the budget. This strong agency prediction has allowed experimentalists in accounting to provide powerful evidence for the presence of social norms in budgeting such as honesty, distributional fairness, and reciprocity (Douthit and Stevens 2015).

The least efficient use of an experimental study is to attempt to simulate a naturally occurring economic setting. The more the experimental setting approaches the naturally occurring setting in realism, the more likely it is to contain measurement problems and potential confounds. The strength of an experimental study is the ability to provide strong measures and manipulations that are able to test causal relations between theoretical variables. Such strong measures and manipulations are unavailable with nonexperimental studies, which typically are only able to capture associations between poorly measured proxies for theoretical constructs. Thus, the strength of experimental research is that it provides an important bridge between the powerful yet highly simplified world of the theorist and the naturally occurring world of the archival researcher. All three forms of scientific inquiry, however, have their strengths and are vitally important to the development of economic theory related to the firm.

THE DEVELOPMENT OF AN EXPERIMENTAL METHODOLOGY

Friedman and Sunder (1994) present a brief history of the emergence of economics as an experimental science. They use their history to address the following questions: (1) Why were innovators able to develop techniques for conducting relevant experiments in economics in the 1960s and 1970s and not before? and (2) Why did mainstream economists begin to acknowledge the relevance of laboratory experiments in the 1980s? In short, Friedman and Sunder attempt to explain the emergence and influence of experimental research in mainstream economics. As someone who joined the experimental economics movement in the early 1990s as a PhD student, and benefitted greatly from the experimental economics faculty and lab at Indiana University, I find this history interesting and always cover it in my own PhD seminars. This history also contributes to the history of the theory of the firm provided in Chapter 3. I discuss it here primarily because it helps explain experimental research methodology in economics and how the neoclassical theory of the firm has become open to social norm theory.

The emergence of economics as an experimental science can be attributed to a perfect storm of influences from experimental psychology, classroom experimental tests of market efficiency, mathematical economics, and game theory. Experimental economics began as a branch of experimental psychology that dealt with issues in economics and business in the 1950s, and was heavily influenced by behavioral researchers such as Herbert Simon (1916–2001) and Sidney Siegel (1916–1961). Simon was a professor of business administration at Carnegie's GSIA in the 1950s who won the Nobel Prize in Economic Science in 1978, and Siegel was an experimental psychologist from Stanford who spent his short career at Pennsylvania State University before his untimely death in 1961. These behavioral researchers were associated with such groups as the RAND Corporation and the Cowles Commission, which were funding research in the postwar era related to the applications of mathematics to economics, management, and human decision-making. These behavioral researchers utilized a broad interpretation of economic rationality that included limitations in information and processing ability, known today as "bounded rationality" or "satisficing."[2]

Simon distinguished between substantive and procedural rationality in experimental studies of decision-making behavior. In particular, he argued that what is rational to the experimenter, given all that she knows, may be quite different from what is rational to the participant in an experiment (Simon 1955). Reflecting on these two types of rationality in experimental studies, Siegel (1959) argued for and provided experimental support for the importance of monetary incentives and procedures designed to maximize learning while avoiding boredom. In a series of experiments with Lawrence Fouraker at Penn State, Siegel documented the importance of salient payoffs and clear instructions in experimental tests of economic decision-making (Siegel and Fouraker 1960). Consistent with this early work, experimental economists have followed the tradition of providing careful instructions, salient payoffs, and sufficient learning in their experimental research. Sufficient learning in experimental markets has come to mean stationary repetition, or repeating a single-period market setting multiple times by replenishing the endowments and resetting the parameters.[3] Despite its origins in experimental psychology, however, this experimental methodology did not transfer over to the experimental tradition in psychology.[4]

Edward Chamberlin (1899–1967) is believed to be the first economist to assign cost and value parameters to participants to create supply and

---

[2] This tradition of using theories in psychology and sociology to study problems in economics and business continues today in the specialty fields of behavioral economics, behavioral accounting, behavioral finance, and organizational behavior. My focus in this chapter, as with the rest of this book, is on research that uses neoclassical economic theory as its foundation and focus.

[3] To avoid the potential for reputation or group effects to form in the experiment, experimental researchers frequently rotate pairings or groupings between periods.

[4] The greatest difficulty I had in running my dissertation experiments in participative budgeting at Indiana was getting the behavioral accountants on my dissertation committee to allow me to include more than one decision period. However, they also pushed me to include a psychometrically valid personality test and a set of exit questionnaire items to capture individual preferences for social norms. These individual preference measures, which are still relatively ignored in experimental economics, yielded important theoretical insights for which I am very grateful.

demand curves in his classroom market experiments at Harvard University in the 1940s. Chamberlin used his market experiments largely to demonstrate his theory of monopolistic competition (Chamberlin 1933) and its superiority over competitive equilibrium theory. His classroom markets did not typically demonstrate convergence to the competitive equilibrium prediction. However, Chamberlin used a weak market institution involving anonymous bilateral search, no stationary repetition, and no salient rewards. The economic theory of competitive equilibrium, beginning with Mill and Marshall, had assumed the presence of financial rewards and perfect information across traders (Ekelund and Hébert 2014). Given the strong influence of competitive market theory at the time, few of Chamberlin's students or colleagues saw scientific value in his classroom experiments (Friedman and Sunder 1994).

Vernon Smith was a graduate student at Harvard in the late 1940s, and he participated in one of Chamberlin's classroom market experiments. Although he was dismissive at the time, Smith later concluded that subjecting neoclassical market theory to experimental testing was a sound methodological idea. When he conducted similar classroom market experiments at Purdue, however, he modified Chamberlin's market institution in a number of important ways. First, all bids and offers were immediately made public rather than requiring bilateral negotiations in private. This market institution, called the double auction market, better captured the underlying assumptions of competitive equilibrium theory and more closely reflected the way capital markets had evolved in practice. Second, Smith relied on the Marshallian notion that markets approach the competitive equilibrium over time as supply and demand remain stationary. Thus, he included stationary repetition in his classroom market experiments. In contrast to Chamberlin's markets, Smith observed transaction prices and final allocations that converged rapidly to the competitive equilibrium prediction. The results from eleven of his classroom market experiments conducted over a span of six years were published in the *Journal of Political Economy* (Smith 1962).

After visiting Stanford in 1961, Smith began to think systematically about applying Sidney Siegel's standards of experimental methodology in his own experiments. Participants in his original classroom markets were not paid, so salient payoffs were absent. In addition to adding salient payoffs, Smith thought about other ways to improve his experimental methodology to advance neoclassical economic theory. He shared his ideas with Charlie Plott, a young theorist at Purdue in the late 1960s who conducted experimental research related to economic public policy. Plott moved to the California Institute of Technology in 1971, and Smith moved to the University of Arizona in 1975. Both Cal Tech and Arizona soon became leading centers of experimental economics in the United States, and both Plott (1982) and Smith (1982) wrote comprehensive reviews of the new experimental methodology in economics. Meanwhile, Reinhard Selten and a group of economists developed experimental methods separately and independently in Germany, and the University of Bonn became another leading center of experimental economics.[5]

In addition to testing static equilibrium predictions and market efficiency, neoclassical economists found their experimental methodology useful for testing game theory predictions introduced by John von Neumann and Oscar Morgenstern (von Neumann and Morgenstern 1944). Early on, mathematicians and economists recognized that the new game theory would require experimental data to help identify relevant equilibrium concepts and select among the frequently multiple equilibria. The presence of multiple equilibria occurs because there are several basic approaches to game theory (e.g., cooperative versus noncooperative forms), and each basic approach has numerous possible equilibria. By the 1950s, therefore, a group of talented mathematicians at Princeton, including John Nash, Lloyd Shapley, and John Milnor began to conduct classroom experiments to illustrate and examine game-theoretical solutions. Soon other mathematicians, economists, and psychologists began to conduct experimental tests of game theory.

Friedman and Sunder (1994) identify developments in game theory as one of the many influences leading mainstream economists to acknowledge the relevance of laboratory experiments in the 1980s. Given that these developments originated from world-class mathematicians at Princeton, the RAND Corporation, and the Cowles Commission, it was difficult for neoclassical economists to ignore the validity and usefulness of this highly experimental source of economic theory. Rather than focus only on static equilibrium predictions based on opportunistic self-interest, however, game theory developed an experimental tradition that opened the economics literature to questions of process and other forms of rationality based on social intelligence and social norm behavior (Camerer 2003). As discussed further below, these experimental tests of game theory revealed persistent

---

[5] Most of the experimental research in the United States retained the rational framework of neoclassical economics while most of the experimental research in Germany incorporated the bounded rationality framework of psychology and sociology (Friedman and Sunder 1994). The former research tradition has been labeled "experimental economics" while the latter tradition has been labeled "behavioral economics."

and recalcitrant behavior consistent with preferences for social norms such as fairness, trustworthiness, and reciprocity. These social norms, which were present long before markets and nation-states, supported the historical development of the merchant culture and its capitalist institutions.

In summary, experimental economics began as a branch of experimental psychology that dealt with issues in economics and business, but it soon developed its own experimental tradition and rigorous methodology. Experimental economics diverged from its foundation in experimental psychology along four dimensions. First, it developed a strong focus on behavior in specific economic institutions such as firms and capital markets. Second, and perhaps more important, it developed a strong focus on preestablished first principles based on neoclassical economic theory. Third, and as a result of the first two, it developed a strong focus on experimental methods designed to make economic incentives and institutions salient to participants. These experimental methods are based on induced-value theory, which attempts to minimize the effects of individual characteristics of participants (Friedman and Sunder 1994).[6] Fourth, experimental economics has developed a strong aversion to deception of any kind. As a rule, deception is avoided because it is both a direct and an indirect threat to the salience of economic incentives and institutions in experimental settings. In contrast, researchers in experimental psychology and behavioral economics use many behavioral theories and frameworks and are generally open to deception in their experimental instructions and manipulations.

In his 2002 Nobel Prize lecture and his follow-up book, *Rationality in Economics: Constructivist and Ecological Forms* (Smith 2008), Vernon Smith identifies two forms of rationality emerging from the evidence in experimental economics. Consistent with Friedrich Hayek (1967, 1988), Smith defines constructivist rationality as "the conscious deductive processes of human reason" (Smith 2008, 26). Constructivist rationality reflects the writings of Descartes and Mill, who argued that human institutions are and ought to be the creation of conscious reason. This form of rationality is reflected in much of traditional neoclassical economic theory, which is derived deductively from a small set of simplifying assumptions and definitions. Smith defines ecological rationality as "home-grown

---

[6] Induced value theory proposes that three conditions suffice to make economic incentives and institutions salient: *Monotonicity* (participants prefer more of the reward medium than less), *Salience* (participants understand the relation between actions and the reward medium), and *Dominance* (changes in participants' utility is dominated by the reward medium, and other influences are negligible).

principles of action, norms, traditions, and 'morality'" (Smith 2008, 36). Ecological rationality reflects the writings of Adam Smith and Hayek, who argued that human institutions are frequently the result of emergent order reflected in human history and evolved human cultures. This form of rationality reflects a type of "social intelligence" that has evolved naturally from our cultural and biological heritage.

The emerging evidence in experimental economics, especially in experimental studies of game theory and the theory of the firm, reflect the robust effects of ecological rationality in economic decision-making. That is, *homo sociologicus* is very evident in this experimental research. It is interesting to note that the neoclassical theory of the firm that emanated from the Chicago school has been heavily dominated by the constructivist rationality of Mill and his narrow view of *homo economicus*.[7] While emphasizing the writings of Adam Smith and Friedrich Hayek related to free markets and the inefficiency of government regulation, the Chicago school largely ignored the writings of Smith and Hayek regarding the emergent order in human institutions, cultures, and social norms. In particular, the neoclassical theory of the firm that came to dominate economics, accounting, and finance, gave little thought to how firms, capital markets, and other capitalist institutions evolved or the importance of culture and social norms in the functioning of such institutions.

Vernon Smith (2008, 25) argues that both constructivist rationality and ecological rationality are critical aspects of economic theorizing:

Roughly, we associate constructivism with attempts to model, formally or informally, rational individual action and to invent or design social systems, and link ecological rationality with adaptive human decision and with group processes of discovery in natural social systems . . . Every business decision is someone's constructivist idea of a best or appropriate action, but whether that decision is ecologically fit is up to socioeconomic forces far beyond the originator. Ecological rationality, however, always has an empirical, evolutionary, and/or historical basis; constructivist rationality need have little, and where its specific abstract propositions lead to some form of implementation, it must survive tests of acceptability, fitness, and/or modification.

Further, Vernon Smith (2008, 25) argues that the two forms of rationality "need not be mutually exclusive, opposed, or incompatible: We can apply reason to understand and model emergent order in human cultures and to evaluate the intelligence and function of such order." As I demonstrate in this book, this is precisely what neoclassical researchers have begun to do in

---

[7] This is particularly interesting, as Mill had little faith in either free markets or unencumbered capitalism (Ekelund and Hébert 2014).

their analytical, experimental, and archival research incorporating social norms into the theory of the firm.

FINDINGS FROM EXPERIMENTAL STUDIES OF NEOCLASSICAL MARKET THEORY

The belief that the static equilibrium prediction from neoclassical market theory required perfect information was common before Vernon Smith's experimental markets at Purdue in the 1950s and 1960s. This belief can be traced back to the writings of W. S. Jevons (1871), the English economist who was instrumental in developing the theory of utility and incorporating it into the political economy of his day (see Chapter 3). Jevons argued that a market was theoretically perfect only when all traders have perfect knowledge of conditions of supply and demand making up market price, and that this was more or less true of organized stock exchanges.[8] Thereafter, the assumption of perfectly competitive markets with perfect information became a common simplifying assumption in formal models of markets and the firm. While this was a common assumption for neo-classical economists, however, Smith (2008, 103) cited it as an example of "a poorly articulated fallacy of constructivism that has done much damage – real and intellectual – to the way economists think about the world." This assumption was particularly damaging to economic theory because it became a "Folk Theorem" that was used to tear down the reasonableness of efficient markets by some economists on the left of the political spectrum and to build an impenetrable and unquestioned temple to market efficiency by some economists on the right.

Vernon Smith's early classroom markets (Smith 1962) yielded two important insights that advanced both constructivist and ecological rationality related to capital markets. The speed with which his double auction markets converged to the competitive equilibrium predictions (price and allocation) suggested that Chamberlin's results were attributable to the use of anonymous bilateral negotiations as the market institution. Thus, the first major insight was the critical importance of institutional structure to market efficiency. The high efficiency of Smith's markets also helps explain why capital markets have generally evolved consistent with double

---

[8] Perfect knowledge assumes that all traders have "common knowledge" of conditions of supply and demand making up market price. Game theorist Robert Aumann (1976) has provided a rigorous definition of common knowledge, which states in essence that if two people have common knowledge of an item then both know it individually, both know that the other knows it, both know that the other knows that they know it, and so on.

auctions in free-market economies. Yet, the value and cost parameters used to create supply and demand curves remained private in Smith's markets. Thus, the second major insight was that market participants did not require perfect knowledge of supply and demand to achieve equilibrium price and allocation predictions. In the face of centuries of neoclassical theory going back to Jevons, all that was needed to achieve the competitive equilibrium prediction was a market institution that better reflected the way capital markets have evolved in free-market economies.

Innovators in economics soon used their new research methodology to test the robustness of Smith's results and to examine the efficiency of other capital market institutions. While at Arizona, Vernon Smith joined with Arlington Williams to develop the first computerized double auction market (Williams 1980) and with Jim Cox began to examine other market institutions such as the sealed-bid auction (also called the call market).[9] Since the publication of Smith's first experimental markets (Smith 1962), thousands of experiments have confirmed the robustness of his double auction results to differing supply-demand curves. The general results from these double auction experiments is that only a few buyers and sellers are required to achieve rapid convergence to efficient equilibrium predictions when there is private supply and demand information and participants are paid according to induced-value theory. Gode and Sunder (1993) demonstrate that this phenomenon is largely due to the power of this emergent market institution and not the intelligence or rationality of traders. In a double auction market with "zero intelligence" computerized traders who choose bids and asks completely at random subject to a no-loss constraint, highly efficient market outcomes are still achieved. Surprisingly, experimental studies have shown that convergence to the competitive equilibrium is only slowed by complete information (Smith 1976).

The early evidence of highly efficient markets, however, was found in experimental markets with stationary repetition and induced supply and demand curves. Smith, Suchanek, and Williams (1988) developed an experimental market setting without stationary repetition and with only one trader type with no induced gains from trade. In their experimental

---

[9] Arlie programmed his computerized markets in PLATO, a computer language that had become archaic by the time I studied experimental economics under him. Experimental markets and game theory experiments today commonly use an easy-to-learn open-source program called Z-tree (Zurich Toolbox for Readymade Economic Experiments) that was originally designed by Urns Fischbacher (Fischbacher 2007) at the University of Zurich's Institute for Empirical Research in Economics.

markets, the traded asset paid a constant dividend in each of fifteen periods so that the intrinsic value of the asset decreased each period, and the asset was worthless after the final period. In dozens of experimental sessions conducted over several years, these markets exhibited frequent bubble-crash behavior where market price rises far above intrinsic value only to crash near the final period. Follow-up studies found similar bubble-crash behavior, even with business professionals (King, Smith, Williams, and Van Boening 1992). More recent studies of this market setting have found that these markets are more prone to bubble as the ratio of cash to shares endowed increases (Caginalp, Porter, and Smith 2001). As the ratio of cash to shares increases, traders interested in speculating on momentum trade have greater capacity to drive up prices. A recent study has also found that reducing the complexity of information regarding intrinsic value increases market efficiency, but only in markets that have a lower ratio of cash to shares endowed and are therefore less prone to bubble (Hobson 2011).

While at Indiana, I conducted a series of experimental asset markets with Ann Gillette, Susan Watts, and Arlie Williams (Gillette, Stevens, Watts, and Williams 1999). The value of the traded asset was the sum of five random draws from a known distribution conducted at the end of every three of fifteen trading periods. Instead of going down at a constant rate and being worthless at the end of the fifteen periods, therefore, the value of the traded asset was the realization of the five random draws. To approximate perfect information, we conducted the dividend draws publicly by having a participant draw a chip from a large beach bucket in the room and gave participants extensive training on the dividend draws prior to the experimental markets.[10] To gather traders' subjective beliefs, we also elicited traders' forecasts of the final asset value at the beginning of each trading period and paid participants based on the accuracy of their forecasts. We conducted thirteen experimental market sessions. Despite the prediction that common knowledge of all market information would result in common expectations and no trade (Milgrom and Stokey 1982, Geanakoplos 1992, Neeman 1996), approximately ten percent of the outstanding shares were traded each period. Both the forecasts and market prices underreacted to the public dividend signals, with prices underreacting more than forecasts. Interestingly, forty-three percent of trades were inconsistent with the traders' forecasts, consistent with speculative trade.

---

[10] Given that I borrowed the beach bucket from my young daughter, who inquired frequently as to when she would get it back, Arlie insisted on adding a footnote (footnote 11) to our published paper thanking her for the use of her beloved bucket.

We added a series of call markets and found that speculative trade was somewhat lower in these markets than in our double auction markets. Finally, we found that trading volume was increasing in the mean absolute forecast revision and decreasing in the contemporaneous dispersion in forecasts.

Upon reviewing the literature, Smith (2008, 62) bemoans our lack of knowledge regarding the ecological rationality of capital markets and the production of a competitive equilibrium (CE). He states, "The alleged 'requirement' of complete, common, or perfect information is vacuous: I know of no predictive theorem stating that when agents have such information their behavior produces a CE, and in the absence of such information their behavior fails to produce a CE." The experimental evidence lends little support for the neoclassical requirement of perfect information based on constructivist rationality. Double auction markets with less than perfect information have been found to converge rapidly and efficiently to the competitive equilibrium price and allocation. In contrast, double auction markets and call markets with fully public, common information have been found to exhibit heterogeneous expectations and speculative trade with prices that frequently vary from the competitive equilibrium prediction. Smith calls for advances in our understanding of the emergent order of capital markets. "What is missing are models of the process whereby agents go from their initial circumstances and dispersed information, using the algorithms and public messages of the institution to update their status, and converge (or fail to converge) to the predicted equilibrium."

Smith (2008, 65) also bemoans our lack of knowledge regarding the role of individual characteristics versus the role of the rules of market institutions in determining market efficiency: "How much of the performance properties of markets are due to characteristics of the individual, and how much to those of institutions? Characteristics of both entities may be passed on to later generations by biological and cultural coevolution. What are the dynamics of these processes?" Finally, Smith (2008, 21–22), bemoans our lack of knowledge regarding the role of culture and social norms in the functioning of markets: "Cultures that have evolved markets have enormously expanded resource specialization, created commensurate gains from exchange, and are wealthier than those that have not (see Scully 1988, Demmert and Klein 2003, Gwartney and Lawson 2003) . . . Markets economize on the need for virtue, but do not eliminate it and indeed depend on it to avoid a crushing burden of monitoring and enforcement cost. If every explicit or implicit contract required external policing resources to ensure efficient performance, the efficiency gains from specialization and exchange would be in danger of being gobbled up by these support costs. In this sense, the information property right rules or norms of moral social engagement – thou shalt not kill, steal, bear false witness, commit adultery, or covet the possessions of thy neighbor – strongly support wealth creation through the increased specialization made possible by personal social exchange and the extended order of markets." Again, this suggests the underlying influence of the merchant culture in generating capitalist institutions and creating wealth.

As I discuss in Chapter 7, the Chicago school's belief in efficient capital markets effectively shut down research related to individual information processing in capital markets as well as research related to trading volume. This belief in efficient capital markets also effectively shut down research related to heterogeneity in investor beliefs (rather than common beliefs) and the role of disclosure quality on such beliefs. More recently, however, researchers in accounting have designed experimental market settings to examine these issues. For example, Barron and Qu (2014) design a two-period repeating experimental market to explore how the quality of public information affects trading volume and market prices in the period prior to the release of the public information. They manipulate the quality of public information at two levels (High and Low Quality) and the asymmetry of private information at two levels (High and Low Asymmetry). Under Low Asymmetry, each of eight traders received one private signal, while under High Asymmetry, four of the eight traders received two private signals and four received none. Barron and Qu find that high-quality public disclosure leads to increased price efficiency and decreases cost of capital in the preannouncement period when information asymmetry is high. Their experimental study suggests that a high-quality information environment characterized by transparent disclosures increases market efficiency to the benefit of both investors and the firm.

FINDINGS FROM EXPERIMENTAL TESTS OF GAME THEORY

Despite the increasing use of mathematical tools in neoclassical economics throughout the nineteenth century, the application of mathematics to economics did not begin in earnest until the late 1930s and 1940s. Part of the new emphasis on mathematics in economics was due to the war effort and part of it was due to the work of The Cowles Commission for Research in Economics. Founded in Colorado Springs in 1932 by businessman and economist Alfred Cowles, the Cowles Commission was moved to the

University of Chicago in 1939 where it joined with a growing group of influential neoclassical economists to become the bastion of mathematical economics.[11] Influential researchers who won Nobel prizes for their research conducted while at the Cowles Commission include Kenneth Arrow, Gérard Debreu, Trygve Haavelmo, Leonid Hurwicz, Lawrence Klein, Tjalling Koopmans, Harry Markowitz, Franco Modigliani, Herbert A. Simon, Joseph E. Stiglitz, and James Tobin.

At the time that John von Neumann and Oskar Morgenstern first published their classic work on game theory and economic behavior in 1944, they had to spend a considerable part of their first chapter defending the use of "the mathematical method" in economics. Von Neumann and Morgenstern (1944, 3) argued that there did not exist any fundamental reason why mathematics should not be used in economics despite the existence of "the human element, of the psychological factors etc...." They developed the formal concept of rational behavior and utility maximization in game theory, but they did not directly address "the measurement of utilities and of preferences" (von Neumann and Morgenstern 1944, 8). Similar to Mill, they applied a narrow definition of *homo economicus* to simplify their mathematical calculations. Although they assumed "that the consumer desires to obtain a maximum of utility or satisfaction and the entrepreneur a maximum of profits," they also assumed "that the aim of all participants in the economic system, consumers as well as entrepreneurs, is money, or equivalently a single monetary commodity."[12]

As would be expected, von Neumann and Morgenstern's classic work on game theory received unparalleled accolades from the mathematical economists at the Cowles Commission (Kuhn 2004). Herbert A. Simon (1945) and Leonid Hurwicz (1945) wrote glowing reviews in the *American Journal of Sociology* and *American Economic Review*, respectively. However, mathematicians and economists at the Cowles Commission followed other economists in generally ignoring game theory for the next few decades. It was left to mathematicians at the RAND Corporation and at von Neumann and Morgenstern's home institution of Princeton University to slowly and quietly push the limits of the new theory in their highly analytical and increasingly experimental research (Kuhn 2004). At the

---

[11] The Cowles Commission was moved to Yale University in 1955, where it was renamed the Cowles Foundation.

[12] Von Neumann and Morgenstern (1944, 10) had a great deal to say about social influences in the social exchange economy, such as, "imitation, advertising, custom, and so on." I return to von Neumann and Morgenstern's expanded view of utility maximization in the social exchange economy in the concluding chapter (Chapter 8).

University of Bonn, meanwhile, Reinhard Selten and his associates pushed the limits of game theory in their experimental research at the laboratory for experimental economics research (BonnEconLab). By the time the Nobel Prize in Economic Science was awarded to John Nash, John Harsanyi, and Reinhard Selten in 1994, experimental game theory had assumed a central position in the development of economic theory.

John Nash expanded the game theory of von Neumann and Morgenstern by adding the insight that self-interested players will adjust their strategies until no player would benefit from changing. Thus, a Nash equilibrium prediction is an iterated-dominance equilibrium that leaves the players no reason to change their choice due to self-interest and the financial incentives of the game. Despite its foundation in a narrow view of *homo economicus*, however, experimental tests of game theory have revealed the presence of *homo sociologicus*. In particular, experimental results from dictator, ultimatum, and trust games have yielded results consistent with preferences for social norms. These experiments have demonstrated the robust influence of human sociality, culture, and social norms on behavior in strategic economic settings. These experimental results are robust and systematic, and so they demonstrate a type of rationality beyond the *constructivist* rationality of traditional game theory. Vernon Smith (2008) has described the emerging results in experimental tests of game theory as powerful evidence of *ecological* rationality arising from social history and experience. Colin Camerer (2003) has coined the term "behavioral game theory" to describe the emerging behavioral regularities from the laboratory that contradict traditional game theory predictions.

In 1950, Melvin Dresher and Merrill Flood began the experimental testing of game theory at the RAND Corporation by conducting an experimental test of the matrix game given below (Roth 1995). The game involved a fixed pair of participants interacting over 100 periods, with Player A picking their choice of row (1 or 2) and Player B picking their choice of column (1 or 2) each period.

−1, 2	½, 1
0, ½	1, −1

The payoffs of the game were in pennies, and each player received the sum of his or her payoffs over the course of the 100 periods. The unique Nash equilibrium prediction is that Player A (row player) would always choose the second row and Player B (column player) would always choose the first column, yielding $0.00 for Player A and $0.50 for Player B over the 100 periods. This Nash equilibrium, while strategically rational in the sense that each player anticipates the opportunistic self-interest of the other, is inefficient in that the cooperative solution would yield a higher profit for both players. If Player A chose the first row and Player B chose the second column, in particular, Player A would receive $0.50 and Player B would receive $1.00 over the 100 periods. This cooperative solution is not the *dominant* solution, however, because it is always in the best interest of each player to defect to reap a higher profit, and this defection is very costly to the other player.[13]

The observed payoffs for this early experimental test of game theory, published in Flood (1952, 1958), were $0.40 for Player A (row player) and $0.65 for Player B (column player). Thus, the two players cooperated enough to improve considerably on the dominant Nash solution ($0.00 for A and $0.50 for B) and yet fell short of the fully cooperative solution ($0.50 for A and $1.00 for B). Dresher and Flood interpreted their results as evidence of a cooperative "split the difference" strategy rather than the Nash equilibrium strategy based on opportunistic self interest. John Nash, however, argued that the study had a fundamental flaw in that "the experiment really amounts to having the players play one large multi-move game" (Flood 1958, 16). Thousands of experimental studies of game theory, however, have yielded the same tendency for players to violate the Nash equilibrium strategy and attempt to cooperate to achieve superior outcomes. Researchers initially labeled these results as irrational or attributed them to simple altruism or "other-regarding preferences." More recently, however, researchers have labeled these results as rational and attributed them to the activation of various social norms (Bicchieri 2006).

Subsequent games have been designed to specifically examine preferences for social norms. Kahneman, Knetsch, and Thaler (1986) designed the first dictator game to examine fairness norms as a constraint on profit-seeking behavior. They gave participants a choice between dictating an even split of $20 with another participant ($10,$10) or an uneven split favoring themselves ($18,$2). Despite the economic incentive to select the split favoring themselves, seventy-six percent of participants chose the even split. A large number of replications and extensions of this dictator game have demonstrated a persistent preference for

---

[13] Given its similarity to a game between two prisoners who are privately asked to confess, variations of this game have been called the *prisoners' dilemma* (Roth 1995).

participants to be fairer than the narrow characterization of *homo economicus*. Since only one player determines the split, however, the dictator game is not a strategic game. Güth, Schmittberger, and Schwarze (1982) designed a strategic game called the ultimatum game where one player (the Proposer) offers a proposed split of an amount and the other player (the Responder) decides either to accept or reject the offer, with both parties receiving nothing if the offer is rejected. Given the assumption of narrow self-interest with preferences for wealth and leisure only, the Nash equilibrium prediction is for the Proposer to offer as close to zero as possible and for the Responder to accept the offer rather than receive nothing. Consistent with preferences for a fairness norm, however, Proposers offered an average of forty percent of the amount, with many offering fifty percent, and Responders rejected small offers of around twenty percent about half of the time.

Again, the results of the ultimatum game in Güth et al. (1982) have been replicated and extended in many subsequent experimental studies. Of particular interest is the direct comparison of dictator games with ultimatum games in Forsythe, Horowitz, Savin, and Sefton (1994). In their study, they compare personal preferences for fairness from the dictator game with strategic beliefs about the other player's preference for fairness from the ultimatum game. They find that dictator offers are much lower than ultimatum offers but dictator offers are still positive, documenting the presence of both *individual* fairness and *strategic* fairness. Researchers have tested the robustness of fairness norms in these two games to repetition, different stakes, anonymity of participants, and culture (Camerer 2003). Although repetition has been found to make little difference, a weak effect has been found for the stakes on the rejection of fixed-percentage offers, and increased anonymity sometimes lowers allocations in dictator games. Interestingly, culture has been found to have a significant effect on fairness norms in both dictator and ultimatum games. Fairness norms are more prevalent in cultures where there are more social exchanges or a higher level of "market integration." These results suggest that social norms support the development and growth of free-market economies, as suggested by the history of the firm in Chapter 2.[14]

---

[14] Interestingly, it is only in relatively simple societies without market exchanges that participants in ultimatum games behave as game theory would suggest. See Camerer (2003) for a more detailed description of these cultural results.

FINDINGS FROM EXPERIMENTAL TESTS OF
PRINCIPAL-AGENT THEORY

There is also a large experimental literature examining principal-agent theory related to corporate governance (Shleifer and Vishny 1997, Prendergast 1999, Bushman and Smith 2001). Corporate governance deals with the fundamental conflict of interest between absentee suppliers of capital and professional managers who manage that capital (Demski 2003). Berg, Dickhaut, and McCabe (1995, hereafter BDM) designed a strategic investment game to capture this fundamental conflict of interest. This game involves an investment decision by the investor followed by a decision regarding the split of the resulting surplus by the manager. Thus, BDM's investment game is an investment decision followed by a dictator game. BDM point out that in traditional game theory settings, "behavior that deviates from self interest is viewed as irrational" (BDM, 122). BDM argue that trust behavior may be rational in economic transactions related to the firm. In particular, they cite Arrow's (1974) contention that transaction costs make trust ubiquitous to almost every economic transaction within the organization. They also point out that self-interested behavior can make everyone worse off in cooperative settings. Finally, they allow for the possibility of social norm behavior, citing Coleman's (1990) definition of a social norm as a socially defined right by others to control an individual's action.

BDM design their investment game so that the only explanation for trust behavior on the part of the investor is expectations for trustworthiness or reciprocity. To control for other potential sources for trust behavior, including repeat game effects such as reputation or threat of punishment, BDM use a double-blind, one-shot experiment. In their original manual investment game experiment, BDM randomly sorted each participant into one of two groups placed in different rooms and gave each participant an endowment of $10 in one dollar bills. Participants in Room A were informed that they would be paired with a participant in Room B and would individually and anonymously transfer any amount of their endowment to their paired participant and keep the remainder. Any amount transferred by a Room A participant was multiplied by three before being delivered to their paired participant in Room B. The Room B participant then decided how much of the tripled amount to return back to the Room A participant and how much to keep. The only explanation for investment on the part of the investor, therefore, is expectations for trustworthiness or reciprocity on the part of the manager.

The Nash equilibrium prediction for BDM's investment game is that Room B participants will keep all of the tripled amount and, knowing this, Room A participants will not transfer any of their endowment to their paired Room B participant. This Nash equilibrium solution, however, is Pareto-inferior in that it only leaves each pair of participants with $20 when any cooperation would improve that amount up to a maximum of $40. BDM find that participants attempt to cooperate and improve upon the Nash equilibrium solution. In particular, thirty of thirty-two Room A participants sent money to their paired Room B participant. The average amount transferred by Room A participants was $5.16, and the average amount returned by Room B participants was $4.66. To directly test the effects of social norms, BDM examine a "history" setting where a new set of twenty-eight pairs of participants received a report summarizing the decisions of the thirty-two pairs of participants in the "no history" setting. In this history setting, the average amount transferred by Room A participants increased marginally to $5.36, and the average amount returned by Room B participants increased significantly to $6.46. This result provided direct evidence that the cooperative behavior in their investment game was driven by expectations for social norm behavior.

BDM conclude that "(t)he ability to include trust and reciprocity as part of the rational choice paradigm would seem to allow better explanations of economic institutions" (BDM, 138). Consistent with Coleman (1990), BDM define trust as the deliberate decision by the trustor to make himself vulnerable to the trustee. This raises the question of whether trust in this experimental setting would be considered a social norm. Bicchieri, Xiao, and Muldoon (2011) directly test whether trust is a social norm by eliciting individuals' expectations about what others would expect one to do in BDM's investment game. In particular, they asked participants in their study what behaviors would bring about punishment from others in the BDM game. Participants expected that most people would not punish untrusting investors. Therefore, participants did not view the trusting behavior reflected in the investor's decision to invest as a social norm. In contrast, participants did view the trustworthy behavior reflected in the manager's decision to return a reasonable amount to the investor as a social norm. Bicchieri et al.'s findings extend the interpretation of BDM's original results by suggesting that, while trust is not a social norm, trustworthiness is a social norm that could influence both investment and return behavior.

Cox (2004) points out that the BDM game does not distinguish between actions motivated by trust and reciprocity and actions motivated by "other-regarding preferences" that are not conditional on the actions or intentions of others. Thus, he utilizes a triadic design that is capable of distinguishing investment and return behavior based on these differing motivations. In particular, Cox incorporates three BDM conditions: the traditional BDM game, a beliefs-control dictator game where Room B participants do not have a return decision to make, and an intentions-control dictator game where Room A participants do not have an investment decision to make. He finds substantial evidence of trustworthy, other-regarding preferences that are not conditional on the actions or intentions of others. To more formally identify what drives trustworthy behavior in the manager, Cox, Kerschbamer, and Neururer (2016) conduct an experiment that decomposes positive returns in the BDM game into four factors: 1) unconditional other-regarding preferences, 2) vulnerability-responsiveness, 3) deal-responsiveness, and 4) gift-responsiveness. They find that the only two causal factors that produce positive returns in the trust game are unconditional other-regarding behaviors and vulnerability-responsiveness behavior. Consistent with Bicchieri et al. (2011), Cox et al. conclude that the social norm of trustworthiness is a motivator of behavior in the BDM game in addition to the social norm of reciprocity.

Experimental researchers have continued to use the BDM investment game to examine determinants of trust and trustworthiness in market and firm behavior. For example, Bruce Davidson and I use the BDM game in our study of the ability of a code of ethics to improve manager behavior and investor confidence (Davidson and Stevens 2013). Applying Bicchieri's (2006) model of social norm activation (see Chapter 4), we predict that a code of ethics will improve manager return behavior and investor confidence to the extent that it activates social norms that control opportunistic behavior in the manager. We find that this social norm activation only occurs when the code incorporates a public certification choice by the manager. Analyses of individual return decisions and exit questionnaire responses support our underlying social norm theory. In a more recent study (Abdel-Rahim, Hales, and Stevens 2018), we use the BDM game to study the effects of financial reporting disaggregation and discretion on manager return and reporting behavior. We find that disaggregation of the manager's financial report into exogenous production costs and discretionary pay, which makes the opportunism of the manager transparent to the investor, increases the amount returned by managers when reporting discretion is absent. When reporting discretion is present, however, managers misclassify some of their discretionary pay as exogenous production costs to appear trustworthy to investors while decreasing the amount returned. This appears to work, however, as it induces investors to keep investing even as managers increase their discretionary pay at the expense of investor returns.

Researchers have also examined the predictions of principal-agent theory in experimental labor markets. These experimental studies, for example, have examined the prediction that the agent will only expect and receive his reservation utility from the principal. Fehr, Gächter, and Kirchsteiger (1997) argue that principal-agent theory has not sufficiently concerned itself with the impact of reciprocity on contracting behavior within the firm. Thus, they design a series of competitive labor market experiments where there is an excess supply of workers and examine the contract offers by principals (firms) and the effort provided by agents (workers). Rather than pay the agent his reservation wage for a relatively low level of effort, principals frequently offer more than the reservation wage and agents reciprocate by providing a higher level of effort. Fehr et al. conclude:

> *Our results indicate, however, that the neglect of reciprocity may render principal agent models seriously incomplete. As a consequence it may limit their predictive power. Moreover, the normative conclusions that follow from models that neglect reciprocity may not be correct.*

A growing number of experimental studies have examined this reciprocity behavior – commonly called gift exchange (e.g., Fehr, Kirchler, Weichbold, and Gächter 1998; Hannan, Kagel, and Moser 2002; Hannan 2005). Kuang and Moser (2009) argue that the effectiveness of optimal agency contracts could be impaired if employees view them as violating reciprocity norms and respond by rejecting the contracts or reducing their effort. To examine this behavioral effect, Kuang and Moser design three labor market experiments that include the optimal agency contract, the reciprocity-based gift-exchange contract used in Hannan (2005), and a hybrid contract that combined the "forcing" feature of the optimal agency contract with the "reciprocity" feature of the gift-exchange contract. Kuang and Moser examine contract acceptance and effort decisions of agents under the first two contracts individually and in a setting where the firm chooses between the two contracts. Kuang and Moser also examine a setting where the firm chooses between all three contracts. Although the optimal agency contract yields more firm profit than the gift-exchange contract, the optimal agency contract yields less and the gift-exchange contract yields more firm profit than standard agency theory predicts. When both contracts are available, however, firm profit is lower on average because employees reject the optimal agency contract more when it is endogenously chosen by the firm and provide lower effort when it is accepted. When all three contracts are available, firms quickly switch to the hybrid contract rather than the optimal agency contract. This behavior is optimal as it yields the highest effort, the highest employee payoff, at least as much firm profit, and the highest combined firm and employee payoff.

FINDINGS FROM EXPERIMENTAL STUDIES
OF PARTICIPATIVE BUDGETING

The largest body of experimental research in managerial accounting involves studies of participative budgeting, where the principal involves the agent in the setting of the budget. These experimental studies examine the effects of contracting and information environments on budget reporting and effort (production) decisions of the agent. Thus, the results of these experimental studies have particular significance for the theory of the firm. In a recent review of the literature, Brown et al. (2009) argue that agency theory is a fruitful theoretical framework for such research, and they recommend that researchers rely more heavily on this economic theory of the firm. Principal-agent models of participative budgeting based on traditional agency assumptions, including opportunistic self-interest and preferences for wealth and leisure only, examine contract solutions to the problem of budgetary slack when the agent has superior information to the principal (Antle and Eppen 1985, Antle and Fellingham 1995). Because of the strong agency prediction that agents will maximize budgetary slack under a slack-inducing pay scheme, experimental researchers have found this setting useful to examine preferences for social norms.

In one of the first experimental studies of participative budgeting, Mark Young (1985) utilizes a manual, single-period experiment to examine the effect of risk aversion and information asymmetry regarding productive capability on budgetary slack. In a nonstrategic setting where the principal is played by an experimenter and the budget of the agent cannot be rejected, Young finds that giving the principal the same information as the agent regarding productive ability leads to self-reported social pressure on an exit questionnaire, and this measure of social pressure is negatively associated with budgetary slack. However, budgetary slack is not significantly different in this experimental condition than in the condition where the agent has private information regarding his productive ability. Budgetary slack is also positively associated with a measure of risk aversion, suggesting that slack is in part a response to uncertainty in the production process. Waller (1988) and Chow, Cooper, and Waller (1988) use Young's experimental setting to examine budgetary slack created under a slack-inducing pay scheme and a truth-inducing pay scheme where agent pay is increasing in the accuracy of the budget. As expected, budgetary slack is lower under the truth-inducing pay scheme. Although the agency prediction is 100 percent slack under the slack-inducing pay scheme, however, Waller (1988) and Chow et al. (1988) document slack levels of only 19.8 percent and 24.0 percent, respectively, under their slack-inducing pay scheme.

In my dissertation experiment (Stevens 2002), I examine why agents do not maximize budgetary slack when given the opportunity to profit from such opportunistic behavior. I believed that the former experimental results could be attributed to the use of manual, single-period experiments. To examine this possibility, I use computerized procedures to carefully control social interactions and multiple production periods (five periods) to increase learning. I also use a letter decoding task to capture productive ability and effort and gather forecasts of production to measure expected production. Consistent with my prior expectations, these experimental procedures allow me to document slack levels that are significantly higher than the prior manual, single-period experiments. Under a total anonymity condition where agents stay in their cubicles and interact only with their computer terminal, average budgetary slack is 60.4 percent. Average budgetary slack is significantly reduced to 25.9 percent, however, when agents hand-deliver a report to the experimenter principal each period that contains the budgets entered into the computer. Having the report also include prior period production does not reduce budgetary slack further and, in fact, increases slack insignificantly to 35.8 percent. My results support Joan Luft's (1997, 200–201) assertion that prior experimental tests lacked the power to distinguish between self-interested and ethical behavior.

Through the use of a preexperiment personality test (Jackson 1994) and items on an exit questionnaire, I generate direct evidence of norm-based behavior on the part of the agent. I find that budgetary slack is negatively associated with a measure of responsibility preferences from the personality test as well as self-reported reputation and ethical concerns in the exit questionnaire. Agents express lower reputation concerns as information asymmetry regarding productive capability increases, thereby reducing the principal's ability to monitor slack levels, but ethical concerns are not diminished with increases in information asymmetry. I interpret these results as follows (Stevens 2002, 153): "These results suggest that reputation is a socially mediated control whereas ethics is an internally mediated control for opportunistic self-interest." In a follow-up study with Jessen

Hobson and Mark Mellon (Hobson, Mellon, and Stevens 2011), however, we find that ethical concerns can also be context-specific. We test the effects of pay scheme and personal values on my measure of ethical concerns regarding budgetary slack, and find that agents who set budgets under the slack-inducing pay scheme judge significant budgetary slack to be unethical on average, whereas participants who set budgets under a truth-inducing pay scheme do not. Controlling for pay scheme, we also find that participants who scored high on *Empathy* and *Traditional Values* on the preexperiment personality test are more likely to judge significant budgetary slack to be unethical.

In Hobson et al. (2011), we use behavioral theories from two different literatures to predict and explain our results. For my dissertation, I combed through the business ethics literature and found theory suggesting that moral reasoning is jointly determined by characteristics of the setting and the individual (Jones 1991). This theory suggests that moral reasoning arises in social settings where self-interest conflicts with a moral duty to others (Bowie and Duska 1990). Because of my focus on the slack-inducing pay scheme in my dissertation, however, I failed to see the potential for a truth-inducing pay scheme to reduce this moral reasoning by aligning the self-interest of the agent with the principal. We discuss this potential in the follow-up study to my dissertation (Hobson et al. 2011, 91):

We argue that a slack-inducing pay scheme will be more likely than a truth-inducing pay scheme to generate a moral frame leading to moral reasoning because it sets economic self-interest against common social norms. Slack-inducing pay schemes, which are common in practice, motivate the subordinate to create budgetary slack by paying a bonus for performance that surpasses the budget (Stevens 2002). Thus, a slack-inducing pay scheme will likely activate moral reasoning by causing the subordinate to focus on the conflict between his economic self-interest and his obligation to be truthful in the budget. In contrast, a truth-inducing pay scheme will be less likely to activate moral reasoning because it sets economic self-interest in harmony with common social norms.

To provide further theoretical support for our predictions and results, we also apply insights from Bicchieri's (2006) model of social norm activation suggesting that situational cues in the participative budgeting setting can make an honesty norm salient and thereby reduce budgetary slack.

More recently, experimental researchers have heeded Brown et al.'s (2009) call to design more powerful participative budgeting experiments that are capable of advancing the theory of the firm. In particular, these researchers have designed budgeting experiments with stark agency predictions and have used them to test alternative behavioral theories that may be useful to extend agency theory. Many of these experimental studies use Bicchieri's model of social norm activation to examine social norm behavior in participative budgeting, which is particularly well-suited for this purpose. First, her rational reconstruction of what constitutes a social norm substitutes a precise concept for an imprecise one, and specifies in what sense one may say that compliance with a norm is rational (Bicchieri 2006, 10–11). Second, her rational reconstruction allows meaningful predictions to be made regarding the effects of situational cues and information on behavior. Third, her model is based on the norm-based behavior arising in experimental tests of game theory. Finally, Bicchieri's model incorporates insights from the literature in social norms, including the insight that social norms may be activated through an automatic route as well as the deliberational route implied by her model.[15]

Evans, Hannan, Krishnan, and Moser (2001) design an experimental setting based on the agency model in Antle and Eppen (1985) to examine how preferences for honesty affect budgetary slack. In Antle and Eppen's single-period model, the owner of a firm hires a manager whose presence is required to implement production. As is commonly assumed, the manager has private information regarding the actual cost of production, which is uniformly distributed. In particular, the manager learns the actual production cost prior to the investment decision of the owner. In contrast, the owner only knows the distribution of possible production costs and the manager's cost report prior to making the investment decision. All other information is common knowledge, including the preferences of the two parties.[16] In their experimental test of the model, Evans et al. find strong support for an honesty norm as well as a fairness norm. Participants setting budgets under a slack-inducing "trust" contract often sacrifice wealth to make honest or partially honest reports, and they do not lie more as the payoff to lying increases. Participants exhibit less honesty, however, under a trust contract that provides a smaller share of the total surplus. The optimal agency contract developed by Antle and Eppen yields more firm profit than does the trust contract that relies on the participants' honesty

---

[15] In introducing her formal model, Bicchieri (2006, 3) states, "The definition of social norm I am proposing should be taken as a rational reconstruction of what a social norm is, not a faithful descriptive account of the real beliefs and preferences people have or of the way in which they in fact deliberate. Such a reconstruction, however, will have to be reliable in that it must be possible to extract meaningful, testable predictions from it."

[16] For a review of agency models of capital investments with private information, see Antle and Fellingham (1997).

preferences.[17] However, a modified version of the optimal agency contract, which makes use of the participants' honesty preferences, yields the highest firm profit.

Rankin, Schwartz, and Young (2008) point out two potential weaknesses in prior experimental studies demonstrating honesty preferences in budgeting settings. First, prior experimental studies had not included a strategic-game setting where the principal is an active participant who is able to reject the agent's budget. Thus, these budget settings resembled a dictator game where the agent had sole decision power over the principal-agent split of the available surplus. Second, prior experimental studies had used budgetary slack as a direct measure of the agent's honesty preferences, even though the agent's budget could also be affected by other social norm preferences such as fairness. Similar to Cox (2004) and Cox et al. (2016), Rankin et al. systematically vary aspects of the agent's budget report and the rejection power of the principal to separate honesty preference effects from the effects of other social norm preferences. They find that less slack is created when the budget report requires a factual assertion than when it only requires a split of the available surplus. However, this effect appears to go away in the strategic setting where the principal is able to reject the agent's budget. Rankin et al. conclude that their results support the theory of "crowding-out," which suggests that extrinsic controls such as a truth-inducing pay scheme or allowing the superior to reject the budget diminishes the agent's intrinsic motivation to display honesty in the budget.

Given that the principal normally has the authority to reject the agent's budget in practice, Rankin et al.'s (2008) results brought the importance of honesty preferences in budgeting into serious doubt.[18] Jeremy Douthit and I developed an experimental budgeting setting to test alternative explanations for Rankin et al.'s honesty results (Douthit and Stevens 2015). Based

[17] Antle and Eppen (1985) demonstrate that the optimal contract in their budgeting setting is a hurdle contract that funds all projects with costs below a threshold but pays the manager for the threshold level of production. The optimal contract solution, therefore, requires the owner to pre-commit to allow the manager to keep the budgetary slack below the threshold and not renegotiate the contract after the manager submits his cost report. This pre-commitment motivates the manager to reveal his private information in the cost report. However, the threshold level of production is at the middle of the possible cost range. Thus, the cost of motivating honest reporting from the manager is budgetary slack and capital rationing (turning down some projects that otherwise would be profitable to the firm).

[18] A private discussion with a prominent experimental researcher shortly after Rankin et al.'s study revealed that she and several of her colleagues had decided that it was no longer fruitful to conduct honesty research in management accounting.

on the game theory literature in ultimatum games and Bicchieri's (2006) social norm theory, we identified three social norms that may be activated and affect budgetary slack in a strategic budgeting setting where the principal has rejection authority: honesty, distributional fairness, and reciprocity. Consistent with Mittendorf's (2006) agency model, we define honesty as a social preference that causes disutility from making false statements. Consistent with game theory incorporating social norm preferences, we define fairness as a social preference that causes disutility from inappropriate allocations of an available surplus (Fehr and Schmidt 1999; Falk, Fehr, and Fischbacher 2003) and we define reciprocity as a social preference that causes positive utility from repaying kind actions with kindness and unkind actions with unkindness (Rabin 1993, Cox and Deck 2005).

We note that Rankin et al. (2008) had made relative pay transparent to both the principal and the agent in their experimental study. Given the dominance of fairness norms in ultimatum games, we argue that this relative pay information may have caused fairness norms to dominate honesty norms in their experiment. Thus, we examine the robustness of Rankin et al.'s honesty results by manipulating the ability of the agent to discern the level of pay that the principal received. We document that honesty has a strong effect on budgetary slack when the salience of a fairness norm is reduced by withholding the relative pay of the principal from the agent. We also document that honesty continues to have a strong effect on budgetary slack when the salience of reciprocity is increased by giving the principal the task of setting the agent's salary. Thus, our results suggest that the previously documented effect of honesty preferences is robust to giving the principal the power to reject the budget. Furthermore, our results suggest that some social norms may be conflicting and some social norms may be complementary in a given economic setting.

Rankin et al. (2008) argued that giving the agent final authority over the budget could cause the agent to frame the budgeting process as a moral dilemma, whereas giving the principal final authority over the budget could cause the agent to frame the budgeting process as a strategic negotiation. In a recent experimental study, we examine the framing effect of endogenous contract selection on budgetary slack (Douthit, Schwartz, Stevens, and Young 2017). In particular, we examine the effect of having the principal select between the two slack-inducing contracts found in Rankin et al.: a trust contract where the principal must accept the budget and a discretion contract where the principal can accept or reject the budget. Because neither contract incorporates a formal control for budgetary slack, we apply insights from Bicchieri's (2006) model of social norm activation to develop our theoretical expectations. We hypothesize and find that budgetary slack is lower for both contracts when they are endogenously selected by the principal than it is when they are exogenously assigned by the experimenter. Consistent with our theoretical predictions, exit questionnaire responses suggest that selecting a trust contract signals trust and expectations of trustworthiness whereas selecting a discretion contract signals distrust and an increased willingness to enforce trustworthiness by rejecting unreasonable budgets. We find that signaling distrust is optimal in our budgeting setting, as the greatest level of efficiency is achieved when the principal endogenously selects the discretion contract, which yields the efficiency of the optimal hurdle contract prescribed under traditional agency assumptions (Antle and Eppen 1985).

The experimental literature in participative budgeting continues to provide new and useful insights regarding norm-based behavior in the firm. The emerging evidence suggests that opportunistic behavior is capable of being controlled in a participative budgeting setting by the activation of social norms such as honesty, fairness, trustworthiness, and reciprocity. A recent study by Douthit and Majerczyk (2017) finds evidence that agents build less budgetary slack when principals are perceived to be legitimate in their role due to superior performance on a letter search task. Thus, legitimate authority may be another social norm that is capable of being activated and reducing opportunistic behavior in principal-agent settings related to the firm.

In summary, the emerging evidence of social norms in experimental research represents the biggest challenge to the culture-free, norm-free core of the neoclassical theory of the firm. This includes evidence emerging in experimental tests of game theory, principal-agent theory, and participative budgeting settings. Early experimental studies provided consistent evidence for other-regarding or social preferences inconsistent with the narrow self-interested assumption in *homo economicus*, but these studies lacked the power to identify particular social norms. Later experimental studies were designed to specifically distinguish self-interested behavior from norm-based behavior, and they had the power to identify particular social norms such as fairness and reciprocity. More recently, experimental studies have used advanced theories of social-norm activation to manipulate various social norms and to identify which norms are substitutionary and which norms are complementary. These studies have also used personality measures to capture individual as well as situational factors that influence social norm activation and behavior. As I discuss in the following chapter, emerging evidence of social norms in archival research also poses a significant challenge to the culture-free, norm-free core of the neoclassical theory of the firm.

7

Emerging Evidence of Social Norms in Archival Research

INTRODUCTION

The theory of the firm that emanated from the Chicago school was built upon the foundation of an emboldened neoclassical economic theory (Khurana 2007). This foundation maintained the narrow definition of *homo economicus* established by Mill and codified by future neoclassical economists as they stretched the limits of mathematical rigor. Thus, this new theory of the firm included the underlying assumptions of opportunistic self-interest, full rationality, and preferences only for wealth and leisure. On this foundation, the Chicago school added a bold new confidence in the efficiency of capital markets. These combined assumptions, as well as the increasing availability of market data and sophisticated data analysis methods, gave birth to a rich new research paradigm. The speed by which this new paradigm swept the three disciplines of economics, accounting, and finance, and the large volume of research that it spawned, has more than proven its usefulness. The underlying assumptions of the new paradigm, however, minimized the importance of individual decision-making and trading volume and left no room for social norms. Emerging evidence from recent archival research, however, has brought these assumptions into question and has opened the door to norm-based behavior in the theory of the firm.

In this chapter, I summarize the emerging evidence of social norm behavior in archival research related to the firm. I begin by discussing key characteristics of theory, research paradigms, and paradigm changes using Popper and Kuhn's classic works on philosophy of science. Next, I describe how the theory of the firm that emanated from the Chicago school represented a paradigm shift. As characterized by Kuhn (1962), the new research paradigm changed what constituted acceptable research and pushed some research issues to the periphery. For example, the new paradigm pushed norm-based behavior out of the discussion space. Next, I discuss the mounting evidence inconsistent with fully efficient markets and the new focus in the literature on market inefficiency. This evidence led some neoclassical researchers to soften their position on efficient markets and opened the door to research related to individual decision-making and trading volume. Recently, archival researchers have used theory related to individual decision-making and trading volume to design archival studies that generate new insights regarding financial markets and the usefulness of financial disclosures to investors. I discuss this growing archival literature.

Next, I discuss archival evidence regarding the effects of financial incentives on manager behavior and the importance of culture and social norms in the management of the firm. The strong research paradigm that came out of the Chicago school discounted the effects of culture and social norms on manager behavior, which gave financial incentives a central role in controlling opportunistic behavior in the firm. I discuss the lack of archival evidence supporting a link between powerful financial incentives and firm performance, as well as the possibility that such incentives can be dysfunctional by crowding out intrinsic motivations and causing excessive risk-taking behavior. Finally, I discuss direct archival evidence suggesting that social norms play an important role in controlling opportunistic manager behavior in the firm.

THEORY, RESEARCH PARADIGMS, AND PARADIGM SHIFTS

As discussed in Chapter 1, Milton Friedman's (1953) methodological essay has been credited with introducing Karl Popper's rigorous philosophy of science to economists (Walters 1987). Popper sought to separate science from pseudoscience by applying insights from the history of science and philosophical logic related to the development of scientific theory. In particular, he sought "to establish the rules, or if you will the norms, by which the scientist is guided when he is engaged in research or in discovery, in the sense here understood" (Popper 1934, 29). These rules focused on the importance of developing strong hypotheses that are capable of "falsifying" or confirming a given theory. Popper's classic work, however, covers much more than his falsification rules, which is why I continue to use it in my PhD seminar on the philosophy of science (in the English version). I consider Popper's classic work one of the best sources of information on scientific theory and the testing of that theory.

Popper (1934, 37-38) states, "Theories are nets cast to catch what we call 'the world'; to rationalize, to explain, and to master it. We endeavor to make the mesh ever finer and finer." In contrast to some of Friedman's (1953) bolder statements, Popper (1934, 50) argues that underlying assumptions are central to a theory and therefore open to testing:

Scientific theories are perpetually changing . . . In spite of this, a tentative system can usually be quite well surveyed as a whole, with all its important consequences. This is very necessary; for a severe test of a system presupposes that it is at the time sufficiently definite and final in form to make it impossible for new assumptions to be smuggled in. In other words, the system must be formulated sufficiently clearly and definitely to make every new assumption easily recognizable for what it is: a modification and therefore a revision of the system.

Popper makes clear that a theory is comprised of a system of underlying assumptions or axioms (assumed truths) and the conclusions or predictions that follow naturally from that system. It is the job of the theorist to formulate and prove theorems, which are the mapping of underlying assumptions or axioms into testable predictions (Smith 2008). It is the job of the empiricist to design rigorous empirical tests of these predictions and the underlying assumptions of the theory. Popper (1934, 51) makes clear, however, that the falsification of a particular prediction or assumption "may sometimes not affect the whole system but only some part of it."

Similar to Adam Smith's assertion that the mind favors simple explanations for scientific phenomena (Smith 1795), Popper argues that theorists collect all the assumptions that are needed, but no more, in forming their theory. Due to the inability of a single observation to rule out the possibility of alternative realities or "black swans," however, Popper discounts the usefulness of inductive reasoning for forming theory. Instead, he emphasizes deductive reasoning or the process of exposing highly general "universal" theories to rigorous testing based on special cases or implications of the theory. This deductive process develops scientific theory through natural selection: "We choose the theory which best holds its own in competition with other theories; the one which, by natural selection, proves itself the fittest to survive. This will be the one which not only has hitherto stood up to the severest tests, but the one which is also testable in the most rigorous way. A theory is a tool which we test by applying it, and which we judge as to its fitness by the results of its applications" (Popper 1934, 91).

Given that Popper discounts the role of inductive reasoning in shaping universal theories, from where does the insight come for developing such theories and their assumptions? Surprisingly, Popper (1934, 8-9) places this insight "outside" of the rational realm of science. He quotes Albert Einstein in stating that there "is no logical path" leading to "those highly universal laws ... from which a picture of the world can be obtained by pure deduction ... They can only be reached by intuition, based upon something like an intellectual love of the objects of experience." Popper (1934, xx) also defends the use of the "historical method" in developing theory, or "trying to find out what other people have thought and said about the problem in hand: why they had to face it: how they formulated it: how they tried to solve it." In the end, Popper (1934, 91) admits that the generation of universal theories and systems of axioms lies outside of his falsification method: "One question, certainly, does remain – a question which obviously cannot be answered by any falsifiable theory and which is therefore 'metaphysical': how is it that we are so often lucky in the theories we construct – how is it that there are 'natural laws'?" It is my personal view that such natural laws can be derived from a combination of "metaphysical" inspiration, as Popper suggests, and inductive reasoning from physical observation, which Popper discounts as severely lacking in logic.

In contrast to Popper's detached view of science, Thomas Kuhn (1962) places science squarely within the realm of scientific community, culture, and social norms. Rather than attribute advances in science to the falsification process of exposing aspects of a universal theory to rigorous testing (its predictions *and* assumptions), Kuhn (1962, 8–10) argues: "Competition between segments of the scientific community is the only historical process that ever actually results in the rejection of one previously accepted theory or in the adoption of another." In place of the traditional view of scientific progress as gradual and linear through the disinterested accumulation of evidence, therefore, Kuhn argues that scientific progress is the result of a competition of ideas that results in periodic, "scientific revolutions." His history of science, similar to Adam Smith's (1795) history of astronomy, supports this view. There is initially strong resistance to new ideas or evidence inconsistent with the current "paradigm," which is "firmly based upon one or more past scientific achievements ... that some particular scientific community acknowledges for a time as supplying the foundation for its further practice." A paradigm shift occurs, therefore, when researchers uncover a new theory or empirical regularity that (1) attracts an enduring group of adherents in the scientific community and (2) is sufficiently open-ended to leave all sorts of new problems to be solved.

Given this social characterization of science, Kuhn (1962, 24) defines "normal science" as mop-up work that a given research paradigm leaves to be done:

> *No part of the aim of normal science is to call forth new sorts of phenomena; indeed those that will not fit the box are often not seen at all. Nor do scientists normally aim to invent new theories, and they are often intolerant of those invented by others. Instead, normal-scientific research is directed to the articulation of those phenomena and theories that the paradigm already supplies.*

This mop-up operation, which is actually quite challenging and interesting to researchers, involves three main activities: (1) determination of significant fact, (2) matching of facts with theory, and (3) further articulation of the theory. The job of training PhD students throughout their doctoral program, therefore, is to prepare them for a career of mop-up work.[1] Throughout the process, however, Kuhn (1962, 52) acknowledges that facts will be found that conflict with the theory or existing paradigm, and they sow the seeds of paradigm shift. "Normal science does not aim at novelties of fact or theory and, when successful, finds none. New and unsuspected phenomena are, however, repeatedly uncovered by scientific research, and radical new theories have again and again been invented by scientists. History even suggests that the scientific enterprise has developed a uniquely powerful technique for producing surprises of this sort."

Kuhn (1962, 52-53) calls these novelties of fact "anomalies." A paradigm shift begins, therefore, "with the awareness of anomaly, i.e., with the recognition that nature has somehow violated the paradigm-induced expectations that govern normal science. It then continues with a more or less extended exploration of the area of anomaly. And it closes only when the paradigm theory has been adjusted so that the anomalous has become the expected." This is consistent with the psychological account of scientific revolutions in Adam Smith's (1795) history of astronomy up to Isaac Newton.[2] Such anomalies only appear, however, against the

---

[1] In my academic experience as both a professor and a coordinator of a PhD program in accounting, I have traditionally been sympathetic toward those more creative students who resist the current research paradigm. Over time, however, I have become less enthusiastic about outright rebellion and more sympathetic toward accounting faculty at Indiana who attempted to keep me firmly planted within the current paradigm in my own PhD program.

[2] Smith (1795, IV.35) acknowledged that Copernicus's radical new theory of the earth revolving around the sun "was almost universally disapproved of, by the learned as well as by the ignorant. The natural prejudices of sense, confirmed by education, prevailed too much with both, to allow them to give it a fair examination."

background provided by the existing paradigm. As Kuhn (1962, 65) concludes, "The more precise and far-reaching that paradigm is, the more sensitive an indicator it provides of anomaly and hence of an occasion for paradigm change. In the normal model of discovery, even resistance to change has a use ... By ensuring that the paradigm will not be too easily surrendered, resistance guarantees that scientists will not be lightly distracted and that the anomalies that lead to paradigm change will penetrate existing knowledge to the core."

A PARADIGM SHIFT AT THE UNIVERSITY OF CHICAGO

The above discussion of theory, research paradigms, and paradigm shifts helps explain the development of the dominant theory of the firm at the University of Chicago in the 1960s. I provided the historical background for this development in Chapter 3. I now provide more detail of this development in the field of accounting to demonstrate how this theory became the new paradigm for archival research in economics, accounting, and finance. As described by Ray Ball and Philip Brown (2014), most research in accounting in the mid-1960s was a priori in nature. In particular, researchers were engaged in normative debates related to the value of current financial reporting methods to investors. Due to the lack of market and accounting theory and the means of testing such theory, the dominant view was that the information provided by the financial statements was of little value to the markets due to the jumbling of various valuation bases such as historical cost (long-lived operating assets), replacement cost (inventories), and fair market value (financial assets and liabilities). There was also a lack of confidence in the efficiency of capital markets, especially given the historic occurrence of bubbles and crashes (see Chapter 2). Thus, even some faculty at the University of Chicago believed that correlating accounting-based earnings with stock prices would be like correlating "garbage (earnings) with garbage (prices)" (Ball and Brown 2014, 8).

The dominant research paradigm in accounting by the 1960s not only lacked meaningful empirical evidence regarding the usefulness of financial disclosures to the capital markets, it also exhibited little desire to gather such evidence. Reviews of the literature often concluded that a priori normative theory rather than descriptive theory was relevant for accounting policy (Wheeler 1970). Furthermore, accounting theorists often claimed that market data related to individual firms did not require elaborate statistical analysis due to the uniqueness of each case

(Chambers 1973). As antiquated as these views appear today, however, they reflect the first major body of market theory in accounting and a well-developed research paradigm. As Ball and Brown (2014, 6) state, "That body of literature constitutes a crucial stage in the development of accounting as an area of serious intellectual inquiry."

As discussed in Chapter 3, the University of Chicago had attracted a growing number of top neoclassical economists to both their economics department and their relatively new business school by the 1960s. While the Cowles Commission had already moved to Yale, the emphasis on mathematical economics continued at Chicago. Furthermore, a generous gift from Merrill Lynch allowed the university to create a unique financial database that gave researchers easy access to massive amounts of market data in a format that facilitated analysis.[3] A "tribe of econometricians" soon developed at Chicago with the ability and resources to analyze the new data (Leeson 2000). Friedman's (1953) view of positive economics was particularly appealing to this new community of market researchers, which was unified and inevitably successful at eclipsing the influence of the Keynesian Neoclassical Synthesis at Harvard and MIT (Johnson 1971). Another key factor in the dominance of the emerging paradigm at Chicago, however, was the prolonged economic distress of the 1970s and 1980s, which caused a decay in the credibility of Keynesianism and "relationship capitalism" and supported the free-market ideas of Milton Friedman and George Stigler.

For archival market research to develop and grow, however, researchers required more than advances in positive economic theory, market data availability, and econometric tools to analyze the data. Researchers also needed confidence in the efficiency of capital markets for archival market research to grow and become fruitful. Thus, another factor that supported the birth of the new research paradigm at Chicago was the development of the efficient market hypothesis (EMH) by Eugene Fama and his colleagues in finance (Fama 1970). The belief that a firm's market price was not "garbage," but fully reflected all public and private information regarding that firm's intrinsic value (i.e., expected future cash flows), facilitated archival market research in economics, accounting, and finance. Based on the EMH, Fama, Fisher, Jensen, and Roll (1969) developed the "event study" method, which became a standard method of analyzing the

---

[3] The Booth School of Business at the University of Chicago used the gift from Merrill Lynch to found the Center for Research in Security Prices (CRSP). CRSP continues to maintain some of the largest proprietary databases for stock market research.

information content of financial disclosures in time. Accounting PhD students at Chicago soon applied the new event study method to analyze the information content of earnings announcements to the market (Beaver 1968, Ball and Brown 1968). What they found caused the new research paradigm to fully penetrate the discipline of accounting.

Ball and Brown (2014, 7) describe the academic environment at Chicago around the time of their classic empirical study of earnings and stock market prices:

The atmosphere at Chicago was electric when we began our research. The environment fairly crackled with innovation. The general attitude to inquiry was to question everything... New ideas about markets were being developed around us by faculty and students in economics and finance. In economics, a constant theme was a fundamental respect for markets and their evolved institutional structures. This line of thinking was informed by the ideas of Hayek, Friedman, Stigler, Coase (all of whom became Nobel Laureates), and many others. It subsequently became mainstream economics, but was excitingly novel at the time.

This description of the academic environment at Chicago in the 1960s reflects the emergence of a new research paradigm in economics, accounting, and finance. Although it is difficult to imagine now, proponents of the existing research paradigm in accounting initially put up stiff resistance to the innovations occurring in financial economics at Chicago. While the EMH was the unchallenged view in the new research paradigm, it had little credence outside of Chicago. Ball and Brown (1968) used the new event study method to address the fundamental research question, "Are accounting income numbers useful?" In particular, they considered both the relevance and the timeliness of income announcements to equity markets. Ball and Brown (2014, 11–12) state that their "priors were so strong that if we had not found an association, if we had not rejected the null hypothesis, then most likely we would have believed there was something wrong with our...design." They did document an association between earnings announcements and long-term price changes, consistent with their priors, but their paper was initially rejected by the lead academic accounting journal at the time, *The Accounting Review*. Thus, they had to publish their award-winning paper in a relatively new and unknown journal out of Chicago, the *Journal of Accounting Research*.

In the hands of neoclassical economists associated with the Chicago school, the theory of the firm took on a decidedly analytical focus that deemphasized the legitimacy of management and public policy. The combination of an increasingly narrow view of *homo economicus* and the EMH reduced both managers and regulators to self-interested opportunists and reduced managerial responsibilities to maximizing share price. Michael Jensen, a PhD student in finance at Chicago during the heady days of the 1960s, played a significant role in pushing the new theory of the firm into the public sphere through his writings in academic journals and practitioner-oriented outlets such as the *Harvard Business Review* and the *Wall Street Journal*. Jensen also integrated the new theory into his MBA courses, first at Rochester and later at Harvard. Agency theory caused students to frame managerial, organizational, and even social issues of the day in terms of narrow self-interest. Jensen has stated that his MBA students found that his courses challenged "some of their deeply held beliefs" (Khurana 2007). Thus, the new research paradigm out of Chicago caused many new ideas to emerge and be taken for granted and many former ideas to be abandoned.

ANOMALIES AND THE NEW FOCUS ON MARKET INEFFICIENCY

The intuition behind the notion of efficient markets can be seen in an early quote from Fama (1965, 56):

In an efficient market, competition among the many intelligent participants leads to a situation where, at any point in time, actual prices of individual securities already reflect the effects of information based both on events that have already occurred and on events which, as of now, the market expects to take place in the future.

This quote reflects the idealization of capital markets by early neoclassical economic theorists (see Chapter 5). The EMH was based on highly competitive markets where there are "many intelligent participants" who are motivated and able to take advantage of any momentary arbitrage opportunities should prices stray from fundamental value. This idealization assumes away market frictions or the presence of participants who may move the market further away from fundamental value due to lower financial knowledge or information or the opportunity for speculative gain (see Chapter 6). Furthermore, this idealization assumes away the inability of investors to trade on their information due to budget constraints or insufficient trading liquidity. The EMH, therefore, is a powerful example of constructivist rationality that abstracts a great deal from reality and ignores the ecological rationality of process or convergence to the competitive equilibrium price (Smith 2008). As I discuss further below, the EMH made considerations of individual decision-making behavior and trading volume irrelevant.

Ball and Brown (1968) provided strong archival evidence that was sufficiently anomalous to challenge the old paradigm, but they also provided evidence that was anomalous to the new paradigm. In particular, while eighty-five to ninety percent of the price adjustment to the earnings news occurred in the twelve months prior to the announcement month, there was a puzzling association between the post-earnings-announcement price movements and the sign of the earnings news. In a result that has been replicated by many subsequent archival studies (e.g., Foster, Olsen, and Shevlin 1984; Bernard and Thomas 1989, 1990), the market's adjustment to the direction of the news in the earnings announcement, particularly bad news, took several months beyond the announcement month. Thus, Ball and Brown's original market study exhibited evidence of post-earnings announcement drift (PEAD), or market underreaction to earnings information and subsequent adjustment to the information over time.

Ball and Brown (2014, 21–22) identify a number of "misinterpretations" of their original study in the literature. One misinterpretation they attempt to correct is the perception that their study demonstrated the superiority of positive empirical research over normative a priori research:

While our research was conducted in the spirit of positive economics, as noted above we viewed it as having distinct normative implications. Recall that the prior literature contained propositions about "what is" (such as the thesis that earnings are meaningless) as well as "what ought to be" propositions emanating from the same way of thinking. Our departure from the mode of research in the prevailing literature was more to do with empirical testing versus a priori theorizing, and not that we adopted a positive versus normative perspective.

In his review of the capital market literature, however, S. P. Kothari (2001, 114) argues that "(m)ost accounting research since Ball and Brown (1968) and Beaver (1968) is positive and the role of accounting theory is no longer normative . . . Unlike previous normative research on accounting theories and optimal accounting policies, positive capital markets research began using changes in security prices as an objective, external outcome to infer whether information in accounting reports is useful to market participants." This new research paradigm gave birth to an explosion of archival capital market studies in accounting examining the effect of financial disclosures on the market, fundamental analysis and stock valuation, and the value relevance of financial reporting. Because the association between accounting earnings and stock market price required a measure of unexpected earnings, this expanding literature included studies of various proxies for expected earnings such as time-series and analyst forecasts (Brown, Griffin, Hagerman, and Zmijewski 1987; Brown 1993).

Kothari (2001, 120) also argues that "in recent years, market efficiency has been subject to significant empirical assault. There is mounting evidence of capital market anomalies, which suggests that capital markets might be inefficient." Kothari's review of the persistent evidence of PEAD and other market inefficiencies leads him to state that "capital markets research in accounting today appears to be in a similar state as accounting theory was prior to 1968" (Kothari 2001, 113). This is indeed surprising coming from a prominent editor of the *Journal of Accounting and Economics*. Kothari (2001, 208) concludes, "Progress is possible in testing market efficiency if attention is paid to the following issues. First, researchers must recognize that deficient research design choices can create the false appearance of market inefficiency. Second, advocates of market inefficiency should propose robust hypotheses and empirical tests to differentiate their behavioral-finance theories from the efficient market hypothesis that does not rely on investor irrationality. The above challenges in designing better tests and refutable theories of market inefficiency underscore the need for accounting researchers trained in cutting-edge research in economics, finance, and econometrics." Interestingly, while Kothari is able to identify the looming threat that the latest archival evidence poses to the EMH, he fails to see the implications of this evidence for market research in individual decision-making or trading volume. This important research has been largely ignored by the Chicago school until very recently.

FINDINGS REGARDING INDIVIDUAL PROCESSING AND TRADING VOLUME

Research paradigms increase the legitimacy of research consistent with the beliefs and assumptions of the paradigm while reducing the legitimacy of research inconsistent with the paradigm. While the new research paradigm out of the Chicago school generated a booming literature in price-related market research that has been impressive in its quality, breadth, and scope, it pushed individual decision-making research out of the top journals and minimized the significance of trading volume research. The reduced legitimacy of individual decision-making research was made clear in an early review of the literature by Gonedes and Dopuch (1974, 106): "Recall that the kind of efficient market considered here is simply a competitive market, a market within which each individual is a price-taker. Given this type of market, any generalizations made about the aggregate behavior of capital market agents on the basis of results from lab/field studies are extremely tenuous. Specifically, given an efficient capital market, studies of the behavior of particular types of investors . . . are not likely to lead to reliable generalizations about the relationship between the production of accounting information and capital market equilibrium."

Given that Dopuch was the editor of the *Journal of Accounting Research* at the time, the review in Gonedes and Dopuch (1974) was a strong signal that individual decision-making research related to financial markets would not be welcome at top accounting journals. As expected, such experimental studies disappeared from top academic journals in accounting until the mid-1990s (Bloomfield 2010). Libby, Bloomfield, and Nelson (2002) attribute the recent resurgence of this experimental research to two factors. First, the persistent evidence of PEAD and other market inefficiencies in the archival capital market literature. Second, the incorporation by researchers of rigorous experimental methods that included some of the incentives and decision processes present in a market setting. Recently, experimental studies have appeared in top accounting journals containing highly controlled market settings that examine individual decision-making and trading volume behavior in addition to market price (e.g., Bloomfield 1996; Bloomfield, Libby, and Nelson 1999; Gillette et al. 1999; Bloomfield and Wilks 2000; Barron and Qu 2014).

Vernon Smith (2008, 62) argues that the competitive equilibrium prediction from neoclassical market theory is an example of constructivist rationality that ignores the ecological rationality of process or convergence to the equilibrium. "What is missing are models of the process whereby agents go from their initial circumstances and dispersed information, using the algorithms and public messages of the institution to update their status, and converge (or fail to converge) to the predicted equilibrium." There can be no market price without trade. Yet we know very little about the underlying trading volume that supports the equilibrium price prediction or the role of liquidity in market price and efficiency. We also do not know how much of the efficiency of markets is due to characteristics of the individual versus characteristics of the market institution. Due to the dominance of the EMH in economics, accounting, and finance, which makes considerations of individual decision-making behavior and trading volume irrelevant, we know very little about the above issues.[4] Even

---

[4] Smith (2008, 62) asserts: "The alleged 'requirement' of complete, common, or perfect information is vacuous: I know of no predictive theorem stating that when agents have

prominent financial theorist Stephen Ross (1989, 94) laments the lack of intuition that neoclassical economic theory has given us regarding trading volume behavior:

(S)urely, there can be nothing more embarrassing to an economist than the ability to explain the price in a market while being completely silent on the quantity . . . in my mind the failure to explain the volume of trade looms as the major dark continent for explorers of this terrain.

Linda Bamber, Orie Barron, and I recently published the only comprehensive review of trading volume research in the literature (Bamber, Barron, and Stevens 2011). We include a brief review of trading volume theory that developed in economics, accounting, and finance beginning in the late 1980s.[5] We attribute the general lack of trading volume theory prior to the late 1980s to the dominance of the efficient market hypothesis (Fama 1970), which left no room for security trading due to informational differences or investor disagreement. Grossman and Stiglitz (1980) were the first to demonstrate analytically the practical impossibility of fully revealing market prices. They showed that when market price fully reveals all public and private information, competitive markets break down because investors can no longer earn a return on their investment in costly private information. Grossman and Stiglitz concluded that it was more useful, from a descriptive and intuitive perspective, for theorists to assume that market prices are only partially revealing. To allow investors to profit from their investment in private information, Grossman and Stiglitz added noise to the market by incorporating uncertainty in the per capita supply of the traded asset. Based on their intuition, a new stream of rational

---

such information their behavior produces a CE (competitive equilibrium), and in the absence of such information their behavior fails to produce a CE . . . I suggest that the idea that agents need complete information is derived from introspective error: As theorists, we need complete information to calculate the CE. But this is not a theory of how information or its absence causes agent behavior to yield, or fail to yield, a CE. It is simply an unmotivated statement declaring, without evidence, that every agent is a constructivist in exactly the same sense as we are as theorists. And the claim that it is 'as if' agents had complete information helps not a whit to understand the wellspring of behavior."

[5] We initiated our project in the late 1990s with the intention of surveying the archival literature in accounting related to trading volume around earnings announcements. There was so little published research on this topic in accounting, however, that we decided to include the literatures in economics and finance. Again, we found so little published research on this topic in these two disciplines that we decided to include theoretical and experimental research in the area. After waiting almost a decade and adding a section on the methodological challenges to conducting such research, we finally had enough content to warrant publication in a top accounting journal. To my knowledge, our paper remains the only published review of trading volume research.

expectations models appeared that assume investors learn from price, but price reveals private information *with noise.*

Results from noisy rational expectations models of capital markets have provided valuable insights regarding trading volume reactions to financial disclosures such as earnings announcements (Verrecchia 2001). For example, assuming a commonly interpreted earnings announcement, Kim and Verrecchia's (1991) model shows that the volume reaction to the announcement is proportional to: (1) the absolute price change at the time of the announcement and (2) the differential precision of preannouncement private information across traders. Thus, differential prior precision generates trading volume reaction that is associated with absolute price change. Kim and Verrecchia's (1997) model adds the potential for an earnings announcement to be differentially interpreted due to differential private information that can only be used in conjunction with the public earnings announcement (such as information gleaned by studying the financial statements in detail). A key result of their model is that adding differential interpretation leads to trading volume reaction that is independent of absolute price change. Based on these analytical models, archival researchers commonly use trading volume associated with absolute price change as a proxy for differential prior precision and trading volume independent of absolute price change as a proxy for differential interpretation of the earnings announcements (Ahmed, Schneible, and Stevens 2003; Barron, Schneible, and Stevens 2018).

In contrast to Ball and Brown (1968), who examined the correlation between annual earnings announcements and abnormal stock returns over the prior twelve months, Beaver (1968) examined both trading volume and price reactions to earnings announcements in the weeks surrounding the announcement date. Despite the lack of trading volume theory at the time, Beaver identified the potential for trading volume reactions to yield unique insights to price reactions. In particular, Beaver argued that trading volume reactions reflected a lack of consensus regarding the appropriate price of the firm's shares. Furthermore, he asserted that trading volume reactions captured changes in the expectations of individual investors while price reactions reflected changes in the average expectations of the market as a whole. Finally, because a given earnings announcement could leave average expectations of the market unchanged yet greatly alter the expectation of individual investors, Beaver (1968, 69–70) concluded that volume reactions could provide more sensitive tests of the usefulness of accounting earnings to the market than could price reactions. Beaver's intuition has turned out to be correct. Bamber and Cheon (1995) find that nearly a quarter of earnings announcements in their sample generate very high trading volume but almost no price reaction. Furthermore, Cready and Hurtt (2002) use market reaction data and related simulations to provide evidence that volume reactions are more powerful indicators of market reactions to earnings announcement than are price reactions.

Recent evidence suggests that trading volume is now the primary measure of the information content of earnings announcements. A doctoral student of mine at Syracuse University, Richard Schneible Jr., could not replicate Linda Bamber's (1986, 1987) *negative* association between trading volume reactions around earnings announcements and firm size. We found that, while the negative firm size effect on price reactions documented by Atiase (1985) persisted in a recent time period, the firm size effect on trading volume reactions had turned *positive*. We took our evidence to Orie Barron, and the three of us began to develop the theory and additional empirical evidence required to interpret this unusual result. We use intuition and supporting empirical evidence to argue that investor diversity has increased over time, particularly for large firms (Barron, Schneible, and Stevens 2018). This leads us to hypothesize that differential precision of preannouncement information around earnings announcements has increased over time, particularly for large firms. Using trading volume associated with absolute price change to proxy for differential prior precision and various institutional investor measures to capture differential acquisition and use of private information, we provide empirical support for our hypothesis. We find that trading volume reactions are more frequent and more heavily concentrated in large firms in recent periods. The increase in large firms' trading volume reactions is so pronounced that the relation between volume reactions and firm size has turned positive.

Recently, some accounting researchers from the Chicago school have questioned the importance of earnings announcements to equity markets due to findings that these announcements now generate relatively small market price reactions (Ball and Shivakumar 2008, Ball 2013). The new evidence in Barron, Schneible, and Stevens (2018), however, demonstrates that trading volume reactions have increased by a factor of six since Linda Bamber's time period (1977–1980). Therefore, almost all of the market reaction to earnings announcements now appears in trading volume. Our evidence suggests that earnings announcements have increased in importance as a source of resolving disagreement between increasingly diverse investors with differential precision of private information. This suggests that the role of financial reporting in leveling the playing field for investors has increased. The new evidence harkens back to a time when theorists and empiricists viewed earnings announcements and other financial disclosures as an important means to reduce the informational disadvantages of smaller, less sophisticated investors. Regulators and policy makers still reflect this view in their efforts to restrict insider trading (Levitt 1998) and promote transparency in financial reporting (Levitt 1999). The current research paradigm has left little role for either trading volume or financial regulation, and it has done little to promote the merchant culture of transparency and accountability.

FINDINGS REGARDING THE EFFECTS OF FINANCIAL INCENTIVES

Just as the neoclassical theory of the firm that emanated from the Chicago school emphasized price reaction research and deemphasized individual processing and trading volume research, it also emphasized the use of financial incentives to control opportunistic behavior within the firm and deemphasized informal controls such as professional culture and social norms. As the influence of institutional economists faded, researchers in economics, accounting, and finance focused increasingly on financial incentives to align the self-interest of agents with principals and thereby control opportunistic behavior. In a review of the agency literature, Canice Prendergast (1999, 7) writes:

Since the interests of workers and their employers are not always aligned, a large theoretical literature has emphasized how firms design compensation contracts to induce employees to operate in the firm's interest. This literature has reached into many areas of compensation and has pointed to a multitude of different mechanisms that can be used to induce workers to act in the interest of their employers. These include piece rates, options, discretionary bonuses, promotions, profit sharing, efficiency wages, deferred compensation, and so on.

In the seminal work on corporate governance, Berle and Means (1932) argued that management ownership in large firms is too small to make managers interested in profit maximization. In what has become known as the Berle-Means thesis, they argued that in large public corporations where shareholders rely on the board of directors to represent their interests, the boards become beholden to the interests of management over time and their supervisory role becomes ineffective. In their review of the finance literature, Shleifer and Vishny (1997) characterize the problem of corporate governance as ensuring that financiers get a return on their financial investment. Shleifer and Vishny argue that this agency problem is a serious one, and that the opportunities for managers to squander investor funds are plentiful and well-documented. Applying the neoclassical theory of the firm and its agency perspective, they focus on incentive contracts to solve this problem. They conclude, similar to Jensen and Murphy (1990), that incentive contracts found in practice are not powerful enough: "(G)iven the large impact of executives' actions on values of firms, why aren't very high powered incentive contracts used more often in the United States and elsewhere in the world?" (Shleifer and Vishny 1997, 774).

In their review of the accounting literature in corporate governance, Bushman and Smith (2001, 238) also emphasize the dominant role of financial incentives in the literature: "The largest body of governance research in accounting concerns the role of financial accounting information in managerial incentive contracts. The heavy emphasis on managerial compensation derives from the widespread use of compensation contracts in publicly traded U.S. corporations, the availability of top executive compensation data in the U.S. as a result of existing disclosure requirements, and the success of principal-agent models in supplying testable predictions of the relations between available performance measures and optimal compensation contracts." Similar to Shleifer and Vishny, Bushman and Smith review archival studies made popular by the EMH and the empirical work of Fama et al. (1969). Bushman and Smith (2001, 321) conclude, however, that "the literature provides mixed results concerning the risk-incentives tradeoff implied by the classic principal-agent model, suggesting that empirical researchers should consider other theoretical structures, such as sorting models, to understand the data."

Interestingly, both Shleifer and Vishny (1997) and Bushman and Smith (2001) argue that legal systems play an important role in corporate governance, and suggest testing corporate governance mechanisms across economies and cultures. Bushman and Smith (2001, 751–752) emphasize the legal protection of a "duty of loyalty" to shareholders: "(T)he courts in Organization for Economic Cooperation and Development (OECD) countries have generally accepted the idea of managers' duty of loyalty to shareholders. There is a good reason for this. The investments by shareholders are largely sunk, and further investment in the firm is generally not needed from them . . . Although the duty of loyalty is accepted in principal in most OECD countries, the strictness with which the courts enforce it varies greatly." Given these authors' loyalty to the neoclassical theory of the firm, with the assumptions of opportunistic self-interest and preferences only for wealth and leisure, they do not mention where this duty comes from or what it entails. In particular, they do not consider the role of professional culture and social norms in keeping management from over-consuming or squandering investor funds.

Joel Demski (2003), an agency theorist in accounting, has raised the Berle-Means thesis as a potential explanation for the relatively high compensation of top executives at US corporations. The specter of corporate boards beholden to the interests of management rather than to share-holders violates a major pillar of the neoclassical theory of the firm. As Bebchuk and Fried (2004, 3) state:

> In the paradigm that has dominated financial economics, which we label the "arm's-length bargaining" approach, the board of directors is viewed as operating at arm's length from executives and seeking to maximize shareholder value. Rational parties transacting at arm's length have powerful incentives to avoid inefficient provisions that shrink the pie produced by their contractual arrangements. The arm's-length contracting approach has thus led researchers to believe that executive compensation arrangements will tend to increase value, which is why we have used the terms, "efficient contracting" or "optimal contracting" to label this approach in some of our earlier work.

Demski (2003) and Bebchuk and Fried (2004) present evidence suggesting that, rather than control manager opportunism and self-interest, corporate boards have designed compensation contracts that enrich top executives and shield them from risk. While the agency literature's assumption of arm's-length independence between the board of directors and management has been tractable and perhaps reassuring for theorists, it has largely failed to account for executive compensation in practice. Both Demski (2003) and Bebchuk and Fried (2004, 4) identify conflicts of interest that cause directors "to support, or at least go along with, arrangements favorable to the company's top executives." These conflicts of interest include large financial rewards for board membership as well as social and psychological factors, including the prestige and reputation that comes from board membership and the desire to maintain collegiality and avoid conflict.

By focusing exclusively on incentive contracting and ignoring important informal controls such as culture and social norms, neoclassical researchers in corporate governance have provided little insight regarding these informal controls and how they interact with incentive contracting. In addition to finding evidence of intrinsic motivations consistent with social norms, experimental research has found evidence that imposing financial incentives can "crowd-out" such motivations (Frey 1994, Frey and Jegen 2001). This evidence suggests that using financial incentives to control opportunistic self-interest may actually increase the tendency for managers to behave opportunistically. Strong financial incentives have also been found to create perverse incentives for managers to manipulate performance measures, suppress bad news, and choose projects and compensation strategies that are less transparent to investors (Bebchuk and Fried 2004). The fact that executive boards and top executives obscure the total amounts of executive pay and the showering of gratuitous benefits on departing executives shows that they are sensitive to perceptions of fairness and trustworthiness from the public.

Another important aspect of financial incentives ignored by neoclassical researchers in corporate governance is the potential for powerful financial incentives to cause excessive risk-taking behavior. Following the subprime mortgage crisis and the government bailout of troubled financial institutions, financial regulators at the Federal Reserve and the US Department of the Treasury attempted to reign in high-powered financial incentives (Lucchetti, Enrich, and Lublin 2009). This effort was predicated on the belief that high-powered financial incentives caused managers to engage in excessive risk-taking at the expense of the health of financial institutions and the overall economy (Hilsenrath 2009). The corporate governance literature, however, is generally silent regarding the potential for financial incentives to cause managers to engage in excessive risk-taking behavior. There are three factors that contribute to this silence. First, corporate governance research is based on agency theory, where the emphasis is on encouraging the agent to behave in a less risk-averse manner in alignment with the interests of shareholders. Second, agency models typically assume constant absolute risk aversion (CARA), so risk aversion is assumed to be unaffected by wealth or the magnitude of the financial incentive (Lambert 2001). Finally, there is an absence of archival data linking financial incentives to excessive risk taking. This last factor is attributable to endogeneity and measurement problems inherent in archival data. For example, it is difficult to attribute risk-taking behavior to financial incentives because both could reflect the same underlying firm strategy (Bushman and Smith 2001). In a recent experimental study with Alisa Brink and Jessen Hobson, however, we find strong evidence that financial incentives can generate excessive risk-taking behavior (Brink, Hobson, and Stevens 2017).

Neoclassical researchers have recently opened the door for the study of social norms in corporate governance and organizational control. In his book, *Theory of Accounting and Control*, Shyam Sunder (1997, 20) includes the importance of social norms in the enforcement of contracts within the firm: "Accounting is one of several necessary parts of the contract enforcement mechanism of a firm. The other parts are common, civil, and criminal law, along with their enforcement and adjudication systems, and the sociocultural norms." In his follow-up book, *Rethinking Financial Reporting: Standards, Norms and Institutions,* Sunder (2016, 52–53) explains how social norms can directly control opportunistic behavior:

> *How can social norms, subjective and incompletely specified, work in the contentious environment of financial reporting where large amounts of money are often at stake? Norms play an important role in common law countries . . . Unlike formal rules and regulations, motivation to conform to social norms is rooted in the anticipation, or even fear, of others' disapproval of deviations from the norms. Social norms tend to become so internalized by individuals that conformity can approach a moral or ethical obligation.*

In a recent review of corporate governance issues in real-world settings, Larcker and Tayan (2013, 8) encourage archival researchers to test various governance practices to see whether or not they work. "Corporate governance is *empirical* in nature. Through standard social science tools (observation, objectivity, and measurement) we can learn which approaches are effective and which are not." After reviewing the evidence and providing practical examples, Larcker and Tayan (2013, 146) conclude that real-world organizations must rely on a broad list of organizational controls, including corporate culture and social norms:

> *(T)he accuracy of financial statements relies on more than just the integrity of the accounting system. It relies on the integrity of the entire organizational system. The rules for describing corporate results are complex and their correct application requires the sound judgment of management. While internal controls are important to safeguarding these results from manipulation or fraud, these controls can only be so effective. If management or employees are intent on getting around them, they will. To prevent this, broad organizational factors—such as culture, leadership, "tone from the top," and a sense of ethical standards—must come into play.*

FINDINGS REGARDING CULTURE AND SOCIAL NORMS

Archival researchers have recently examined the effect of corporate culture and social norms on corporate governance and organizational control. Early research examined opportunistic financial reporting by managers, and in the process documented another market anomaly inconsistent with the EMH. This research found evidence that managers manipulated earnings to surpass earnings targets attached to annual bonuses (Healy 1985), and that the market was at least partially misled by such earnings manipulation (Sloan 1996, Collins and Hrigar 2000). More recently, archival researchers have extended this literature by showing that companies that have CEOs with a higher proportion of their pay tied to company share prices have higher levels of earnings management (Bergstresser and Philippon 2006). In particular, CEOs with high-powered financial incentives use discretionary components of earnings more aggressively to affect reported performance. These results provide further evidence of opportunistic reporting by management and increase the importance of corporate governance mechanisms to control this opportunistic behavior at the expense of investors.

In the face of this evidence, archival researchers have recently examined corporate governance mechanisms related to culture and social norms to control opportunistic reporting by management. Bamber, Jiang, and Wang (2010) note that neoclassical economic theory leaves no role through which idiosyncratic differences among managers can affect corporate reporting. They test the hypothesis that such idiosyncratic differences are reflected in voluntary disclosure choices of the firm. After controlling for firm fixed effects, time-specific fixed effects, and economic determinants of voluntary disclosure identified in previous research, Bamber et al. find that managers exert economically significant individual-specific influence over five attributes of management earnings forecasts: the frequency of forecasts, forecast precision, news conveyed by the forecast, and the bias in and accuracy of the forecast. They find that military experience leads managers to favor more precise forecasts that guide expectations down, consistent with conservatism and valuing honesty and integrity. Managers promoted from accounting and finance also exhibit more precise and conservative forecast disclosures. This evidence is consistent with individual managers differing in internalized social norms or social norm sensitivity.

Researchers have also used large sample archival studies to examine the effects of culture and religion on the financial reporting behavior of the firm. Dyreng, Mayew, and Williams (2012) argue that the religious adherence of the population surrounding a firm's headquarters reflects the social environment in which managers operate. In particular, interactions with religious individuals increase in locations where a large fraction of the population is religious, and this interaction is likely to expose managers to the influence of social norms that control opportunistic reporting behavior. Using the level of religious adherence in the county of a US firm's headquarters as a proxy for these social norms, Dyreng et al. find that higher levels of religious adherence are associated with both lower likelihood of financial restatement and less risk that financial statements misrepresent the financial condition of the firm. Firms located in areas of high religious adherence are less likely to engage in tax sheltering and are more forthcoming with bad news in their voluntary disclosures. These results hold overall and separately for both Catholic and Protestant religious adherence.

In concurrent and complementary work, McGuire, Omer, and Sharp (2012) also examine the relation between religious social norms and financial reporting. They provide three main reasons that such research is important: (1) social norms are known to have a strong influence on human behavior and so they represent a mechanism for reducing agency costs, (2) examining the strength of local religious social norms could help to identify firms that are more or less likely to engage in actions that are costly to shareholders, and (3) evidence on how local social norms influence corporate policies can provide useful insights to standard-setters, investors, and regulators. To measure religious social norms, they use a unique database comprised of responses to interviews conducted by the Gallup organization. McGuire et al. find that religious social norms act as an alternative monitoring mechanism over corporate financial reporting, especially when external monitoring is low. In particular, they find that firms headquartered in areas with strong religious social norms experience lower incidences of financial reporting irregularities.

Corporations have always used a mix of financial and nonfinancial measures to facilitate organizational control (Johnson and Kaplan 1987). More recently, however, firms have increasingly used a system of financial and nonfinancial measures to support strategic goals called the balanced scorecard (Kaplan and Norton 1996). The balanced scorecard includes forward-looking measures to help management focus on long-term strategic goals as well as short-term financial goals. The balanced scorecard also allows management to focus on social and environmental goals as a means to achieve long-term financial goals (Horngren, Datar, and Rajan 2018). Corporations have also begun to supplement their annual financial reports with separate corporate social responsibility (CSR) reports demonstrating the firm's performance on a wide range of social and environmental goals. This reflects the increasing scrutiny and pressure on managers to incorporate socially responsible business practices into the way they run their corporations (Campbell 2007, Moser and Martin 2012, Christensen 2016).

While agency theorists continue to argue whether companies should invest in CSR activities, and whether such activities represent a net positive or negative effect for shareholders, archival researchers have begun to examine the effect of CSR activities and reporting on the behavior of the firm. Moser and Martin (2012, 799) argue that "it is important to understand the extent to which the demand for CSR activities is driven by non-shareholder constituents and whether the related disclosures may therefore serve different or broader purposes than other traditional corporate financial disclosures." One important purpose of CSR activities and disclosures is to communicate a firm's underlying culture and social norms, and the emerging results from archival studies support this purpose. In particular, recent CSR studies support the importance of culture and social norms in corporate governance and organizational control.

Dhaliwal, Li, Tsang, and Yang (2011) examine whether the initiation of voluntary disclosure of CSR activities results in a reduction in the firm's cost of capital. They find that initiating firms with superior social responsibility performance enjoy a subsequent reduction in their cost of equity capital, attract dedicated institutional investors and analyst coverage, and allow analysts following their firm to achieve lower absolute forecast errors and dispersion. Dhaliwal et al. use their results to explain the rapid growth in CSR reporting in the United States and around the world. Kim, Park, and Wier (2012) examine whether firms that exhibit CSR reporting also behave in a socially responsible way in their financial reporting, thereby delivering more transparent and reliable financial information to investors. They find that socially responsible firms are less likely to manage earnings through discretionary accruals, manipulate real operating activities, and be the subject of SEC investigations. Kim et al. (2012, 790) conclude that their results are consistent "with the notion that CSR activities are motivated by managers' incentives to be honest, trustworthy, and ethical."

Davis, Hecht, and Perkins (2003) model the effects of others' behavior, enforcement, and social norms on the dynamics of taxpayer compliance. Their analytical results suggest that taxpayer compliance is dependent upon whether the population is initially compliant or noncompliant and upon changes in social norms for compliance. Consistent with the general intuition of their model, CSR activities and reporting have also been found to effect tax compliance behavior. Hoi, Wu, and Zhang (2013) find evidence that firms with excessive "irresponsible activities" on their CSR report are more aggressive in avoiding taxes, lending credence to the idea that corporate culture affects tax avoidance. Davis, Guenther, Krull, and Williams (2016) investigate the relation between CSR ratings of US public corporations and both the amount of taxes paid by the firm and the amount of tax lobbying initiated by the firm. They find that CSR is negatively related to five-year cash-effective tax rates and positively related to tax lobbying expenditures, suggesting that socially responsible firms do not view the payment of corporate taxes as complementing CSR activities.

Archival studies have found a positive effect of CSR reporting on a wide array of opportunistic behavior such as insider trading, bribery, and kickbacks. Gao, Lisic, and Zhang (2014) argue that while a firm's commitment to social good helps build a positive image, and this benefits the firm in various ways, it imposes additional costs on management engaging in activities that conflict with the appearance of doing social good. Informed trading is one activity that is often considered greedy and an unfair expropriation of uninformed investors' wealth. In addition to the potential for CSR to increase the social costs of insider trading, Gao et al. argue that a firm's CSR orientation can be a signal of executives' tendency to be a good citizen. They find that executives of CSR-conscious firms profit significantly less from insider trading and are less likely to trade prior to future news than are executives of non-CSR-conscious firms. Christensen (2016) investigates whether CSR helps protect firm value by preventing the occurrence of high-profile misconduct such as bribery, kickbacks, discrimination, etc. Using lawsuits related to CSR issues that are reported in international business news articles, he finds that firms that report on CSR are less likely to engage in high-profile misconduct in the following year. Furthermore, Christensen finds that when high-profile misconduct does occur, CSR-reporting firms experience a less negative stock price reaction. He concludes that CSR reporting protects shareholders by controlling opportunistic behavior and strengthening a firm's reputation.

In summary, the culture-free, norm-free core of the neoclassical theory of the firm has also come under assault from emerging evidence in large sample archival studies. This chapter has demonstrated that the strong view of market efficiency promoted by the research paradigm out of Chicago, which reduced the responsibility of management to increasing stock price and made individual decision-making and trading volume irrelevant, is in full retreat. In response to more moderate views of market efficiency, researchers in economics, accounting, and finance have returned to examining individual information processing and trading volume behavior in market settings. These researchers have also returned to examining corporate governance and organizational control mechanisms that involve corporate culture and social norms. Despite the inherent difficulties of generating evidence from archival data – including the overall lack of control for potential confounds and the necessity of relying on noisy empirical proxies for theoretical constructs – these researchers have uncovered strong evidence that social norms play an important role in controlling opportunistic behavior in the firm. This growing body of archival research supports the importance of social norms demonstrated in recent formal models (see Chapter 5) and in experimental research related to the firm (see Chapter 6).

8

Conclusion: "Where do we go from here?"

In addressing the topic of social norms and the theory of the firm, I have taken a foundational approach that provides historical, theoretical, and empirical insights. The insights contained in this book, however, are necessarily limited in that they reflect my own attempt to address this topic throughout a career of research and teaching that began the day I stepped onto the campus of Indiana University in 1989. Nevertheless, the search for new insights in this important area goes on. I am confident that we will learn much more about social norms and the theory of the firm in the years ahead. (I know that I have much more research planned.) It is my hope that this book clears away some of the hindrances and biases that have blocked this important research initiative in the past. After demonstrating that many of the previous objections to incorporating social norms into the theory of the firm are spurious, and that this approach has the potential to yield new and useful insights, an important question remains: "Where do we go from here?"

It is common for researchers within a given scientific community to ignore evidence inconsistent with the received research paradigm (Kuhn 1962). In the past, persistent evidence of behavior inconsistent with the narrow behavioral assumptions of *homo economicus* has given rise to specialty subdisciplines such as behavioral economics, behavioral accounting, and behavioral finance. Researchers have even developed a behavioral theory of the firm (Cyert and March 1963). All too often, however, adding the descriptor "behavioral" to a field or discipline has meant abandoning rational expectations and the powerful tools of neoclassical theory. The failure of these subdisciplines to develop rich theoretical frameworks with broad generalizability has limited the contribution of this approach. My research and that of many others within the neoclassical economic tradition suggests that such disciplinary fission is unnecessary when it comes to incorporating social norms into the theory of the firm. In particular, a growing number of researchers have concluded that social norms can be incorporated into the neoclassical theory of the firm to the benefit of theory, practice, and public policy.

The historical background provided in this book (see Chapters 2–4) demonstrates the importance of social norms to free-market capitalism and the development and control of the firm. This historical background also reveals that prominent classical and neoclassical economists have consistently expressed the possibility for social norms to influence behavior in economic settings related to the firm. I have uncovered many "bread crumbs" left by such prominent economists for researchers to follow. For example, I have found that Adam Smith's first book provided a fully developed moral theory that incorporates the role of social norms in developing standards of behavior and the moral conscience (Smith 1759/1790). Furthermore, I have found that his second book on political economy contained a broad view of economic man that incorporated these social norms (Smith 1776/1791). It was John Stuart Mill, not Adam Smith, who developed the narrow behavioral assumptions of *homo economicus* that dominate neoclassical economic theory today. Yet even Mill (1836, 323) acknowledged the potential for economists to incorporate social and moral aspects of human nature to expand his political economy.

When economists did incorporate social norms into the theory of the firm, however, they often repudiated the mathematical tools of neoclassical economic theory. This caused the great *Methodenstreit*, or "battle of the methods," between institutional and neoclassical economists that engulfed Europe in the late nineteenth century and eventually spilled over to the United States. This conflict drove issues of culture and social norms out of the neoclassical theory of the firm, first in economics departments and later in university-based business schools. Among the staunchest defenders of neoclassical economics, however, were Carl Menger and Friedrich von Wiesner of the Austrian school of economics. These neoclassical economists pushed the envelope of the utility function to include subjective valuation for noneconomic goods and eventually incorporated behavioral constraints from social institutions such as law, morals, contracts, property rights, habits, and customers (Ekelund and Hébert 2014, 350). Even Alfred Marshall, the British economist who was instrumental in building the neoclassical synthesis at Cambridge University toward the end of the nineteenth century, was open to incorporating social institutions and norms, provided they occurred with sufficient regularity within economic life. More recently, leading neoclassical economists such as Kenneth Arrow and Vernon Smith have urged researchers to incorporate social norms into neoclassical economic theory.

The most rigorous neoclassical economic theory related to the firm is game theory. In particular, principal-agent theory is a special form of game theory (see Chapters 5 and 6). Yet even John von Neumann and Oscar Morgenstern left bread crumbs for researchers to follow in their initial introduction of game theory. Von Neumann and Morgenstern (1944, 9–12) compare the theory of utility maximization offered by the Austrian school of economics with economic decisions made by Robinson Crusoe on his isolated island. They state, "The chief objection against using this very simplified model of an isolated individual for the theory of a social exchange economy is that it does not represent an individual exposed to the manifold social influences. Hence, it is said to analyze an individual who might behave quite differently if his choices were made in a social world where he would be exposed to factors of imitation, advertising, custom, and so on..." Von Neumann and Morgenstern argue that in a real social exchange economy, behavior is affected by *social influences*. That is, participants in a social exchange economy are influenced by what they expect others to do and what they themselves are expected to do. At the very founding of game theory, therefore, we see Bicchieri's (2006) emphasis on behavioral expectations to explain norm-based behavior in experimental tests of game theory.

Given the historical evidence that neoclassical economists were generally aware of the "simplifying" and "idealizing" nature of their behavioral assumptions and were open to incorporating social norms into the theory of the firm, why did they not engage in this research initiative long ago? Why were issues of culture and social norms excluded from the neoclassical tradition in economics, accounting, and finance? Much of the continued resistance to incorporating social norms into the theory of the firm can be attributed to the powerful influence of the research paradigm developed by the Chicago school. As suggested by Fourcade and Khurana (2013), the neoclassical theory of the firm that emanated from the Chicago school was instrumental in transforming all three major disciplines. The writings and influence of prominent scholars associated with the Chicago school – including Milton Friedman, George Stigler, and Michael Jensen – caused the theory of the firm to become increasingly dismissive of market inefficiencies and social preferences outside of Mill's narrow conception of *homo economicus*.

After spending a semester at Glasgow University studying Adam Smith, it has become increasingly clear to me that the Chicago school misinterpreted the writings of the father of classical economics in building their powerful new research paradigm. In particular, these neoclassical economists took strong positions that were not always supported by the very economic tradition and evidence they used as building materials. Further research appears warranted regarding how the Chicago school misinterpreted Adam Smith's writings in the building of the neoclassical theory of the firm. Returning to his social norm theory in *The Theory of Moral Sentiments* appears to be a useful starting point for incorporating social norms into the theory of the firm. I, for one, plan to conduct further research regarding the social norm theory present in Adam Smith's writings and its implications for the theory of the firm.

Neoclassical economists at the Chicago school built their powerful research paradigm on a pessimistic view of human nature (opportunistic self-interest) and an idealized view of capital markets (fully revealing and efficient). Due to persistent evidence inconsistent with fully efficient markets, neoclassical researchers have relaxed the assumption of fully efficient markets and have developed rational expectations models with only partially revealing market prices. This has opened up the literature to research related to individual information processing and trading volume. Sadly, we still know far too little about the role of markets in gathering together the expectations of differently informed traders and the effect of financial information disclosures on those expectations. The relatively new literature in individual information processing and trading volume is already yielding new and useful insights (Bamber, Barron, and Stevens 2011). Relaxing the assumption of fully efficient markets, however, should also open up the literature again to the role of managers in directing and controlling the firm. In particular, it is time again for neoclassical researchers to fully consider the "visible hand" of management control.

Persistent evidence of norm-based behavior in experimental and archival studies suggests that the "nexus of contracts" view of the firm is incomplete. Theorists initially interpreted this norm-based behavior as reflecting economic benefits somewhere in the future, consistent with narrow self-interest. This interpretation, however, could not explain norm-based behavior emerging in single-period experimental settings. Next, theorists incorporated this evidence by assuming that managers had stable "other-regarding preferences" or preferences for simple reciprocity. More recent theory has incorporated evidence suggesting that norm-based behavior is context specific and can be activated by situational cues and information present in the economic setting. This theory maintains a role for manager "type" or "social norm sensitivity" in the manager, but it also gives the economic setting a role in making specific social norms salient. The evidence for social norm activation is growing, but we still know little regarding how traditional contracting solutions interact with norm-based motivations and behavior. We also know little regarding how social norm preferences should be modeled within the utility function of either the agent or the principal. Much more research is needed in these areas, and neoclassical researchers will be needed to lead the way.

Researchers in the behavioral subdisciplines (behavioral economics, behavioral accounting, and behavioral finance) have too often joined early neoclassical theorists in viewing norm-based behavior as irrational because it does not fit constructivist views of rational self-interest. For example, behavioral researchers have labeled norm-based behavior such as honesty "predictably irrational" simply because it is financially costly in the short run. From the perspective of ecological rationality, however, norm-based behavior is perfectly rational as it has proven its fitness across social history and culture. The fact that norm-based behavior is systematic and predictable is a strong indication that it is rational, and there is a strong tradition in moral philosophy suggesting that moral norms are activated precisely in economic settings where financial self-interest conflicts with group or societal interests. My experimental research confirms that pre-senting economic agents with such conflicts of interest activates social norms that control opportunistic behavior. More research appears war-ranted regarding this alternative form of rationality based on social history and culture.

In this book, I have focused on the neoclassical theory of the firm that emanated from the Chicago school and its powerful research paradigm. Incorporating social norms into this theory of the firm, however, will require insights from norm-based research in other disciplines and research paradigms. Having traveled this journey for so long, I am some-what familiar with the terrain. I have learned that multidisciplinary research is a two-way street. Other research paradigms have their own strong assumptions and methodological preferences. Researchers in psy-chology, for example, have a low tolerance for mathematical modeling and a high tolerance for behavioral heuristics and biases. Researchers in moral philosophy, on the other hand, have a low tolerance for empirical methods but a high tolerance for complex philosophical theories with normative implications. These research paradigms seem far apart from the neoclassi-cal economic paradigm, yet there are ample opportunities for cross-pollination of ideas if researchers from these disparate paradigms become more familiar with each other's work.

My own theoretical and experimental research has convinced me that the neoclassical theory of the firm is fully capable of incorporating social norms. Similar to the development of experimental methods in economics, however, this research initiative may evolve in a way that is unique to other research traditions. I believe that Posner's (2000) game-theoretic approach to social norms, which assumed that social norms are simply behavioral regularities used to signal one's type and thereby reap future economic rewards, was a useful first approach in that it maintained the tools of rational choice theory. As I discussed in Chapter 4, his signaling model focuses on the reputational source of behavioral regularities to the exclusion of their cognitive and emotional sources. Posner (2000, 46) states that his model ignores such cognition and emotion because they "are just not well enough understood by psychologists to support a theory of social norms, and repeated but puzzled acknowledgements of their importance would muddy the exposition of the argument without providing any off-setting benefits." As Posner admitted, however, his model provided few testable implications and was therefore of limited use to empirical researchers.

More recently, researchers have developed a theory of social norm activation that incorporates behavioral expectations and yet is faithful to rational choice theory. Consistent with the emerging evidence in game theory experiments, this theory characterizes social norms as conditional preferences that can be activated by situational cues and information present in an economic setting (Bicchieri 2006). Researchers have found this social norm theory useful in designing and interpreting experimental tests of game theory and the theory of the firm. This growing body of experimental research is capable of providing new and useful insights not only to the disciplines of economics, accounting, and finance, but also to the related disciplines of organizational behavior and business ethics (Blay et al. 2017). Advances in this body of research, however, will require further developments in theory, experimental evidence, and archival evidence. For example, further research is needed to determine whether social norm preferences meet the traditional conditions for rationality, including complete, consistent, and transitive preferences over a range of options (Posner 2000, 13).

In addition to being open to insights from social norm research in other disciplines, neoclassical researchers should also regain their commitment to the development of both positive and normative theory. The neoclassical theory of the firm has had a minimal influence on public policy due to both its underlying assumptions (opportunistic self-interest and fully efficient markets) and its emphasis on positive theory. The abandonment of normative theory has been particularly harmful to the disciplines of accounting and finance, where regulators and policy-makers have been left to develop policy with very little guidance from theorists and empiricists. In addition to increasing the descriptive power of the theory, incorporating social norms into the theory of the firm enhances the theory's ability to make affective prescriptions for policy makers. In particular, it allows the theory to make policy recommendations that incorporate norm-based behavior and support capitalist institutions and social norms.

Experimental and archival research has revealed the presence of the historic merchant culture that gave birth to free-market capitalism. This culture promotes private property rights and unparalleled civil liberties, yet protects those rights and liberties through a network of social norms, including transparency and accountability. These social norms nourish the growth of markets and firms and are supported by other social institutions such as the family, religion, and education. By ignoring social norms, the neoclassical theory of the firm has been unable to support this merchant culture and may have inadvertently put capitalist institutions and economies at risk. For example, history has shown that a lack of transparency and accountability has frequently given rise to an opportunism culture, which eventually requires the monarchy culture of heavy regulation and big government. History has also shown, however, that both the opportunism and monarchy cultures are vulnerable to corruption, which sows the seeds of their own destruction.

I am encouraged by the growing openness to social norm theory among neoclassical researchers from the Chicago research tradition. Early in my career I had the privilege of presenting my dissertation paper at Washington University and had a private meeting with Nick Dopuch. He complimented my experimental design and said that he found my examination of reputation and ethics interesting. He also said that he liked my use of traditional agency theory throughout the paper and asked if I had submitted it yet for publication. I admitted to my esteemed colleague that my paper had recently been rejected from the top accounting journal he had helped found at the University of Chicago. In response, he asked me why I bothered to send the paper to that journal, given its demonstrated bias against experimental research. He seemed genuinely disappointed that the top journal he helped found was generally closed to experimental research testing the limits of neoclassical theory. In more recent conversations with prominent researchers from the Chicago tradition, however,

I have found an increasing openness to expand the neoclassical research paradigm. I am confident that the same neoclassical tradition that relaxed its view of fully efficient capital markets to make room for individual information processing and trading volume will eventually relax its view of *homo economicus* to make room for norm-based behavior.

References

Abdel-Rahim, H., and D. Stevens. 2018. The effect of information system precision on honesty in managerial reporting: A re-examination of information asymmetry effects. *Accounting, Organizations and Society*, 64(1): 31–43.

Abdel-Rahim, H., J. Hales, and D. Stevens. 2018. Financial Reporting Disaggregation and Discretion Effects on Manager Opportunism: An Experimental Examination of Trustworthiness and Honesty. Georgia State University Working Paper.

Abernathy, W., and R. Hayes. 1980. Managing our way to economic decline. *Harvard Business Review*, (July–August): 67–77.

Adams, D., and E. Maine. 1998. *Business Ethics for the 21st Century*. Mountain View, CA: Mayfield Publishing.

Ahmed, A., R. Schneible, and D. Stevens. 2003. An empirical analysis of the effects of online trading on stock price and trading volume reactions to earnings announcements. *Contemporary Accounting Research*, 20(3): 413–439.

Alchian. A., and H. Demsetz. 1972. Production, information costs, and economic organization. *American Economic Review*, 62(5): 777–795.

Allen, R. 2009. *The British Industrial Revolution in Global Perspective*. Cambridge, UK: Cambridge University Press.

Alvey, J. 2007. The 'new view' of Adam Smith and the development of his views over time. In *New Perspectives on Adam Smith's The Theory of Moral Sentiments*, Geoff Cockfield, Ann Firth, and John Laurent (eds.). Cheltenham, UK: Edward Elgar Publishing, 66–83.

American Association of Collegiate Schools of Business. 1933. *Proceedings of the Fifteenth Annual Meeting*. Fifteenth Annual Meeting of the AACSB, Lexington, KY, Summer.

American Association of Collegiate Schools of Business. 1936. *Proceedings of the Eighteenth Annual Meeting*. Eighteenth Annual Meeting of the AACSB, Boston, MA, April 22, 23, 24, and 25.

Antle, R., and G. Eppen. 1985. Capital rationing and organizational slack in capital budgeting. *Management Science*, 31(2): 163–174.

Antle, R., and J. Fellingham. 1995. Information rents and preferences among information systems in a model of resource allocation. *Journal of Accounting Research*, 33(Supplement): 41–58.

Antle, R., and J. Fellingham. 1997. Models of capital investments with private information and incentives: A selective review. *Journal of Business Finance and Accounting*, 24(7–8): 887–908.

Arce, D. 2006. Taking corporate culture seriously: Group effects in the trust game. *Southern Economic Journal*, 73(1): 27–36.

Arce, D. 2007. Is agency theory self-activating? *Economic Inquiry*, 45(4): 708–720.

Arrow, K. 1962. The economic implications of learning by doing. *Review of Economic Studies*, 29(3): 155–173.

Arrow, K. 1974. *The Limits of Organization*. New York, NY: Norton, York.

Arrow, K. 1985. The economics of agency. In *Principals and Agents: The Structure of Business*, J. W. Pratt and R. J. Zeckhauser (eds.). Boston, MA: Harvard Business School Press, 37–51.

Atiase, R. 1985. Predisclosure information, firm capitalization, and security price behavior around earnings announcements. *Journal of Accounting Research*, 23(1): 21–36.

Aumann, R. 1976. Agreeing to disagree. *The Annals of Statistics*, 4(6): 1236–1239.

Backhouse, R. 2009. Friedman's 1953 essay and the marginalist controversy. In *The Methodology of Positive Economics: Reflections on the Milton Friedman Legacy*. Uskali Mäki (ed.). Cambridge, UK: Cambridge University Press, 217–240.

Baiman, S. 1990. Agency research in managerial accounting: A second look. *Accounting, Organizations and Society*, 15(4): 341–371.

Ball, R. 2013. Accounting informs investors and earnings management is rife: Two questionable beliefs. *Accounting Horizons*, 27(4): 847–853.

Ball, R., and L. Shivakumar. 2008. How much new information is there in earnings? *Journal of Accounting Research*, 46(5): 975–1016.

Ball, R., and P. Brown. 1968. An empirical evaluation of accounting income numbers. *Journal of Accounting Research*, 6(2): 159–178.

Ball, R., and P. Brown. 2014. Ball and Brown (1968): A retrospective. *The Accounting Review*, 89(1): 1–26.

Bamber, L. 1986. The information content of annual earnings releases: A trading volume approach. *Journal of Accounting Research*, 24(1): 40–56.

Bamber, L. 1987. Unexpected earnings, firm size, and trading volume around quarterly earnings announcements. *The Accounting Review*, 62(3): 510–532.

Bamber, L., O. Barron, and D. Stevens. 2011. Trading volume around earnings announcements and other financial reports: Theory, research design, empirical evidence, and directions for future research. *Contemporary Accounting Research*, 28(2): 431–471.

Bamber, L., and Y. Cheon. 1995. Differential price and volume reactions to accounting earnings announcements. *The Accounting Review*, 70(3): 417–441.

Bamber, L., J. Jiang, and I. Wang. 2010. What's my style? The influence of top managers on voluntary corporate financial disclosure. *The Accounting Review*, 85(4): 1131–1162.

Barbalet, J. 2005. Smith's sentiments (1759) and Wright's passions (1601): The beginnings of sociology. *British Journal of Sociology*, 56(2): 171–189.

Barbalet, J. 2007. The moon before the dawn: A seventeenth-century precursor of Smith's *The Theory of Moral Sentiments*. In *New Perspectives on Adam Smith's*

The Theory of Moral Sentiments. Geoff Cockfield, Ann Firth, and John Laurent (eds.). Cheltenham, UK: Edward Elgar Publishing, 84–105.

Barron, O., O. Kim, S. Lim, and D. Stevens. 1998. Using analysts' forecasts to measure properties of analysts' information environment. *The Accounting Review,* 73(4): 421–433.

Barron, O., and H. Qu. 2014. Information asymmetry and the *ex ante* impact of public disclosure quality on price efficiency and the cost of capital: Evidence from a laboratory market. *The Accounting Review,* 89(4): 1269–1297.

Barron, O., R. Schneible, and D. Stevens. 2018. The changing behavior of trading volume reactions to earnings announcements: Evidence of the increasing use of accounting earnings news by investors. *Contemporary Accounting Research,* Forthcoming.

Baumol, W. 1959. *Business Behavior, Value and Growth.* New York, NY: Macmillan.

Beauchamp. T., and N. Bowie. 2004. Ethical theory and business practice. In *Ethical Theory and Business,* 7th edition. T. Beauchamp and N. Bowie (eds.). Upper Saddle River, NJ: Pearson Prentice Hall.

Beaver, W. 1968. The information content of annual earnings announcements. *Journal of Accounting Research,* 6(Supplement): 67–92.

Bebchuk, L., and J. Fried. 2003. Executive compensation as an agency problem. *Journal of Economic Perspectives,* 17(3): 71–92.

Bebchuk, L., and J. Fried. 2004. *Pay Without Performance: The Unfulfilled Promise of Executive Compensation.* Cambridge, MA: Harvard University Press.

Bebchuk, L., and J. Fried. 2005. Executive compensation at Fannie Mae: A case study of perverse incentives, nonperformance pay, and camouflage. *Journal of Corporate Law,* 30(4): 807–822.

Bennis, W., and J. O'Toole. 2005. How business schools lost their way. *Harvard Business Review,* (May): 96–104.

Berg, J., J. Dickhaut, and J. McCabe. 1995. Trust, reciprocity, and social history. *Games and Economic Behavior,* 10(1): 122–142.

Bergstresser, D., and T. Philippon. 2006. CEO incentives and earnings management. *Journal of Financial Economics,* 80(3): 511–529.

Berle, A., and G. Means. 1932. *The Modern Corporation and Private Property.* New York, NY: Macmillan.

Bernard, V., and J. Thomas. 1989. Post-earnings-announcement drift: Delayed price response or risk premium? *Journal of Accounting Research,* 27(Supplement): 1–36.

Bernard, V., and J. Thomas. 1990. Evidence that stock prices do not fully reflect the implications of current earnings for future earnings. *Journal of Accounting and Economics,* 13(4): 305–340.

Bernstein, M. 2001. *A Perilous Progress: Economists and Public Purpose in Twentieth-Century America.* Princeton, NJ: Princeton University Press.

Bernstein, W. 2004. *The Birth of Plenty: How the Prosperity of the Modern World Was Created.* New York, NY: McGraw-Hill.

Berry, C. 2003. Sociality and socialization. In *The Cambridge Companion to The Scottish Enlightenment.* Alexander Broadie (ed.). Cambridge, UK: Cambridge University Press, 243–257.

Berry, C. 2006. Smith and science. In *The Cambridge Companion to Adam Smith.* K. Haakonssen (ed.). New York, NY: Cambridge University Press, 112–135.

Bicchieri, C. 2006. *The Grammar of Society: The Nature and Dynamics of Social Norms.* New York, NY: Cambridge University Press.

Bicchieri, C., E. Xiao, and R. Muldoon. 2011. Trustworthiness is a social norm, but trusting is not. *Politics, Philosophy and Economics*, 10(2): 170–187.

Blay, A., E. Gooden, M. Mellon, and D. Stevens. 2017. The usefulness of social norm theory in empirical business ethics research: A review and suggestions for future research. *Journal of Business Ethics*, Forthcoming.

Blay, A., E. Gooden, M. Mellon, and D. Stevens. 2018. Can social norm activation improve audit quality? Evidence from an experimental audit market. *Journal of Business Ethics*, Forthcoming.

Bloomfield, R. 1996. The interdependence of reporting discretion and informational efficiency in laboratory markets. *The Accounting Review*, 71(4): 493–511.

Bloomfield, R. 2010. Traditional vs. Behavioral Finance. Cornell University Johnson School Research Paper Series #22-2010.

Bloomfield, R., R. Libby, and M. Nelson. 1999. Confidence and the welfare of less-informed investors. *Accounting, Organizations and Society*, 24(8): 623–647.

Bloomfield, R., and T. Wilks. 2000. Disclosure effects in the laboratory: Liquidity, depth, and the cost of capital. *The Accounting Review*, 75(1): 13–41.

Bowie, N., and R. Duska. 1990. *Business Ethics*, 2nd edition. Englewood Cliffs, NJ: Prentice Hall.

Bowie, N., and R. Freeman. 1992. Ethics and agency theory: An introduction. In *Ethics and Agency Theory: An Introduction*, N. E. Bowie and R. E. Freeman (eds.). New York, NY: Oxford University Press, 3–22.

Brandt, R. 1979. *A Theory of the Good and the Right.* Oxford, UK: Clarendon Press.

Brennan, M. 1994. Incentives, rationality and society. *Journal of Applied Corporate Finance*, 7(2): 31–39.

Brink, A., J. Hobson, and D. Stevens. 2017. The effect of high power financial incentives on excessive risk-taking behavior: An experimental examination. *Journal of Management Accounting Research*, 29(1): 13–29.

Broadie, A. 2003. Introduction. In *The Cambridge Companion to The Scottish Enlightenment.* Alexander Broadie (ed.). Cambridge, UK: Cambridge University Press, 1–7.

Brown, J., J. Evans, and D. Moser. 2009. Agency theory and participative budgeting experiments. *Journal of Management Accounting Research*, 21(1): 317–345.

Brown, L. 1993. Earnings forecasting research: Its implications for capital markets research. *International Journal of Forecasting*, 9(3): 295–320.

Brown, L., P. Griffin, R. Hagerman, and M. Zmijewski. 1987. An evaluation of alternative proxies for the assessment of unexpected earnings. *Journal of Accounting and Economics*, 9(2): 159–193.

Buckle, H. 1864. *History of Civilization in England.* New York, NY: D. Appleton and Co.

Burgstahler, D. 1987. Inference from empirical research. *The Accounting Review*, 62(1): 203–214.

Burk, K. 2007. *Old World, New World: Great Britain and America from the Beginning.* New York, NY: Atlantic Monthly Press.

Burns, J. 2009. *Goddess of the Market: Ayn Rand and the American Right.* New York, NY: Oxford University Press.

Bushman, R., and A. Smith. 2001. Financial accounting information and corporate governance. *Journal of Accounting and Economics*, 32(1–3): 237–333.

Caginalp, G., D. Porter, and V. Smith. 2001. Financial bubbles: Excess cash, momentum, and incomplete information. *Journal of Psychology and Financial Markets*, 2(2): 80–99.

Camerer, C. 2003. *Behavioral Game Theory: Experiments in Strategic Interaction*. Princeton, NJ: Princeton University Press.

Campbell, J. 2007. Why would corporations behave in socially responsible ways? An institutional theory of corporate social responsibility. *Academy of Management Review*, 32(3): 946–967.

Campbell, R., and A. Skinner. 1981. General Introduction. In *An Inquiry into the Nature and Causes of the Wealth of Nations*, the Glasgow Edition, R. H. Campbell and A. S. Skinner (eds.). Indianapolis, IN: Liberty Fund, Inc., 1–60.

Campbell, T. 1971. *Adam Smith's Science of Morals*. London, UK: Alan & Unwin Ltd.

Chamberlin, E. 1933. *The Theory of Monopolistic Competition: A Re-orientation of the Theory of Value*. Cambridge, MA: Harvard University Press.

Chambers, R. 1973. Observation as a method of inquiry—The background of securities and obscurities. *Abacus*, 9(2): 156–175.

Chandler, A. Jr. 1977. *The Visible Hand: The Managerial Revolution in American Business*. Cambridge, MA: Belknap Press.

Chow, C., J. Cooper, and W. Waller. 1988. Participative budgeting: Effects of a truth-inducing pay scheme and information asymmetry on slack and performance. *The Accounting Review*, 63(1): 111–122.

Christensen, D. 2016. Corporate accountability reporting and high-profile misconduct. *The Accounting Review*, 91(2): 377–399.

Clarke, P. 2007. Adam Smith, religion and the Scottish Enlightenment. In *New Perspectives on Adam Smith's The Theory of Moral Sentiments*. Geoff Cockfield, Ann Firth, and John Laurent (eds.). Cheltenham, UK: Edward Elgar Publishing, 47–65.

Coase, R. 1937. The nature of the firm. *Economica*, 4(16): 386–405.

Cockfield, G., A. Firth, and J. Laurent. 2007. Introduction. In *New Perspectives on Adam Smith's The Theory of Moral Sentiments*. Geoff Cockfield, Ann Firth, and John Laurent (eds.). Cheltenham, UK: Edward Elgar Publishing, 1–10.

Coleman, J. 1990. *Foundations of Social Choice Theory*. Cambridge, MA: Harvard University Press.

Collins, D., and P. Hribar. 2000. Earnings-based and accrual-based market anomalies: One effect or two? *Journal of Accounting and Economics*, 29(1): 101–123.

Commons, J. 1932. The problem of correlating law, economics, and ethics. *Wisconsin Law Review*, 3: 3–26.

Cournot, A. 1838. *Researches into the Mathematical Principles of the Theory of Wealth*, N. T. Bacon (Trans.). New York, NY: A. M. Kelley, 1960.

Cox, J. 2004. How to identify trust and reciprocity. *Games and Economic Behavior*, 46(2): 260–281.

Cox, J., and C. Deck. 2005. On the nature of reciprocal motives. *Economic Inquiry*, 43(3): 623–635.

Cox, J., R. Kerschbamer, and D. Neururer. 2016. What is trustworthiness and what drives it? *Games and Economic Behavior*, 98: 197–218.

Cready, W., and D. Hurtt. 2002. Assessing investor response to information events using return and volume metrics. *The Accounting Review*, 77(4): 891–909.

Crowther, D., and C. Carter. 2002. Legitimating irrelevance: Management education in higher education institutions. *The International Journal of Educational Management*, 16: 268–278.

Cyert, R., and J. March. 1963. *A Behavioral Theory of the Firm.* Englewood Cliffs, NJ: Prentice-Hall.

Davidson, B., and D. Stevens. 2013. Can a code of ethics improve manager behavior and investor confidence? An experimental study. *The Accounting Review*, 88(1): 51–74.

Davis, A., D. Guenther, L. Krull, and B. Williams. 2016. Do socially responsible firms pay more taxes? *The Accounting Review*, 91(1): 47–68.

Davis, J., G. Hecht, and J. Perkins. 2003. Social behaviors, enforcement, and tax compliance dynamics. *The Accounting Review*, 78(1): 39–69.

Demmert, H., and D. Klein. 2003. Experiment on entrepreneurial discovery: An attempt to demonstrate the conjecture of Hayek and Kirzner. *Journal of Economics and Behavioral Organization*, 50(3): 295–310.

Demski, J. 2003. Corporate conflicts of interest. *Journal of Economic Perspectives*, 17(2): 51–72.

Demski, J., and G. Feltham. 1978. Economic incentives in budgetary control systems. *The Accounting Review*, 53(2): 336–359.

Dhaliwal, D., O. Li, A. Tsang, and Y. Yang. 2011. Voluntary nonfinancial disclosure and the cost of equity capital: The initiation of corporate social responsibility reporting. *The Accounting Review*, 86(1): 59–100.

Dobbin, R., and D. Zorn. 2005. Corporate malfeasance and the myth of shareholder value. In *Political Power and Social Theory*, Volume 17, D. E. Davis (ed.). Greenwich, NY: Emerald Group Publishing Limited, 179–198.

Douthit, J., and D. Stevens. 2015. The robustness of honesty concerns on budget proposals when the superior has rejection authority. *The Accounting Review*, 90(2): 467–493.

Douthit, J., and M. Majerczyk. 2017. Subordinate perceptions of the superior and agency costs: Theory and evidence. Georgia State University Working Paper.

Douthit, J., S. Schwartz, D. Stevens, and R. Young. 2017. The effect of endogenous contract selection on budgetary slack: An experimental examination of trust, distrust, and trustworthiness. Georgia State University Working Paper.

Dyreng, S., M. Hanlon, and E. Maydew. 2010. The effects of executives on corporate tax avoidance. *The Accounting Review*, 85(4): 1163–1189.

Dyreng, S., W. Mayew, and C. Williams. 2012. Religious social norms and corporate financial reporting. *Journal of Business Finance and Accounting*, 39(7–8): 845–875.

Ekelund, R., and R. Hébert. 2014. *A History of Economic Theory & Method, Sixth Edition.* Long Grove, IL: Waveland Press.

Elster, J. 1989. Social norms and economic theory. *Journal of Economic Perspectives*, 3(4): 99–117.

Emmons, W., and G. Sierra. 2004. Incentives askew? *Regulation*, 27(4): 22–28.

Evans, J., R. Hannan, R. Krishnan, and D. Moser. 2001. Honesty in managerial reporting. *The Accounting Review*, 76(4): 537–559.

Falk, A., E. Fehr, and U. Fischbacher. 2003. On the nature of fair behavior. *Economic Inquiry*, 41(1): 20–26.

Fama, E. 1965. The behavior of stock-market prices. *Journal of Business*, 38(1): 34–105.

Fama, E. 1970. Efficient capital markets: A review of theory and empirical work. *Journal of Finance*, 25(2): 383–417.

Fama, E., L. Fisher, M. Jensen, and R. Roll. 1969. The adjustment of stock prices to new information. *International Economic Review*, 10(1): 1–21.

Fannie Uncovered. September 23, 2004. *Wall Street Journal*, Review and Outlook. Retrieved from: http://www.wsj.com.

Fehr, E., S. Gächter, and G. Kirchsteiger. 1997. Reciprocity as a contract enforcement device: Experimental evidence. *Econometrica*, 65(4): 833–860.

Fehr, E., E. Kirchler, A. Weichbold, and S. Gächter. 1998. When social norms overpower competition: Gift exchange in experimental labor market. *Journal of Labor Economics*, 16(2): 324–351.

Fehr, E., and K. Schmidt. 1999. A theory of fairness, competition, and cooperation. *Quarterly Review of Economics*, 114(3): 817–868.

Financial Crisis Inquiry Commission. 2011. *The Financial Crisis Report: Final Report of the National Commission on the Causes of the Financial and Economic Crisis in the United States*. New York, NY: Public Affairs.

Firth, A. 2007. Adam Smith's moral philosophy as ethical self-formation. In *New Perspectives on Adam Smith's The Theory of Moral Sentiments*. Geoff Cockfield, Ann Firth, and John Laurent (eds.). Cheltenham, UK: Edward Elgar Publishing, 106–123.

Fischbacher, U. 2007. z-Tree: Zurich toolbox for ready-made economic experiments. *Experimental Economics*, 10(2): 171–178.

Fischer, P., and S. Huddart. 2008. Optimal contracting with endogenous social norms. *American Economic Review*, 98(4): 1459–1475.

Fligstein, N. 1990. *The Transformation of Corporate Control*. Cambridge, MA: Harvard University Press.

Flood, M. 1952. Some experimental games. Research Memorandum RM-789, RAND Corporation, June.

Flood, M. 1958. Some experimental games. *Management Science*, 5(1): 5–26.

Forsythe, R., J. Horowitz, N. Savin, and M. Sefton. 1994. Fairness in simple bargaining experiments. *Games and Economic Behavior*, 6(3): 347–369.

Foster, G, C. Olsen, and T. Shevlin. 1984. Earnings releases, anomalies, and the behavior of security returns. *The Accounting Review*, 59(4): 574–603.

Fourcade, M., and R. Khurana. 2013. From social control to financial economics: The linked ecologies of economics and business in twentieth century America. *Theory and Society*, 42(2): 121–159.

Frank, R., T. Gilovich, and D. Regan. 1993. Does studying economics inhibit cooperation? *Journal of Economic Perspectives*, 7(2): 159–171.

Frey, B. 1994. How intrinsic motivation is crowded out and in. *Rationality and Society*, 6(3): 334–352.

Frey, B., and R. Jegen. 2001. Motivation crowding theory. *Journal of Economic Surveys*, 15(5): 589–611.

Friedman, D., and S. Sunder. 1994. *Experimental Methods: A Primer for Economists*. New York, NY: Cambridge University Press.

Friedman, M. 1953. The methodology of positive economics. In *Essays in Positive Economics*. Chicago, IL: Chicago University Press.

Friedman, M. 1970. The social responsibility of business is to increase its profits. *New York Times Magazine* (September 13).

Friedman, M., and R. Friedman. 1998. *Two Lucky People: Memoirs*. Chicago, IL: Chicago University Press.

Gao, F., L. Lisic, and I. Zhang. 2014. Commitment to social good and insider trading. *Journal of Accounting and Economics*, 57(2): 149–175.

Geanakoplos, J. 1992. Common knowledge. *Journal of Economic Perspectives*, 6(1): 53–82.

Ghoshal, S. 2005. Bad management theories are destroying good management practices. *Academy of Management Learning and Education*, 4(1): 75–91.

Gillette, A., D. Stevens, S. Watts, and A. Williams. 1999. Price and volume reactions to public information releases: An experimental approach incorporating traders' subjective beliefs. *Contemporary Accounting Research*, 16(3): 437–479.

Gode, D., and S. Sunder. 1993. Allocative efficiency of markets with zero intelligence traders: Markets as a partial substitute for individual rationality. *Journal of Political Economy*, 101(1): 119–137.

Gonedes, N., and N. Dopuch. 1974. Capital market equilibrium, information production, and selecting accounting techniques: Theoretical framework and review of empirical work. *Journal of Accounting Research*, 12 (Supplemental): 48–129.

Gordon, R. 1948. Short-period price determination in theory and practice. *American Economic Review*, 38 (June): 265–288.

Gordon, R., and J. Howell. 1959. *Higher Education for Business*. New York, NY: Columbia University Press.

Griswold, C. 1999. *Adam Smith and the Virtues of Enlightenment*. New York, NY: Cambridge University Press.

Grossman, S., and J. Stiglitz. 1980. On the impossibility of informationally efficient markets. *American Economic Review*, 70(3): 393–408.

Güth, W., R. Schmittberger, and B. Schwarze. 1982. An experimental analysis of ultimatum bargaining. *Journal of Economic Behavior and Organization*, 3(4): 367–388.

Gwartney, J., and R. Lawson. 2003. The concept and measurement of economic freedom. *European Journal of Political Economy*, 19(3): 405–430.

Haakonssen, K. 2006. Introduction: The coherence of Smith's thought. In *The Cambridge Companion to Adam Smith*, Knud Haakonssen (ed.). New York, NY: Cambridge University Press, 1–21.

Haakonssen, K., and D. Winch. 2006. The legacy of Adam Smith. In *The Cambridge Companion to Adam Smith*, Knud Haakonssen (ed.). New York, NY: Cambridge University Press, 366–394.

Hands, D. 2009. Did Milton Friedman's positive methodology license the formalist revolution? In *The Methodology of Positive Economics: Reflections on the Milton Friedman Legacy*. Uskali Mäki (ed.). Cambridge, UK: Cambridge University Press, 143–164.

Hannan, L. 2005. The combined effect of wages and firm profit on employee effort. *The Accounting Review*, 80(1): 167–188.

Hannan, L., J. Kagel, and D. Moser. 2002. Partial gift exchange in experimental labor market: Impact of subject population differences, productivity differences, and effort requests on behavior. *Journal of Labor Economics*, 20(4): 923–951.

Haskell, T. 1977. *The Emergency of Professional Social Science: The American Social Science Association and the Nineteenth-Century Crisis of Authority*. Urbana, IL: University of Illinois Press.

Hayek, F. 1967. *Studies in Philosophy, Politics, and Economics*. Chicago, IL: University of Chicago Press.

Hayek, F. 1988. *The Fatal Conceit*. Chicago, IL: University of Chicago Press.

Hayes, R., and S. Wheelwright. 1984. *Restoring our Competitive Edge: Competing Through Manufacturing*. New York, NY: John Wiley & Sons.

Healy, P. 1985. The effect of bonus schemes on accounting decisions: *Journal of Accounting and Economics*, 7(1–3): 85–107.

Heilbroner, R. 1999. *The Worldly Philosophers: The Lives, Times, and Ideas of the Great Economic Thinkers*. New York, NY: Simon & Schuster.

Hilsenrath, J. 2009. Plan aims to curb dangerous risk. *The Wall Street Journal*, Friday, October 23.

Hobson, J. 2011. Do the benefits of reducing accounting complexity persist in markets prone to bubble? *Contemporary Accounting Research*, 28(3): 957–989.

Hobson, J., Mellon, M., and D. Stevens. 2011. Determinants of moral judgments regarding budgetary slack: An experimental examination of pay scheme and personal values. *Behavioral Research in Accounting*, 23(1): 87–107.

Hoi, C., Q. Wu, and H. Zhang. 2013. Is corporate social responsibility (CSR) associated with tax avoidance? Evidence from irresponsible CSR activities. *The Accounting Review*, 88(6): 2025–2059.

Horngren, C., S. Datar, and M. Rajan. 2018. *Horngren's Cost Accounting: A Managerial Emphasis*, 16th edition. Hoboken, NJ: Pearson.

Hurwicz, L. 1945. Review (The Theory of Economic Behavior). *American Economic Review*, 35(5): 909–925.

Isaacson, W. 2003. *Benjamin Franklin: An American Life*. New York, NY: Simon & Schuster.

Jackson, D. 1994. *Jackson Personality Inventory—Revised Manual*. Port Huron, MI: Sigma Assessment Systems, Inc.

Jensen, M. 1983. Organization theory and methodology. *The Accounting Review*, 58(2): 319–339.

Jensen, M. 2001. Corporate budgeting is broken—let's fix it. *Harvard Business Review*, (November): 94–101.

Jensen, M. 2002. Value maximization, stakeholder theory, and the corporate objective function. *Business Ethics Quarterly*, 12(2): 235–256.

Jensen, M. 2008. Forward. In *Moral Markets: The Critical Role of Values in the Economy*. Paul J. Zak (ed.). Princeton, NJ: Princeton University Press, ix–x.

Jensen, M., and W. Meckling. 1976. Theory of the firm: Managerial behavior, agency costs and ownership structure. *Journal of Financial Economics*, 3(4): 305–360.

Jensen, M., and K. Murphy. 1990. Performance pay and top management incentives. *Journal of Political Economy*, 98(2): 225–263.

Jevons, W. 1871. *The Theory of Political Economy*. London, UK: Penguin, 1970.

Johnson, H. 1971. The Keynesian Revolution and the Monetarist Counter-Revolution. *American Economic Review*, 61(2): 91–106.

Johnson, H., and R. Kaplan. 1987. *Relevance Lost: The Rise and Fall of Management Accounting*. Boston, MA: Harvard Business School Press.

Jones, T. 1991. Ethical decision making by individuals in organizations: An issue-contingent model. *Academy of Management Review*, 16(2): 366–395.

Kahneman, D., J. Knetsch, and R. Thaler. 1986. Fairness as a constraint on profit seeking: Entitlements in the market. *American Economic Review*, 76(4): 728–741.

Kaplan, R., and D. Norton. 1996. *The Balanced Scorecard: Translating Strategy into Action*. Boston, MA: Harvard Business School Press.

Khurana, R. 2007. *From Higher Aims to Hired Hands: The Social Transformation of American Business Schools and the Unfulfilled Promise of Management as a Profession*. Princeton, NJ: Princeton University Press.

Khurana, R., and J. Spender. 2012. Herbert A. Simon on what ails business schools: More than "A problem in organizational design." *Journal of Management Studies*, 49(3): 619–639.

Kim, O., and R. Verrecchia. 1991. Trading volume and price reactions to public announcements. *Journal of Accounting Research*, 29(2): 302–321.

Kim, O., and R. Verrecchia. 1997. Pre-announcement and event-period private information. *Journal of Accounting and Economics*, 24(3): 395–419.

Kim, Y., M. Park, and B. Wier. 2012. Is earnings quality associated with corporate social responsibility? *The Accounting Review*, 87(3): 761–796.

King, R., V. Smith, A. Williams, and M. Van Boening. 1992. The robustness of bubbles and crashes in experimental stock markets. In *Nonlinear Dynamics and Evolutionary Economics*. I. Prigogine, R. Day, and P. Chen (eds.). Oxford, UK: Oxford University Press, 183–200.

Koford, K., and M. Penno. 1992. Accounting, principal-agent theory, and self-interested behavior. In *Ethics and Agency Theory: An Introduction*. Norman Bowie and R. Edward Freeman (eds.). New York, NY: Oxford University Press, 127–142.

Kohlberg, L. 1969. Stage and sequence: The cognitive-developmental approach to socialization. In *Handbook of Socialization Theory and Research*, D. Goslin, (ed.). Chicago, IL: Rand McNally, 347–480

Kohlberg, L. 1976. Moral states and moralization: The cognitive developmental approach. In *Moral development and behavior*, T. Lickona (ed.). New York: Holt, Rinehart & Winston, 31–53.

Kothari, S. 2001. Capital markets research in accounting. *Journal of Accounting and Economics*, 31(1–3): 105–231.

Kuang, X., and D. Moser. 2009. Reciprocity and the effectiveness of optimal agency contracts. *The Accounting Review*, 84(5): 1671–1694.

Kuhn, H. 2004. Introduction. In *Theory of Games and Economic Behavior: Sixtieth-Anniversary Edition*. Princeton, NJ: Princeton University Press.

Kuhn, T. 1962. *The Structure of Scientific Revolutions*. Chicago, IL: University of Chicago Press.

Lakoff, G. 2009. *The Political Mind: A Cognitive Scientist's Guide to Your Brain and Its Politics*. New York, NY: Penguin Books.

Lambert, J. 1891. *Two Thousand Years of Guild Life*. Hull, England: A. Brown & Sons.

Lambert, R. 2001. Contracting theory and accounting. *Journal of Accounting and Economics*, 32(1–3): 3–87.

Larcker, D., and B. Tayan. 2013. *A Real Look at Real World Corporate Governance*. San Bernardino, CA: David Larcker and Brian Tayan.

Leeson, R. 2000. *The Eclipse of Keynesianism: The Political Economy of the Chicago Counter Revolution*. New York, NY: Palgrave Macmillan.

Levitt, A. 1998. A question of integrity: Promoting investor confidence by fighting insider trading. Speech given at the SEC Speaks Conference, February 27.

Levitt, A. 1999. Quality information: The lifeblood of our markets. Speech given at The Economic Club of New York, October 18.

Libby, R., R. Bloomfield, and M. Nelson. 2002. Experimental research in financial accounting. *Accounting, Organizations and Society*, 27(8): 775–811.

Lowenstein, R. 2000. *When Genius Failed: The Rise and Fall of Long-Term Capital Management*. New York, NY: Random House.

Lucchetti, A., D. Enrich, and J. Lublin. 2009. Fed hits banks with sweeping pay limits: Thousands of firms affected in plan meant to discourage risky bets; Small-town institutions "pay for the sins" of big players. *The Wall Street Journal*, Friday, October 23.

Luft, J. 1997. Fairness, ethics and the effect of management accounting on transaction costs. *Journal of Management Accounting*, 9: 199–216.

MacKenzie, D. 2006. *An Engine, Not a Camera. How Financial Models Shape Markets*. Cambridge, MA: MIT Press.

Maddison, A. 1995. *Explaining the Economic Performance of Nations*. Cheltenham, UK: Edward Elgar Publishing.

Maddison, A. 2001. *The World Economy: A Millennial Perspective*. Paris, France: Organization for Economic Cooperation and Development.

Mäki, U. 2009a. Reading *the* methodological essay in twentieth-century economics: Map of multiple perspectives. In *The Methodology of Positive Economics: Reflections on the Milton Friedman Legacy*. Uskali Mäki (ed.). Cambridge, UK: Cambridge University Press, 47–67.

Mäki, U. 2009b. Unrealistic assumptions and unnecessary confusions: rereading and rewriting F53 as a realist statement. In *The Methodology of Positive Economics: Reflections on the Milton Friedman Legacy*. Uskali Mäki (ed.). Cambridge, UK: Cambridge University Press, 90–116.

Marchand, R. 1998. *Creating the Corporate Soul: The Rise of Public Relations and Corporate Imagery in American Big Business*. Berkeley, CA: University of California Press.

Marris, R. 1964. *The Economic Theory of Managerial Capitalism*. New York, NY: Free Press.

Marsden, G. 1994. *The Soul of the American University: From Protestant Establishment to Established Nonbelief*. New York, NY: Oxford University Press.

Marshall, A. 1890 (8th ed. 1920). *Principles of Economics*. London, UK: Macmillan.

Marshall, A. 1925. *Memorials of Alfred Marshall*, A. C. Pigou (ed.). London, UK: Macmillan.

Mayer, T. 2009. The influence of Friedman's methodological essay. In *The Methodology of Positive Economics: Reflections on the Milton Friedman Legacy*. Uskali Mäki (ed.). Cambridge, UK: Cambridge University Press, 119–142.

McGuire, S., T. Omer, and N. Sharp. 2012. The impact of religion on financial reporting irregularities. *The Accounting Review*, 87(2): 645–673.

Mehta, P. 2006. Self-interest and other interests. In *The Cambridge Companion to Adam Smith*, Knud Haakonssen (ed.). New York, NY: Cambridge University Press, 246–269.

Miles, E. 2016. *The Past, Present, and Future of the Business School*. Basingstoke, UK: Palgrave Macmillan.

Milgrom, P., and N. Stokey. 1982. Information, trade and common knowledge. *Journal of Economic Theory*, 26(1): 17–27.

Mill, J. 1836. On the definition of political economy. In *Collected Works of John Stuart Mill: Essays on Economics and Society*, J. M. Robson (ed.). Toronto, ON: University of Toronto Press, 1967.

Mill, J. 1848. *Principles of Political Economy*, W. J. Ashley (ed.). New York, NY: A. M. Kelly, 1965.

Mitnick, B. 1974. The theory of agency: The concept of fiduciary rationality and some consequences. Unpublished Ph.D. dissertation, Department of Political Science, University of Pennsylvania. University Microfilms No. 74-22, 881.

Mitnick, B. 1992. The theory of agency and organizational analysis. In *Ethics and Agency Theory: An Introduction*, Norman Bowie and R. Edward Freeman (eds.). New York, NY: Oxford University Press, 75–96.

Mittendorf, B. 2006. Capital budgeting when managers value both honesty and perquisites. *Journal of Management Accounting Research*, 18: 77–95.

Moody, J. 1946. *The Long Road Home: An Autobiography*. New York, NY: Macmillan.

Morgan, M. 2006. Economic man as model man: Ideal types, idealization and caricatures. *Journal of the History of Economic Thought*, 28(1): 1–27.

Morse, J., and A. Bower. December 30, 2002. Sherron Watkins: The party crasher. *Time*, 160 (27). Retrieved from: http://content.time.com/time/magazine/article/0,9171,1003992,00.html.

Moser, D., and P. Martin. 2012. A broader perspective on corporate social responsibility research in accounting. *The Accounting Review*, 87(3): 797–806.

Neeman, Z. 1996. Common beliefs and the existence of speculative trade. *Games and Economic Behavior*, 16(1): 77–96.

Noe, T., and M. Rebello. 1994. The dynamics of business ethics and economic activity. *American Economic Review*, 84(3): 531–547.

Nohria, N. 2002. *Changing Fortunes: Remaking the Industrial Corporation*. New York, NY: Wiley & Sons.

Noreen, E. 1988. The economics of ethics: A new perspective on agency theory. *Accounting, Organizations and Society*, 13(4): 359–369.

North, D. 1991. Institutions. *Journal of Economic Perspectives*, 5(1): 97–112.

North, D., and B. Weingast. 1989. Constitutions and commitment: The evolution of institutions governing public choice in seventeenth-century England. *Journal of Economic History*, 49(4): 803–832.

Ouchi, W. 1981. *Theory Z: How American Business Can Meet the Japanese Challenge*. Reading, MA: Addison-Wesley.

Özler, Ş. 2012. Adam Smith and dependency. *Psychoanalytic Review*, 99(3): 333–358.

Parker, R. 1986. The development of the accountancy profession in Britain in the early twentieth century. *Academy of Accounting Historians Monograph*. Tuscaloosa, AL: University of Alabama.

Partnoy, F. 2003. *Infectious Greed: How Deceit and Risk Corrupted the Financial Markets.* London, UK: Profile Books.

Pedersen, O. 1997. *The First Universities: Studium Generale and the Origins of University Education in Europe.* Cambridge, UK: Cambridge University Press.

Penno, M. 2017. A theory of assurance: Balancing costly formal control with tone at the top. University of Iowa Working Paper.

Perelman, M. 1989. Adam Smith and dependent social relations. *History of Political Economy,* 21(3): 503–520.

Pfeffer, J., and C. Fong. 2002. The end of business schools? Less success than meets the eye. *Academy of Management Learning and Education,* 1(1): 78–95.

Phillipson, N. 2010. *Adam Smith: An Enlightened Life.* New Haven & London: Yale University Press.

Pierson, F. 1959. *The Education of American Businessmen: A Study of University-College Programs in Business Administration.* New York, NY: McGraw-Hill.

Pincus, S. 2009. *1688: The First Modern Revolution.* New Haven, CT: Yale University Press.

Plott, C. 1982. Industrial organization theory and experimental economics. *Journal of Economic Literature,* 20(4): 1485–1527.

Podolny, J. 2009. The buck stops (and starts) at business school. *Harvard Business Review* (June): 62–67.

Popper, K. 1934. *The Logic of Scientific Discovery.* New York, NY: Routledge Classics, 2002.

Porter, L., and L. McKibbin. 1988. *Management Education and Development: Drift or Thrust into the 21st Century?* New York, NY: McGraw-Hill.

Posner, E. 2000. *Law and Social Norms.* Cambridge, MA: Harvard University Press.

Pratt, J., and R. Zeckhauser. 1985. Principals and agents: An overview. In *Principals and Agents: The Structure of Business,* J. W. Pratt and R. J. Zeckhauser (eds.). Cambridge, MA: Harvard University Press, 1–35.

Prendergast, C. 1999. The provision of incentives in firms. *Journal of Economic Literature,* 37(1): 7–63.

Rabin, M. 1993. Incorporating fairness into game theory and economics. *The American Economic Review,* 83(5): 1281–1302.

Rajan, R., and L. Zingales. 2004. *Saving Capitalism from the Capitalists: Unleashing the Power of Financial Markets to Create Wealth and Spread Opportunity.* Princeton, NJ: Princeton University Press.

Rankin, F., S. Schwartz, and R. Young. 2008. The effect of honesty and superior authority on budget proposals. *The Accounting Review,* 83(4): 1083–1099.

Raphael, D., and A. Macfie. 1982. Introduction. In *The Theory of Moral Sentiments,* 6th edition, D. D. Raphael and A. L. Macfie (eds.). Indianapolis, IN: Liberty Fund, Inc., 1–52.

Rasmusen, E. 1990. *Games and Information: An Introduction to Game Theory.* Cambridge, MA: Basil Blackwell, Inc.

Readings, B. 1996. *The University in Ruins.* Cambridge, MA: Harvard University Press.

Reder, M. 2009. Appraisal of evidence in economic methodology. In *The Methodology of Positive Economics: Reflections on the Milton Friedman Legacy,* Uskali Mäki (ed.). Cambridge, UK: Cambridge University Press, 165–188.

Reeder, J. 1997. Introduction. In *On Moral Sentiments: Contemporary Responses to Adam Smith*. J. Reeder (ed.). Bristol, UK: Thoemmes Press, vii–xxi.

Reuben, J. 1996. *The Making of the Modern University: Intellectual Transformation and the Marginalization of Morality*. Chicago, IL: University of Chicago Press.

Revell, J. 2003. Mo'money, fewer problems; Is it a good idea to get rid of the $1 million CEO pay ceiling? *Fortune*, March 31: page 34.

Ripley, A. December 30, 2002. Cynthia Cooper: The night detective. *Time*, 160 (27). Retrieved from: http://content.time.com/time/magazine/article/0,9171,1003990,00.html.

Romer, P. 1986. Increasing returns and long-run growth. *Journal of Political Economy*, 94(5): 1002–1037.

Ross, S. 1973. The economic theory of agency: The principal's problem. *American Economic Review*, 63(2): 134–139.

Ross, S. 1989. Discussion: Intertemporal asset pricing. In *Theory of Valuation*, S. Bhattacharya and G. Constantinides (eds.). Totowa, NJ: Rowman & Littlefield. 85–96.

Roth, A. 1995. Introduction to experimental economics. In *The Handbook of Experimental Economics*, John H. Kagel and Alvin E. Roth (eds.). Princeton, NJ: Princeton University Press.

Samuelson, L. 2005. Economic theory and experimental economics. *Journal of Economic Literature*, 43(1): 65–107.

Samuelson, P. 1947. *Foundations of Economic Analysis*. Cambridge, MA: Harvard University Press.

Sass, S. 1982. *The Pragmatic Imagination: A History of the Wharton School, 1881–1981*. Philadelphia, PA: University of Pennsylvania Press

Scaff, L. 2011. *Max Weber in America*. Princeton, NJ: Princeton University Press.

Schumpeter, J. 1954. *History of Economic Analysis*, E. B. Schumpeter (ed.). New York, NY: Oxford University Press.

Scott, R. 1995. *Institutions and Organizations*. Thousand Oaks, CA: Sage.

Scully, G. 1988. The institutional framework and economic development. *Journal of Political Economy*, 96(3): 652–662.

Sen, A. 1977. Rational fools: A critique of the behavioral foundations of economics theory. *Philosophy and Public Affairs*, 6(4): 317–344.

Serrano, D., and J. Bonilla. 2009. The politics of positivism: Disinterested predictions from interested agents. In *The Methodology of Positive Economics: Reflections on the Milton Friedman Legacy*. Uskali Mäki (ed.). Cambridge, UK: Cambridge University Press, 189–213.

Shils, E., and P. Altbach. 1997. *The Order of Learning: Essays on the Contemporary University*. New Brunswick, NJ: Transaction.

Shleifer, A., and R. Vishny. 1997. A survey of corporate governance. *The Journal of Finance*, 52(2): 737–783.

Siegel, S. 1959. Theoretical models of choice and strategy behavior: Stable state behavior in the two-choice uncertain outcome situation. *Psychometrika*, 24(4): 303–316.

Siegel, S., and L. Fouraker. 1960. *Bargaining and Group Decision Making-Experiments in Bilateral Monopoly*. New York, NY: McGraw-Hill.

Simon, H. 1945. Review. *American Journal of Sociology*, 50(6): 558–560.

Simon, H. 1955. A behavioral model of rational choice. *Quarterly Journal of Economics*, 69(1): 99–118.

Sinclair, T. 2005. *The New Masters of Capital: American Bond Rating Agencies and the Politics of Creditworthiness*. Ithaca, NY: Cornell University Press.

Skapinker, M. 2008. Why business ignores the business schools. *Financial Times*, January 8.

Sliwka, D. 2007. Trust as a signal of a social norm and the hidden costs of incentive schemes. *The American Economic Review*, 97(3): 999–1012.

Sloan, R. 1996. Do stock prices fully reflect information in accruals and cash flows about future earnings? *The Accounting Review*, 71(3): 289–316.

Smith, A. 1759 (6th ed., 1790). *The Theory of Moral Sentiments*, the Glasgow Edition, D. D. Raphael and A. L. Macfie (eds.). Indianapolis, IN: Liberty Fund, Inc., 1982.

Smith, A. 1762–1763. *Lectures on Jurisprudence*, the Glasgow Edition, R. L. Meek, D. D. Raphael, and P. G. Stein (eds.). Indianapolis, IN: Liberty Fund, 1982.

Smith, A. 1776 (6th ed., 1791). *An Inquiry Into The Nature and Causes of the Wealth of Nations*, the Glasgow Edition, R. H. Campbell and A. S. Skinner (eds.). Indianapolis, IN: Liberty Fund, Inc., 1981.

Smith, A. 1795. The history of astronomy. In *Essays on Philosophical Subjects*, the Glasgow Edition, W. P. D. Wightman (ed.). Indianapolis, IN: Liberty Fund, Inc., 1982.

Smith, V. 1962. An experimental study of competitive market behavior. *Journal of Political Economy*, 70(2): 111–137.

Smith, V. 1976. Experimental economics: Induced value theory. *American Economic Review*, 66(2): 274–279.

Smith, V. 1982. Microeconomic systems as an experimental science. *American Economic Review*, 72(5): 923–955.

Smith, V. 2003. Constructivist and ecological rationality in economics. *Les Prix Nobel*, Stockholm, SE: Nobel Foundation. Reprinted in *American Economic Review*, 93(3): 465–508.

Smith, V. 2008. *Rationality in Economics: Constructivist and Ecological Forms*. New York, NY: Cambridge University Press.

Smith, V., G. Suchanek, and A. Williams. 1988. Bubbles, crashes, and endogenous expectations in experimental spot asset markets. *Econometrica*, 56(5): 1119–1151.

Snowdon, B., and H. Vane. 1999. *Conversations with Leading Economists*. Cheltenham, UK: Edward Elgar Publishing.

Soll, J. 2014. *The Reckoning: Financial Accountability and the Rise and Fall of Nations*. New York, NY: Basic Books.

Song, H. 1995. Adam Smith as an early pioneer of institutional individualism. *History of Political Economy*, 27(3): 425–448.

Spence, M., and R. Zeckhauser. 1971. Insurance, information and individual action. *American Economic Review*, 61(2): 380–387.

Squires, S., C. Smith, L. McDougall, and W. Yeack. 2003. *Inside Arthur Andersen: Shifting Values, Unexpected Consequences*. Upper Saddle River, NJ: Prentice Hall.

Stevens, D. 2002. The effects of reputation and ethics on budgetary slack. *Journal of Management Accounting Research*, 14: 153–171.

Stevens, D. 2011. Rediscovering Adam Smith: How *The Theory of Moral Sentiments* can explain emerging evidence in experimental economics. Adam Smith Working Papers Series 2011:04, University of Glasgow, UK.

Stevens, D., and A. Thevaranjan. 2010. A moral solution to the moral hazard problem. *Accounting, Organizations and Society*, 35(1): 125–139.

Stigler, G. 1961. The economics of information. *Journal of Political Economy*, 69(3): 213–225.

Stigler, G. 1971a. Smith's travels on the ship of the state. *History of Political Economy*, 3 (2): 265–277.

Stigler, G. 1971b. The theory of economic regulation. *The Bell Journal of Economics and Management Science*, 2(1): 3–21.

Stigler, G. 1982. *The Economist as Preacher and Other Essays*. Chicago, IL: University of Chicago Press.

Sunder, S. 1997. *Theory of Accounting and Control*. Mason, OH: South-Western Cengage Learning.

Sunder, S. 2016. Rethinking financial reporting: Standards, norms and institutions. *Foundations and Trends in Accounting*, 11(1–2): 1–118.

Tenbrunsel, A., and D. Messick. 1999. Sanctioning systems, decision frames, and cooperation. *Administrative Science Quarterly*, 44(4): 684–707.

Thomas, C. 2002. The rise and fall of Enron: When a company looks too good to be true, it usually is. *Journal of Accountancy*, 193(4): 41–48.

Thorpe, D. 2007. Science and its applications in The Theory of Moral Sentiments. In *New Perspectives on Adam Smith's The Theory of Moral Sentiments*, Geoff Cockfield, Ann Firth, and John Laurent (eds.). Cheltenham, UK: Edward Elgar Publishing, 124–140.

Toffler, B. 2003. *Final Accounting: Ambition, Greed, and the Fall of Arthur Andersen*. New York, NY: Broadway Books.

Verrecchia, R. 2001. Essays on disclosure. *Journal of Accounting and Economics*, 32 (1–3): 97–180.

Veysey, L. 1965. *The Emergence of the American University*. Chicago, IL: University of Chicago Press.

Von Neumann, J., and O. Morgenstern. 1944. *Theory of Games and Economic Behavior*. Princeton, NJ: Princeton University Press.

Waller, W. 1988. Slack in participative budgeting: The joint effect of a truth-inducing pay scheme and risk preferences. *Accounting, Organizations and Society*, 13(1): 87–98.

Walters, A. 1987. Friedman, Milton. In *The New Palgrave Dictionary of Economics*, Vol 2. London, UK: Macmillan.

Watts, R., and J. Zimmerman. 1978. Towards a positive theory of the determination of accounting standards. *The Accounting Review*, 53(1): 112–134.

Watts, R., and J. Zimmerman. 1986. *Positive Accounting Theory*. Englewood Cliffs, NJ: Prentice Hall, Inc.

Wheeler, J. 1970. Accounting theory and research in perspective. *The Accounting Review*, 45(1): 1–10.

Wightman, W. 1982. Introduction. In *Essays on Philosophical Subjects*, the Glasgow Edition, W. P. D. Wightman (ed.). Indianapolis, IN: Liberty Fund, Inc., 5–27.

Williams, A. 1980. Computerized double-auction markets: Some initial experimental results. *Journal of Business*, 53(3): 235–258.

Williamson, O. 1964. *The Economics of Discretionary Behavior: Managerial Objectives in a Theory of the Firm.* Englewood Cliffs, NJ: Prentice-Hall.

Williamson, O. 1975. *Markets and Hierarchies: Analysis and Antitrust Implications: A Study in the Economics of Internal Organization.* New York, NY: Free Press.

Williamson, O. 1993. Opportunism and its critics. *Managerial and Decision Economics*, 14(2): 97–107.

Williamson, O. 2009. Friedman (1953) and the theory of the firm. In *The Methodology of Positive Economics: Reflections on the Milton Friedman Legacy*, Uskali Mäki (ed.). Cambridge, UK: Cambridge University Press, 241–256.

Wilson, E. 1998. *Consilience.* New York, NY: Alfred A. Knopf.

Wittrock, B. 1993. The modern university: The three transformations. In *The European and American University since 1800*, S. Rothblatt and B. Wittrock (eds.). Cambridge, UK: Cambridge University Press.

Young, M. 1985. Participative budgeting: The effects of risk-aversion and asymmetric information on budgetary slack. *Journal of Accounting Research*, 23(2): 829–842.

Index

academic journals, 13, 49, 64, 81–2, 171–2
accountability
  double-entry accounting and, 24
  free-market capitalism and, 23, 31
  merchant culture and, 23, 31, 44
  transparency, 89
  transparency and, 25–6, 31, 44
accounting. *See* double-entry accounting
  financial, 23, 61, 177
  management/managerial, 14–15, 33, 49,
    153
  positive, 81–2, 85
accounting control. *See* financial control
accounting firms
  business consulting and, 37
  competition between, 37
  emergence of, 36–7
  Metcalf Committee Report and, 37
  opportunism culture and, 37
accounting scandals, 39
accounting schools
  in Great Britain, 29–30
  in Netherlands, 25
  in northern Italy, 24
  professional norms and, 29
adverse selection, 112
agency theory. *See also* principal-agent theory
  accounting and, 79
  assumptions and implications, 79–84
  corporate finance and, 79
  financial incentives and, 82–3, 176
  information asymmetry and, 80
  information economics and, 80
  management responsibility and, 46
  organizational behavior and, 79
  participative budgeting and, 153

  revitalized neoclassical economic theory
    and, 79–80
agents. *See also* principals
  conformists, 126
  economic, 9, 15
  ethical, 115–16
  firm, 111–13, 152–3, 176
  market, 172–3
  opportunistic, 112, 115–16, 125–6
Alchian, Armen, 73
altruism, 85, 147
American Accounting Association (AAA), 119
American Association of Collegiate Schools of
  Business (AACSB), 51–2, 60, 109
American Association of Public Accountants,
  35
American Economic Association (AEA), 53,
  57
Amsterdam, 25, 29
Andersen, Arthur, 37
anomalies, 11, 15, 125, 165–6, 171, 180
anonymity, 148, 154
Antwerp, 25
Arce, Daniel, 124–5
archival market research
  efficient market hypothesis (EMH) and,
    167–8
  event study method and, 167–8
  evidence of social norms in, 180–5
Arrow, Kenneth, 109–11, 123, 145, 149
Arthur Andersen (firm), 37–9, 43
assumptions. *See* behavioral assumptions
asymmetric information. *See* information
  asymmetry
Atiase, Rowland, 175
automobile industry, 33